The Executive's
Book of Quotations

THE EXECUTIVE'S
BOOK OF QUOTATIONS

JULIA VITULLO-MARTIN
J. ROBERT MOSKIN

New York   Oxford
Oxford University Press
1994

Oxford University Press

Oxford   New York   Toronto
Delhi   Bombay   Calcutta   Madras   Karachi
Kuala Lumpur   Singapore   Hong Kong   Tokyo
Nairobi   Dar es Salaam   Cape Town
Melbourne   Auckland   Madrid

and associated companies in
Berlin   Ibadan

Copyright © 1994 by Julia Vitullo-Martin and J. Robert Moskin

Published by Oxford University Press, Inc.,
200 Madison Avenue, New York, New York 10016

Oxford is a registered trademark of Oxford University Press

Library of Congress Cataloging-in-Publication Data

The executive's book of quotations / Julia Vitullo-Martin, J. Robert
Moskin [editors].
    p.   cm.
Includes index.
ISBN 0-19-507836-5
1. Business—Quotations, maxims, etc.   I. Vitullo-Martin, Julia,
1946–   II. Moskin, J. Robert, 1923–
PN6084.B87D55   1994
650—dc20   93–26647
                                                            CIP

246897531
Printed in the United States of America
on acid-free paper

For Tom,
our computer consultant,
and Lynn,
our communications consultant

PREFACE

This book will give executives and managers the precise quotation they need when they speak or write for any kind of audience. It offers more than 5,000 quotations that have been chosen specifically for use by business people, nonprofit executives, and government managers—and those who help them prepare their writings and speeches. It makes finding the perfect quotation easy.

Executives repeatedly have to communicate their ideas and wishes to people of widely differing backgrounds, experiences, and expectations. They have to talk to other executives, employees, customers—even competitors. They need to make their case to public policy makers, the media, and the general public.

For the executive with a talk to prepare or a report to write, the apt quote is invaluable. It can enliven any presentation; it can make an idea crystal clear; it can move an audience. It may even get a laugh.

Included here are only quotations that have passed the test: "Will it be useful to the executive who is writing for publication or speaking before an audience?" They range from sage advice to epigrams, *bon mots,* witticisms, and jibes. They talk the language of many different audiences. Their sources are as varied as Plato and Casey Stengel; they come from chewing gum king William Wrigley to management gurus Tom Peters and Robert Waterman and from Chinese proverbs to John Maynard Keynes. Most of the quotations are serious; some are veined with humor.

Quotations are like pepper, to be sprinkled judiciously. They should be used only when the quotation makes a point more precisely, colorfully, or authoritatively than you are able to with your own words. Overused, they can get between you and your audience. Used with care, they can brighten your talk and writing. These will.

This book is a unique compilation. It is designed for today's reader, writer, and speaker. It is fresh, not another edition of an aged work. This book originated from the authors' private hoards of quotations studiously collected over decades and supplemented by two years of research specifically for this volume. And they were assembled from vast numbers of speeches, books, newspapers, movies, and poetry.

Finding a Quote

This book is organized to lead you to the exact quote for your need. The quotations are arranged under 500 topics, alphabetically from "Ability" and "Avarice" to "Winners" and "Youth." If you need a quotation about "Investing" or "Firings" or "Power" or "Sex," or "Trust," simply turn to that word.

The topics are listed in the Contents at the beginning of the book. Begin your search for a quote by running your eye over this list to find your topic.

In the back of the volume are two additional indexes designed to make the book even more useful to you. The Index of Names lists alphabetically the names of the people who are either quoted or named in the quotes. You may want a quotation by Warren Buffett or J. P. Morgan, John W. Gardner or Tom Peters, Tallulah Bankhead or Dorothy Parker.

The final index—perhaps the most useful—is the Index of Cross-Topics. It increases your range of choice. Each quotation is presented under only one topic, even if it relates to more than one idea. The Index of Cross-Topics points you to other topics under which you might find a useful quote. For example, General Omar Bradley's quotation "In war there is no prize for the runner-up" is included under the topic "War." It could as aptly be categorized under "Losing" or "Determination." Thus, you will find "War" listed as a cross-topic under "Losing" and "Determination."

Attributions and Sources

Each quotation is accompanied by the most accurate attribution possible. Knowing the speaker is essential for a full appreciation of most quotes. "If you can't be captain, don't play" is clear enough, but becomes even more valuable when the speaker is Joseph P. Kennedy. Sometimes, the context is also vital information. "Pet rocks" means nothing until you learn that it was said by H. Ross Perot about his fellow board members at General Motors.

Each quotation also carries as accurate a source as was available to the compilers. In most cases the original source is given, but sometimes original sources are difficult—even impossible—to track down. And often a secondary source is interesting and significant, as when Clark Clifford quotes Yeats or Walter Wriston quotes Aristotle. If an executive has used a classic quote well, both may be cited.

Many speakers have had more than one position for which they are known. Speakers are identified by the position at the time of the quote when that is useful. Otherwise they are identified by the position for which they are best known. Some writers, usually giants such as Aristotle and St. Augustine, are listed without titles.

Browsing

This book is intended to be used by a specific person for a specific, and usually serious, purpose. But it has also evolved into a book to browse in. Thus, the user is warned that it will be easy to be diverted by other marvelous quotes along the way in the search for a specific quotation.

Here are just a few examples:

Sun Tzu's advice on strategy: "Appear at points which the enemy must hasten to defend, march swiftly to places where you are not expected."

Stan Musial's advice on how to solve a difficult problem, hitting a spitball: "Hit it on the dry side."

Oil man Clint Murchison's observation on investing: "Money is like manure. If you spread it around, it does a lot of good."

McDonald's late chairman Ray Kroc's advice on keeping a youthful perspective: "When you're green, you're growing; when you're ripe, you rot."

Casey Stengel on losing: "When you're losing, everyone commences to play stupid."

Nebraska Furniture Mart CEO Rose Blumkin's guidelines: "Sell cheap and tell the truth."

This is, then, a book to be used and enjoyed. Flipping these pages will often bring you an insight—and a smile. The quotations in this volume will make your speeches brighter and writing more cogent. They will put your point across and make you more effective and remembered longer.

New York   J. V.-M.
June 1993   J. R. M.

CONTENTS

The Executive's
Book of Quotations

THE EXECUTIVE'S
BOOK OF QUOTATIONS

ABILITY

"Ability is the art of getting credit for all the home runs someone else hits." CASEY STENGEL, baseball manager (*The Gospel According to Casey*, p. 18)

"Even a blind hog can find an acorn."
BILL CLINTON, then Governor of Arkansas, wrote this on the score sheet for a game of hearts won by *Newsweek*'s Mark Miller, who had more often lost (William Safire, the *New York Times Magazine*, December 13, 1992)

"One does what one can, not what one can't."
Attributed to AGATHA CHRISTIE, responding to why she wrote only mystery novels, not literary ones, as quoted by Ruth Gordon playing a Christie-like character in a "Colombo" episode, *Try and Catch Me* (screenplay by Gene Thompson and Paul Tuckahoe)

ACCOUNTING

"The three C's explain it all: Their members are either comatose, co-opted, or corrupt."
JOSEPH GRUNDFEST, retiring as a commissioner of the Securities and Exchange Commission, on why corporate audit committees don't work (*Fortune*, January 1, 1990)

"Bloom, do me a favor. Move a few decimal points around. You can do it. You're an accountant. You're in a noble profession. The word 'count' is part of your title."
ZERO MOSTEL asking Gene Wilder to cook the books in *The Producers* (screenplay by Mel Brooks)

"Nowadays, you hear a lot about fancy accounting methods, like LIFO and FIFO, but back then we were using the ESP method, which really sped things along when it came time to close those books. It's a pretty basic method: if you can't make your books balance, you take however much they're off by and enter it under the heading ESP, which stands for Error Some Place."

SAM WALTON, founder and CEO, Wal-Mart stores (*Sam Walton*, p. 53)

"A sensitive, creative artist with a fine sense of double-entry bookkeeping." ALEXANDER WOOLLCOTT, writer, on film producer Sam Goldwyn
(*Hollywood Quotations*, p. 32)

ADVANTAGE

"Some folks no doubt figured we were a little fly-by-night—you know, in the discount business today but out selling cars or swampland tomorrow. I think that misunderstanding worked to our advantage for a long time, and enabled Wal-Mart to fly under everybody's radar until we were too far along to catch."

SAM WALTON, founder and CEO, Wal-Mart stores (*Sam Walton*, p. 79)

"I never will really know where I could have gotten on my own. Everyone likes to know what he could do against competition with no unfair advantage." PETER GRACE, JR., who became the head
of W. R. Grace & Co. at age 32 (interview, 1981)

"*Cui bono fuerit*?" ("Who benefits?")

Cui bono was the principle on which the Roman judge, LUCIUS CASSIUS
LONGINUS (2nd century B.C.) decided his cases; the person benefiting
from the crime was most likely to have committed it

ADVERTISING

"Mr. Murdoch, your readers are our shoplifters."

MARVIN TRAUB, chairman, Bloomingdale's, declining Rupert Murdoch's
request that Bloomingdale's advertise in the *New York Post*, 1983
(told to Donna E. Shalala at dinner by Traub)

"People don't buy from clowns."

CLAUDE HOPKINS, called "the father of modern advertising" by DAVID
OGILVY, former chairman, Ogilvy and Mather, who quotes this warning
with which he came to disagree strongly (*Ogilvy on Advertising*, p. 103)

"Once upon a time, the head of a big corporation went into Cartier's and ordered a diamond bracelet for his wife, 'Send the bill to my office,' said he. Nothing doing—Cartier had never heard of his corporation. The next morning he instructed his agency to prepare a corporate advertising campaign."

DAVID OGILVY, former chairman, Ogilvy and Mather
(*Ogilvy on Advertising*, p. 117)

"Word-of-author-advertising."

DR. MONROE FRIEDMAN, professor of psychology, Eastern Michigan
University, on the number of brand names used by writers
(*New York Times*, December 6, 1992)

"The only thing that looked like a firm work offer was an idea for an American Express commercial. This would focus on me-as-the-President's-daughter, and I just couldn't do it, no matter how poor I was. Besides, I couldn't imagine how they would make it seem plausible. Put me in front of the White House and have me say, 'You don't know me—and they don't either'?"

PATTI DAVIS, daughter of President Ronald Reagan
(*The Way I See It*, p. 301)

"It is not necessary to advertise food to hungry people, fuel to cold people, or houses to the homeless."

JOHN KENNETH GALBRAITH, economist
(*American Capitalism*, 1957)

"Let me just pull something out of a hat here and see if it hops for us."

ALAN HEWITT talking advertising in *Days of Wine and Roses*
(screenplay by J. P. Miller)

"Just advertising departments with legs and high heels."

RICHARD AVEDON, photographer, describing top fashion editors in a
comment made at Diana Vreeland's memorial service
(*New York*, March 27, 1992)

"Of all the vocations depicted, the one that had the highest recall was always the cowboy."

JACK LANDRY, marketing director, Philip Morris,
and, for 30 years, brand manager of Marlboro
(*Esquire*, December 1991, p. 60)

"You can tell the ideals of a nation by its advertisements."

NORMAN DOUGLAS, British writer (*South Wind*, 1917, chapter 6)

"The wrong advertising can actually *reduce* the sales of a product. I am told that George Hay Brown, at one time head of marketing

research at Ford, inserted advertisements in every other copy of
the *Reader's Digest*. At the end of the year, the people who had *not*
been exposed to the advertising had bought more Fords than
those who had."

> David Ogilvy, former chairman, Ogilvy and Mather
> (*Ogilvy on Advertising*, p. 9)

"Advertising is a valuable economic factor because it is the
cheapest way of selling goods, particularly if the goods are
worthless."

> Sinclair Lewis, novelist (*New York Times*, April 18, 1943)

"The codfish lays ten thousand eggs,
The homely hen lays one.
The codfish never cackles
To tell you what she's done—
And so we scorn the codfish
While the humble hen we prize,
It only goes to show you
That it pays to advertise!"

> David Ogilvy, former chairman, Ogilvy and Mather
> (*Ogilvy on Advertising*, p. 172)

ADVERTISING SLOGANS

"Your mother wears Nike."

> Campaign for British Knights sneakers targeted at teenagers
> by Donny Deutsch, New York advertiser
> (*New York Times*, October 14, 1992)

"Reach for a Lucky instead of a sweet."

> Albert Lasker, the great advertising man, encouraging women to smoke
> to lose weight (*Wall Street Journal*, Centennial Edition, 1989)

"If you ain't eating Wham, you ain't eating ham."

> Louise Beavers, housekeeper, giving a career-saving slogan to
> employer Cary Grant in *Mr. Blandings Builds His Dream House*
> (screenplay by Norman Panama and Melvin Frank)

ADVICE

"Tomorrow there'll be another tidal wave, so keep your snorkel
above the water level."

> President George Bush, quoting advice his mother gave him about
> staying calm while learning to snorkel (*Public Broadcast System*, 1989)

"Watch the turtle. He only moves forward by sticking his neck out."

> Saying on a pillow, quoted by Louis V. Gerstner, Jr., chairman, IBM
> (*New York Times*, March 27, 1993)

"Don't panic."

> Douglas Adams (*Hitch Hiker's Guide to the Galaxy*, 1979, preface)

"The ideal attitude is to be physically loose and mentally tight."

> Arthur Ashe, tennis player (*New York Times*, February 8, 1993)

"*Carpe diem*." ("Seize the day.")

> Horace (*Odes*)

"Don't bunt. Aim out of the ball park. Aim for the company of the immortals."

> David Ogilvy, former chairman, Ogilvy and Mather
> (*Ogilvy on Advertising*, p. 21)

"Put your ass into the ball, Mr. President."

> Sam Snead, pro golfer, to Dwight D. Eisenhower
> (Winokur, *Friendly Advice*, p. 117)

"Sleep with the right people."

> Lillian Hellman, playwright, to Marianne Wiggins,
> who had just said that she owed her career
> as a fledgling writer to Hellman's inspiration
> (*The Nation*, November 16, 1992)

"When you're building mountains, it's best not to look at those God has already made."

> Ron Toomer, president and ceo, Arrow Dynamics, an amusement-ride
> manufacturer, who keeps his drafting table back from his office
> windows that overlook Utah's Wasatch mountain range
> (*American Way Magazine*, December 1, 1992)

"Don't pay any attention to what they write about you. Just measure it in inches."

> Andy Warhol, artist, to Tama Janowitz, writer, in 1986
> (*New York Times*, September 2, 1992)

"Hit it on the dry side."

> Attributed to Stan Musial, baseball player, on spitballs

"They need to ask people, 'How do you like your car?' I would bet not one in 10 of them has done that."

> John A. Dalles, former GM car owner who now drives a Honda Accord
> (*New York Times*, September 23, 1992)

"Whatever you do, don't end up doing this."

A baker and father to William Serrin, who became a labor reporter for
the *New York Times* and an author (*Newsweek*, October 11, 1992)

"Run to daylight."

VINCE LOMBARDI, coach, Green Bay Packers (*Run to Daylight: Vince
Lombardi's Diary of One Week with the Green Bay Packers*, 1963)

"Protect yourself."

RALPH DeNUNZIO, chairman, Kidder, Peabody and Co., to investment
banker Michael Siegel on learning that Siegel's trading profits had come
from inside information (Stewart, *Den*, picture 9)

"Don't tell your problems to people: 80 percent don't care; and
the other 20 percent are glad you've got them."

LOU HOLTZ, football coach at the University of Notre Dame
("Tonight Show," January 7, 1992)

"If you can stand it, do it."

THOMAS J. WATSON, JR., CEO, IBM, to sons who ask if they
should join their fathers in business (*Father Son & Co.*, p. xi)

"When a fielder gets the pitcher into trouble, the pitcher has to
pitch himself out of a slump he isn't in."

CASEY STENGEL, baseball manager (*The Gospel According to Casey*, p. 71)

"Don't let 'em scare you."

Anchor DAN RATHER to speechwriter Peggy Noonan as she left CBS for
the White House (Noonan,*What I Saw at the Revolution*, p. 38)

"Avoid slickness at all costs."

REESE SCHONFELD, first president, Cable News Network, who argued that
the reality of their live programs should always be on display
(Peters, *Liberation*, p. 33)

"You must start with a bang."   Attributed to RICHARD STRAUSS, instructing
young composers on how to begin an orchestration

"When you arrive at a fork in the road, take it."

YOGI BERRA, catcher, New York Yankees (*It Ain't Over*, p. 7)

"Don't wear an ascot unless you've been there."

HAL RUBENSTEIN and JIM MULLEN, "Iron, John: How to Get Dressed
Better" (*New York Times Magazine*: "Men's Fashions of the Times,"
September 13, 1992)

"If you have to have a policy manual, publish the 'Ten Commandments.'"

ROBERT TOWNSEND, former CEO, Avis, management consultant
(*Further Up the Organization*, 1984)

"Be there."

C. P. SNOW, writer, basic political advice when trouble arises
(*Strangers and Brothers*, 1940)

"*Duc, sequere, aut de via decede.*" ("Lead, follow, or get out of the way.")

HENRY BEARD (*Latin for Even More Occasions*, p. 6)

"Run to the bank, Walter, run to the bank."

Warren E. Buffett, CEO, Berkshire Hathaway, to Walter Annenberg who had asked whether he should accept Rupert Murdoch's offer of $3 billion cash for his Triangle publications, which included the *Daily Racing Form* and *TV Guide* (Shawcross, *Murdoch*, p. 313)

"If 80 percent of your sales come from 20 percent of all items, just carry those 20 percent."

STEW LEONARD, grocer (*Wall Street Journal*, October 16, 1992)

"When you have nothing to say, sing it."

DAVID OGILVY, former chairman, Ogilvy and Mather, recommending jingles in some instances (*Ogilvy on Advertising*, p. 111)

"You could look it up."

CASEY STENGEL's refrain; his skill as a baseball manager was based in part on his ability to remember who could hit whom and what had happened before (*The Gospel According to Casey*, p. 32)

"If I were you, I'd close the show and keep the store open nights."

Attributed to GEORGE S. KAUFMAN, playwright, to Alfred Bloomingdale, who had backed a flop musical

"In life as in a football game, the principle to follow is: Hit the line hard; don't foul and don't shirk, but hit the line hard."

THEODORE ROOSEVELT (*The Strenuous Life*, 1900)

"Always associate with your superiors."

MRS. JOHN D. ROCKEFELLER, JR., to son Nelson
(quoted in Isaacson, *Kissinger: A Biography*, p. 91)

"Don't let him make any major decisions until he is entirely well. You don't make good decisions when you're sick. I was recovering from pneumonia when I made the decision not to burn the tapes."

> Former President RICHARD NIXON to Lyn Nofziger on President Reagan (*Nofizger*, 1992)

"Don't fight forces; use them."

> R. BUCKMINISTER FULLER, futurist (*Shelter*, 1932)

"A few times throw over there and give him a lousy move so he thinks it's your good move."

> WATTY CLARK, left-handed Dodger pitcher, advising the young Harry Eisenstadt to avoid any set routine in throwing to first base against base-runners (*The Gospel According to Casey*, p. 61)

"Be not afraid of any man no matter what his size;
When danger threatens, call on me, and I will equalize."

> Inscription on a Colt Revolver (Patton, *Made in USA*, p. 50)

ADVICE—FINANCIAL

"Buy on the rumor; sell on the news."

> Wall Street saying

"Democracy in economics, aristocracy in thought."

> GEORGE W. RUSSELL (known as A.E.), Irish writer (quoted in Van Wyck Brooks, *A Writer's Notebook*, 1957)

"Think left, live right."

> Post-1960s proverbial version of A.E.'s adage

"Think rich. Look poor."

> ANDY WARHOL, artist (Hackett, *The Andy Warhol Diaries*, 1989)

"Achetez aux canons, vendez aux clairons."
(Buy on the cannons, sell on the trumpets.)

> French adage to buy when the cannons are pummelling your country and sell when the enemy is routed; often cited by economic Contrarians

"Buy when there's blood in the streets."

> Attributed to BARON GUY DE ROTHSCHILD, banker

ADVICE—LEGAL

"I don't know as I want a lawyer to tell me what I cannot do. I hire him to tell me how to do what I want to do."

> J. P. MORGAN, financier, responding to his lawyer's advice (quoted in Tarbell, *The Life of Elbert H. Gary*, 1925, p. 81)

"Never, never, never, on cross-examination ask a witness a question you don't already know the answer to, was a tenet I absorbed with my baby food. Do it, and you'll often get an answer you don't want, an answer that might wreck your case."
GREGORY PECK, as Atticus Finch, the lawyer-hero, in To Kill a Mockingbird
(screenplay by Horton Foote)

"Too bad it didn't happen further down the street—in front of the May Company. From *them*, you can collect! Couldn't you have dragged yourself another 20 feet?"
WALTER MATTHAU giving legal advice to Howard McNear in
The Fortune Cookie (screenplay by Billy Wilder and I. A. L. Diamond)

"How not to turn the juice into wine."
Title of booklet of explicit instructions accompanying sparkling white
Taylor grape juice during Prohibition

"You've got to guard against speaking more clearly than you think."
Senator HOWARD H. BAKER, JR., repeating his father's advice to him after
his first trial (Washington Post, June 24, 1973)

"He that goes to law holds a wolf by the ears."
ROBERT BURTON, English clergyman
(Anatomy of Melancholy, 1621–57)

AFRICAN-AMERICANS

"A lot of African-Americans are very hesitant to talk about the struggle. They're almost embarrassed to talk about being poor. But talking about the struggle gives you strength, it gives you character. Sometimes we want to forget our heritage, which infuriates me because it's rich. You can build off of it. You can use it to get you through adversity. That's the way I use it."
BUCK WILLIAMS, power forward, Portland Trail Blazers basketball team,
on the work ethic he learned from his parents
(Wall Street Journal, June 11, 1992)

"I am a man of substance, of flesh and bone, fiber and liquids—and I might even be said to possess a mind. I am invisible, understand, simply because people refuse to see me."
RALPH ELLISON, writer (The Invisible Man, 1952, prologue)

"If you are born in America with a black skin, you're born in prison."
MALCOLM X, political leader (interview, June 1963)

"Whether I like it or not, it seems clear that blacks who succeed have a special obligation to try to live exemplary lives."

> ARTHUR ASHE, tennis player (Ashe and Rampersad, *Days of Grace*, 1993)

AGENTS

"Michael has developed a spiderweb of connections, though I don't mean that in a sinister sense. He realizes that his assets are relationships. He is always meshing—his agents, his clients, the studios, the networks, the small production companies. He has a capacity to relate to whole bunches of people in that web—and he always realizes that a twang over here has repercussions over there. So much of Mike's life is about sizing people up, seeing where the weaknesses are. He makes fewer mistakes in the area of people than anyone I know."

> ALFRED CHEECHI, co-chairman, NWA, Inc., the parent company of
> Northwest Airlines, on Michael Ovitz of the Creative Arts
> Agency, who brokered the acquisition of MCA by Matsushita
> (Bruck, "The World of Business," *The New Yorker*, October 9, 1991)

"A Packard? A Cadillac? And Jack, what would my commission be—a bicycle?"

> Attributed to IVAN KAHN, agent, on being told by Jack L. Warner that his
> client, Joe E. Brown, would only get the gift of a car to be in Max
> Reinhardt's *A Midsummer Night's Dream*

"There goes the sonuvabitch who takes 90 percent of my money."

> Hollywood line about the agent seeing a star actor walk by;
> New York line about the agent seeing a star writer walk by

"If God had an agent, the world wouldn't be built yet. It'd only be about Thursday."

> JERRY REYNOLDS, player personnel director, Sacramento Kings,
> commenting on how agents slow down negotiations
> (*Newsweek*, December 25, 1991)

"Mother, I am married to an American agent."

> CLAUDE RAINES to Madame Konstantin about Ingrid Bergman
> in *Notorious* (screenplay by Ben Hecht)

AGGRESSION

"He told the referees they didn't know what they were doing and just picked up the ball after a running play and moved it back . . .

I remember thinking, 'If the refs are intimidated by this guy, I'd better be.'"

> CALVIN HILL, Cleveland Browns fullback, on Chicago Bears linebacker
> Dick Butkus (*Sports Illustrated*, 1980)

"Being aggressive is a lot less risky in the end. Are you going to eat your lunch, or have your lunch eaten for you?"

> WILLIAM T. ESREY, chairman and CEO, The Sprint Corporation
> (*New York Times*, August 23, 1992)

"On matters of intonation and technicalities, I am more than a martinet—I am a martinetissimo."

> Attributed to LEOPOLD STOKOWSKI, conductor

"Be an aggressor. Don't sit back and wait to react."

> ALAN PAGE, justice, Minnesota Supreme Court; former
> defensive lineman, Minnesota Vikings, Chicago Bears, and
> University of Notre Dame (*Fortune*, May 18, 1992)

"I got chewed up. I thought of myself as aggressive until I went to Washington, but I didn't know what aggressive was. Washington is a city in which there's enormous turf fighting, in which internal politics can be rough and bitter. I did not know how to operate in that kind of environment, in part because I have no subtlety and in part because I'm basically a kind of nice human being."

> DONNA E. SHALALA, Secretary of Health and Human Services, on her
> early days in Washington as Assistant Secretary for Policy at HUD
> (*New York Daily News*, August 19, 1980)

AGING

"This is what fifty looks like. We've been lying so long, who would know?"

> GLORIA STEINEM, editor, *Ms.* magazine,
> after someone commented she didn't look 50 (interview, 1984)

"When the body gets worn out, the soul gets in shape."

> POPE JOHN XXIII (Michaels, *Pope John XXIII*, p. 17)

"I have no hatred for anybody, anymore. But your question reminds me of the story of an old fellow about my time of life who attended a prayer meeting at which the preacher spoke of brotherly love. When the preacher asked if there was anyone in the congregation who could honestly say he did not have a single enemy, this old fellow stood up and said, 'Right here, parson. I don't have one enemy.'

"The preacher commended him on the exemplary life he must have led, and then asked him to explain how he had come to be so universally beloved that he hadn't a single enemy. 'I outlived the bastards!' the old party shouted."

> President HERBERT HOOVER, on his 80th birthday, responding to a question about whether he was bitter about having been pilloried during and after his White House years (Hyman, *Washington Wind and Wisdom*, p. 36)

"Gray hair might look good on a CEO but not on an assistant vice-president. The thinking is that people who are not chiefs—people who are still at mid-level when they're in their fifties—must not be so good."

> ANNE C. VLADECK, a lawyer who has represented dismissed employees, summarizing corporate attitudes (*New York*, March 29, 1993)

"I'm in my anecdotage."

> CLARE BOOTHE LUCE, writer, at age 77 (*Town and Country*, January 1981)

"Here I am at the end of the road and at the top of the heap."

> POPE JOHN XXIII, on succeeding Pope Pius XII (*Time*, November 24, 1958)

"The machines and I date from World War II. All of us are too gear-stripped and rickety for a move. These are the kinds of thoughts I have in the final weeks before the end. Youth is here at the plant. I'm going to lose the lease on that as well."

> D. KEITH MANO, novelist and fourth-generation owner of a cement powder manufacturing plant that had to shut down on losing its lease in a gentrifying Long Island City, New York, neighborhood (*Business World*, *New York Times Magazine*, June 6, 1986)

"The older they get the better they were when they were younger."

> JIM BOUTON, major league pitcher (*Ball Four*, 1970)

"When you get old, everything is hurting. When I get up in the morning, it sounds like I'm making popcorn."

> LAWRENCE TAYLOR, 33 year-old linebacker, New York Giants (*Sports Illustrated*, October 26, 1992)

"I remember now that the toughest birthday I ever faced was my fortieth. It was a big symbol because it said goodbye, goodbye,

goodbye to youth. But I think that when one has passed through that age it's like breaking the sound barrier."

NORMAN CORWIN, writer and director, at age 82
(*Newsweek*, December 7, 1992)

"I'm not Walt Disney anymore."

WALT DISNEY, founder and CEO, Disney Co., 1965
(Greene, *The Man Behind the Magic*, p. 164)

"Remember what they say: after 40, it's patch, patch, patch."

WILLIAM J. MARTIN, M.D., professor of medicine, Indiana University
(to author, 1993)

"Too old to rock 'n' roll and too young to fly."

Lord KING, former chairman, British Airways, on Richard Branson, CEO,
Virgin Air (*New York Times*, February 28, 1993)

"I believe Moses was 80 when God first commissioned him for public service."

President RONALD REAGAN, on running for president at age 73
(address in Dixon, Illinois, February 6, 1984)

"I got up on the rack, drained the oil, and put in some additive. That's the trouble with a make and model my age, it's hard to get parts."

JOHN RIGGINS, Washington Redskins running back, on his back treatment
at age 35 (*Seattle Post-Intelligencer*, 1984)

"You've heard of golden parachutes for the boss? Now we'll need platinum handcuffs for the employees."

PAT CHOATE, vice president of policy analysis, TRW,
and author, on the economy's need to retain older workers
given, among other things, fewer young workers
entering the work force
(*Fortune*, January 30, 1989)

"I feel exactly the same as I've always felt: a lightly reined-in voracious beast."

JACK NICHOLSON, actor, on being 55
(*Newsweek*, December 7, 1992)

"Middle age is when you're faced with two temptations and you choose the one that will get you home by 9 o'clock."

President RONALD REAGAN, on his 66th birthday
(*Washington Post*, February 7, 1977)

AGREEMENT

"Agree, for the law is costly."

WILLIAM CAMDEN, English historian (*Remains*, 1603)

"If you don't agree with what I'm saying, then it isn't necessarily what I mean."

Agent to screenwriter Larry Gelbart
(Randall and Mindlin, *Which Reminds Me*, p. 155)

"Just because I disagree with you doesn't mean I'm disagreeable."

SAM GOLDWYN, film producer (Marx, *Goldwyn*, 1976)

"I desire what is good; therefore everyone who does not agree with me is a traitor."

Attributed to GEORGE III of England

ALCOHOL

"Imagine the outcry from the black community if a brewer were to market a liquor entitled Martin Luther King Beer, or from the Christian community for a Jesus Christ White Wine."

GREGG BOURLAND, chairman, Cheyenne River Sioux tribe in South
Dakota, on Hornell Brewing's naming its new malt liquor Crazy Horse
(*Fortune*, June 15, 1992)

"Always do sober what you said you'd do drunk. That will teach you to keep your mouth shut."

ERNEST HEMINGWAY, writer (Winokur, *Friendly Advice*, p. 34)

"It's a naive domestic Burgundy without any breeding, but I think you'll be amused by its presumption."

JAMES THURBER, humorist, caption for a *New Yorker* cartoon
(March 27, 1939)

"I like my convictions undiluted, same as I do my bourbon."

GEORGE BRENT in *Jezebel* (screenplay by Clements Ripley, Abem Finkel,
and John Huston)

"Get me the brand, and I'll send a barrel to my other generals."

President ABRAHAM LINCOLN on being told that General Grant drank
too much whiskey (remark at a cabinet meeting, 1864)

ALWAYS

"Always stay in with the outs."

DAVID HALBERSTAM, writer

"Always make an audience suffer as much as possible."
Attributed to ALFRED HITCHCOCK, filmmaker

"Always do right! This will gratify some and astonish the rest."
MARK TWAIN, to the Young People's Society, Greenpoint Presbyterian
Church, Brooklyn, New York, 1901 (a favorite quote of Harry S Truman)
(McCullough, *Truman*, p. 403)

"Son, always give em a good show, and travel first class."
WALTER HUSTON, to his son John (quoted in *John Huston*, documentary by
Joni Levin, producer, and Frank Martin, director)

AMBITION

"Some of us are becoming the men we wanted to marry."
GLORIA STEINEM, editor, *Ms.* magazine (*Ms.*, July/August, 1982)

"I want to put a ding in the universe."
STEVEN JOBS, pitchman for the Apple computer designed by his friend
Steve Wozniak; this *ding* refers to spiritual powers—to make the
computer a *Ding an sich*, a thing in itself, whose sheer potential to do
things overrode the importance of anything it could actually do
(Patton, *Made in USA*, p. 346)

"I want to be at the table and a player when they move the pieces
around in America."
RUPERT MURDOCH, chairman, News Corporation,
on wanting to buy *Time* magazine in 1989 (Shawcross, *Murdoch*, p. 353)

"I ain't going to be a preacher or lawyer. I'm going to be a
businessman and make my pile."
"BUCK" DUKE, then a dirt-poor North Carolina schoolboy, boasting to his
teachers, before amassing an enormous fortune in tobacco and power
(*Wall Street Journal*, Centennial Edition, 1989)

"We can teach a kid to hit; we can teach a kid to throw. The one
thing we can't teach is desire. I look for kids with desire."
TOM GREENWADE, New York Yankees baseball scout who found Mickey
Mantle and others (*Look*, April 15, 1958)

"A female Fred Astaire."
LIZA MINNELLI, actress, responding to fashion designer Halston's query
about what she wanted to look like (*Simply Halston*, p. 121)

"I started at the top and worked my way down."
Attributed to ORSON WELLES, actor and director

"The noble Brutus
Hath told you Caesar was ambitious;
If it were so, it was a grievous fault;
And grievously hath Caesar answered it."

SHAKESPEARE (*Julius Caesar*, III)

"I hitched my wagon to an electron rather than the proverbial star."

DAVID SARNOFF, chairman, RCA (*New York Times*, April 4, 1958)

"I wanted to be czar."

CHARLES M. SCHWAB, investor, U.S. Steel,
after his extravagant lifestyle had taken its toll on his fortune; he died
penniless in 1939 (*Wall Street Journal*, Centennial Edition, 1989)

"To strive, to seek, to find, but not to yield."   ALFRED TENNYSON ("Ulysses")

"Ambition—the foulest strumpet of all."

CHARLES LAUGHTON as Bligh in *Mutiny on the Bounty*
(screenplay by Talbot Jennings, Jules Furthman, and Carey Wison)

"Ambition is the last refuge of the failure."

OSCAR WILDE, writer (*Phrases and Philosophies for
the Use of the Young*, 1894)

"When that the poor have cried, Caesar hath wept;
Ambition should be made of sterner stuff."

SHAKESPEARE (*Julius Caesar*, III, ii, 97)

"In men of the highest character and noblest genius there is to be found an insatiable desire for honor, command, power, and glory."

CICERO (*De Officis*, 1)

AMERICA

"In the 18th century, Voltaire said that every man had two countries: his own and France. In the 20th century, that has come to be true of the United States."

RUPERT MURDOCH, chairman, News Corporation
(speech, New York City, November 9, 1989)

"My generation has made America the most affluent country on earth. It has tackled, head-on, a racial problem, which no nation on earth in the history of mankind has dared to do. It has

publicly declared war on poverty and it has gone to the moon;
it has desegregated schools and abolished polio; it has presided
over the beginning of what is probably the greatest social and
economic revolution in man's history. It has begun these things,
not finished them. It has declared itself, and committed itself,
and taxed itself, and damn near run itself into the ground in the
cause of social justice and reform."

> K. Ross Toole, professor of history, University of Montana,
> who also noted he was "tired of the tyranny of spoiled brats"
> (quoted in Wriston, *Risk and Other Four-Letter Words*, p. 6)

"The 20th century was the American Century. The 21st century
will also be the American Century."

> Mishone, aide to former Japanese Prime Minister Nakasone
> (*The Economist*, special issue on Japan, 1988)

"We've been Gapped, linened, and Lancomed."

> Peggy Noonan, speechwriter, on the sameness in American life
> (*New York Times*, August 23, 1992)

"The universal nation."

> Ben Wattenberg, political analyst
> (*Wall Street Journal*, October 28, 1992)

"A man went looking for America and couldn't find it
anywhere."

> Underline advertising the movie *Easy Rider* (1969)

"America has many contradictions, but none greater than the fact
that it was founded by puritans and yet invented tolerance. The
tension between the busy-bodies of 1620 and the free spirits of
1776 has often marked American history: the puritan had the
upper hand in Prohibition, the permissive had it at Woodstock."

> Editorial (*The Economist*, July 20, 1991)

"When I was a graduate student at Harvard, I learned about
showers and central heating. Ten years later, I learned about
breakfast meetings. These are America's three great contributions
to civilization."

> Mervyn A. King, professor, London School of Economics
> (*New York Times*, March 5, 1987)

"Of course, America had often been discovered before, but it had
always been hushed up."

> Oscar Wilde, writer
> (*Personal Impressions of America*, 1883)

"What has become of the descendants of the irresponsible adventurers, the scapegrace sons, the bond servants, the redemptionists and the indentured maidens, the undesirables, and even the criminals, which made up, not all, of course, but nevertheless a considerable part of, the earliest emigrants to these virgin countries? They have become the leaders of the thought of the world, the vanguard in the march of progress, the inspirers of liberty, the creators of national prosperity, the sponsors of universal education and enlightenment."

> WILLIAM RANDOLPH HEARST, newpaper publisher, testifying before the American Crime Study Commission, May 19, 1929

"Don't get the idea I'm one of these goddamn radicals. Don't get the idea I'm knocking the American system."

> Al Capone, gangster, interview c. 1929 with Claud Cockburn
> (*In Time of Trouble*, 1956, chapter 16)

"In America the geography is sublime, but the men are not; the inventions are excellent, but the inventors one is sometimes ashamed of."

> Ralph Waldo Emerson, essayist (*The Conduct of Life*, VII, 1860)

ANALYSIS

"Never let your data get in the way of your analysis."

> THEODORE J. LOWI, John L. Senior professor of political science, Cornell University (to author, 1968)

"Mush has a strength all of its own."

> ROBERT LEITMAN, senior vice president, Louis Harris and Co., on the staying power of soft analysis (to author, 1986)

ANARCHY

"Tap the energy of the anarchist and he will be the one to push your company ahead."

> ANITA RODDICK, founder and CEO, Body Shop (Peters, *Liberation*, p. 595)

"So much of economic success—Silicon Valley, Taipei, Hong Kong, Guangdong, Hollywood—has to do with anarchy. The 'magic' of Silicon Valley lies as much in the bars and the squash courts as in Stanford University's fertile labs. It is the anarchy itself that 'produces' the high volume of chance connections, the oft-told motivational fables. It is the energy from the critical

mass—a statistical artifact, product of the law of large numbers—
that makes Silicon Valley what it is, and makes it almost
uncopyable."
                           TOM PETERS, business consultant (*Liberation*, p. 500)

"Things fall part; the centre cannot hold;
Mere anarchy is loosed upon the world. . . .
The best lack all conviction, while the worst
Are full of passionate intensity."
               WILLIAM BUTLER YEATS, Irish poet ("The Second Coming," as cited in
                    Clark Clifford memoir, *Counsel to the President*, p. 567)

ANGST

"This shouldn't cause any tsoris."
               JAMES A. BAKER III, Secretary of State, commenting on a procedural
               matter to a member of the Israeli team during the negotiations leading to
               the Madrid conference in 1991 (quoted by William Safire, *New York Times*,
               who noted that "This epochal understanding of Yiddish angst by a
               starchy diplomat from Texas augured well for the opening of the face-to-
               face meetings between Israelis and Arabs.")

ANSWERS

"Stuff."
               BILL CLINTON, President-elect, answering a reporter who asked what he
               had been working on (*Newsweek*, December 14, 1992)

"The Trinitron TV. Why? Because we bet the company on that
basic technology, and in 23 years nobody else has been able to
match it."
               MASARU IBUKA, founder and honorary chairman, Sony, who invented
               the pocket-sized transistor radio, the VCR, and the Walkman, naming his
               favorite product (*Fortune*, February 24, 1992)

"Surgery."
               JOHN HUSTON, director, who'd had several rounds of surgery, when asked
               to what he attributed his longevity (quoted by actor Robert Mitchum in
               John Huston, documentary by Joni Levin, producer,
               and Frank Martin, director)

"Investments. I guess you would say investments."
               PAUL MELLON, of the Pittsburgh Mellons, whose horse won the 1993
               Kentucky Derby, responding to a British reporter's question of how he
               made a living (*New York Times*, May 2, 1993)

"Out to the airports."
               New York detective, on being asked where the waterfront hoods had
               gone (*New York Daily News*, August 2, 1987)

"T-bills."   Retail consultant, when asked what traditional department stores should
do to generate profits (*New York Times*, December 30, 1991)

"Insomnia."
An executive's response to ITT CEO Harold Geneen's 3:00 A.M. question
about what management talent was most important to success at ITT,
known for round-the-clock meetings (*The Nation*, November 17, 1984)

"No, but they gave me one anyway."
ELDEN CAMPBELL, center for the Los Angeles Lakers, on being asked if he
had earned a degree from Clemson University
(*The Economist*, December 5, 1992)

"Then we would have to take only half the boos each."
TOM KELLY, Minnesota Twins manager, on why he made pitcher Pat
Mahomes walk off the field with him while the Twins were losing 17–1
to the Detroit Tigers (*Sports Illustrated*, May 10, 1993)

"Well, no, that would be like being put in charge of the Maginot
Line."
FELIX ROHATYN, investment banker, responding to a journalist's query
about whether he would like to be Secretary of the Treasury
during the Carter Administration (interview, 1978)

"The people. Could you patent the sun?"
JONAS E. SALK, American virologist, on being asked who owned the
patent on his polio vaccine (Bolton, *Famous Men of Science*, p. 282)

"It was involuntary. They sank my boat."
President JOHN F. KENNEDY's answer to "How did you become a war
hero?" (quoted in Schlesinger, *A Thousand Days*, 1965)

"I have, sir; just like you would a load of potatoes."
HUEY P. LONG responding to "Governor, do you mean to tell us that you
bought and paid for our Representatives?" (*Official Journal of the House of
Representatives*, State of Louisiana, March 20, 1929)

"Cowboy."   A LEO BURNETT copywriter answering Burnett's "What's the most
masculine type of man?" Burnett said his job was to make the "sissified"
Marlboro cigarette macho (*New York Times Style*, October 13, 1992)

"Honey, I just forgot to duck."
JACK DEMPSEY, telling his wife by telephone from his dressing room why
he lost the heavyweight title to Gene Tunney (September 23, 1926)

"Humility in the presence of a good idea."
ALBERT LASKER, the great advertising man, when asked what was the best
asset a person could have (Ogilvy, *Ogilvy on Advertising*, p. 16)

"I've had the luxury of getting cold-cocked in the face every two and a half years. That forces me to consider my place in the universe."

> TOM HANKS, on being asked whether he considered himself a master of the universe like his *Bonfire* character, investment banker Sherman McCoy (Salamon, *The Devil's Candy*, p. 397)

"Because we were schmucks, that's why."

> WALTER YETNIKOFF, president, CBS Records, in response to why CBS missed signing Janet Jackson—her album *Control* sold 8 million copies— after its success with Michael (*Hit Men*, p. 187)

"By air conditioning."

> Warren Beatty's BUGSY SIEGEL, responding to a fellow gangster's saying, "Ben, I don't get it. The Hoover Dam and fucking are connected how?" Siegel's plan to build Las Vegas came in part from his realization that electricity would be available in a state that permitted gambling, in the movie, *Bugsy* (screenplay by James Toback)

"What's left of her."

> Attributed to TALLULAH BANKHEAD, actress, when asked late in life if she were Tallulah Bankhead

"His gloves, dear: never been hit by an eye in me life."

> Prizefighter TERRY DOWNES, answering a woman reporter who asked whether he watched an opponent's eyes or gloves (Sherrin, *Cutting Edge*, p. 204)

"Because it had gotten him out of every hole he'd ever been in."

> Henry Ford to President Woodrow Wilson, relating Ford's favorite Model-T joke on why a man had asked to be buried with his Model T (Patton, *Made in USA*, p. 177)

APPRECIATION

"Please arrange ovation."

> GLORIA SWANSON, actress, wiring Paramount Studio on her return from France

"If I'd gotten this much applause in Hollywood, I never would have left."

> President RONALD REAGAN to Tip O'Neill during his first address to Congress (January 1981)

"When I drive, the fans still wave to me, and all of their fingers show."

> WAYNE FONTES, Detroit Lions coach, saying his job is not in jeopardy (*Sports Illustrated*, September 30, 1991)

"I appreciate your welcome. As the cow said to the Maine farmer, 'Thanks for a warm hand on a cold morning.'"

> President JOHN F. KENNEDY (speech, 1960)

ARROGANCE

"There but for the grace of God, goes God."

HERMAN J. MANKIEWICZ, screenwriter, on Orson Welles
(New York Times, October 11, 1985)

"Early in life I had to choose between honest arrogance and hypocritical humility. I chose honest arrogance and have seen no occasion to change."

FRANK LLOYD WRIGHT, architect (Frank Lloyd Wright, p. 376)

ART

"Being good in business is the most fascinating kind of art."

ANDY WARHOL, artist (Observer, March 1, 1987)

"The artist can like hedonism but he himself cannot be a hedonist."

DAVID HOCKNEY, artist (New York Times, January 21, 1993)

"The only works of art America has given are her plumbing and her bridges."

MARCEL DUCHAMP, cubist-futurist painter (quoted in Gies,
Bridges and Men, p. 306)

ARTISTS

"True artists, whatever smiling faces they may show you, are obsessive, driven people—whether driven by some mania or driven by some high, noble vision."

JOHN GARDNER (The Art of Fiction, 1984)

"Real artists ship."

Attributed to STEVEN P. JOBS, founder, Apple Computer, and quoted by
Nicholas Callaway, founder, Callaway Editions, a publisher who
combines printed books with compact disks
(New York Times, October 19, 1992)

"The world will never be happy until all men have the souls of artists—I mean when they take pleasure in their jobs."

Attributed to AUGUSTE RODIN, sculptor

"We are a business concern and not patrons of the arts."

Attributed to DAVID O. SELZNICK, producer, 1938

ASSETS

"The movie business is the only business in the world where the assets go home at night."

Attributed to Dorothy Parker, writer

"Activist shareholders come forth to do battle for control of mismanaged corporations and to put the assets of these corporations to better uses."

T. Boone Pickens, raider of Gulf Oil, Phillips Petroleum, Unocal Corp.,
and other firms (Olive, Business Babble, p. 4)

ATTENTION

"Breaking the attention span at a company that doesn't have layers of management is a big-time cost. It can kill you."

John Wallace, chairman, Wallace Co., a family-owned distributor of
industrial pipes and valves in Houston, criticizing the effort that went
into winning a Baldridge award in 1990; they entered Chapter 11
in 1991 (Fortune, March 9, 1992)

"He has a short attention span. You sort of have to edit your friendship into sound bites."

Candice Bergen, actress, on Herbert Allen, investment banker and
chairman, Allen and Co. Inc. (Esquire, June 1991)

"When things haven't gone well for you, call in a secretary or a staff man and chew him out. You will sleep better and they will appreciate the attention."

President Lyndon B. Johnson (quoted in People, February 2, 1987)

"I have always believed in Mark Twain's philosophy that you should put all your eggs in one basket and watch that basket."

Stew Leonard, grocer, resisting pressures to open a second store
beyond his first in Norwalk, Connecticut; persuaded by his son,
he eventually opened one in Danbury
(Wall Street Journal, October 16, 1992)

"Proceed. You have my biased attention."

Justice Learned Hand, to an attorney who asked to review a motion
already heard (recalled on his death, August 18, 1961)

"Pay no attention to that man behind the curtain . . . the . . . uh Great Oz has spoken!"

Frank Morgan to Judy Garland in The Wizard of Oz
(screenplay by Noel Langley, Florence Ryerson, and Edgar Allen Woolf)

AUTHORITY

"It ain't nothin' until I call it."
BILL KLEM, legendary baseball umpire
(Harwell, *Ernie Harwell's Diamond Gems*, 1991)

"And keep in mind, I'm the guy who signs your paychecks."
GEORGE STEINBRENNER, owner, New York Yankees,
after asking his team to vote for drug testing in 1985
(Coffey, *The Wit & Wisdom of George Steinbrenner*, p. 63)

"The buck stops with the guy who signs the checks."
RUPERT MURDOCH, chairman, News Corporation (*All About Money*, p. 261)

AUTOMOBILE

"Henry Ford did not initially build a car equipped with seat belts or air bags, nor one designed to meet environmental standards. Now the need to protect safety and the environment makes it necessary for consumers to pay much higher prices—allegedly for cars but in fact the automobile buyer is paying in part for clean air. Without this externality, the price of the car would of course be much lower. But by including clean air in the price—which is probably the best way to exact payment—we obscure the enormous increase in productivity achieved in the output of automobiles."
JUANITA KREPS, Duke University economist, former Secretary of
Commerce (quoted by Wriston, *Risk and Other Four-Letter Words*, p. 125)

"If Detroit is right . . . there is little wrong with the American car that is not wrong with the American Public."
JOHN KETAS (Sherrin, *Cutting Edge*, p. 53)

AVARICE

"Avarice, the spur of industry."
DAVID HUME (*Essays. Of Civil Liberty*, 1741)

"The avarice of mankind is insatiable."
ARISTOTLE (*Politics*)

BAD

"I believe my bookie, who says business has never been so bad, more than I believe the President."
JERRY DELLA FEMINA, president, Della Femina, McNamee Inc.
(*New York Times*, November 5, 1991)

"You're telling us things are so bad because they are so good and they will get better as soon as they get worse?"

John Sununu, then governor of New Hampshire, to James Baker,
then Secretary of the Treasury, who said "yes'
(*The 776 Stupidest Things Ever Said*, Doubleday, 1993)

"When we got into office, the thing that surprised me most was to find that things were just as bad as we'd been saying they were."

President John F. Kennedy
(speech at White House, May 27, 1961)

"Bad times have a scientific value. These are occasions a good learner would not miss."

Ralph Waldo Emerson, essayist (*The Conduct of Life*,
"Considerations by the Way," 1860)

"I'm not a bad man, just a very bad wizard."

Wizard in *The Wizard of Oz* (screenplay by Noel Langley,
Florence Ryerson, and Edgar Allen Woolf)

"He won't hit anything bad but don't give him anything good."

Advice given to pitcher Bobby Shantz on how to pitch to Ted Williams.
(quoted by George F. Will, *New York Times Book Review*, April 7, 1991)

"When a man's partner is killed, he's supposed to do something about it. It doesn't make any difference what you thought of him. He was your partner, and you're supposed to do something about it. As it happens, we're in the detective business. Well, when one of your organization gets killed, it's — it's bad business to let the killer get away with it. Bad all around. Bad for every detective everywhere."

Humphrey Bogart to Mary Astor in *The Maltese Falcon*
(screenplay by John Huston)

BANKERS AND FINANCIERS

"Lifelong practices make {bankers} the most romantic and least realistic of men. It is so much their stock in trade that their position should not be questioned, that they do not even question it themselves until it is too late. Like the honest citizens they are, they feel a proper indignation at the perils of the wicked world in which they live—when the perils mature; but they do not foresee them."

John Maynard Keynes, economist
(*The General Theory of Employment, Interest and Money*, 1936)

"I had assumed that the financial elements like the banks and major bondholders would have a very strong desire to save the company. In fact, they often wished to be rid of the problem and wanted to move toward liquidation. Once they are secured they don't care."

> RYAL R. POPPA, CEO, Storage Technology, on the rescue process
> (*New York Times*, March 20, 1992)

"Bankers think of black-owned businesses as beauty salons and barbecue stands."

> PATSY BROWN, general contractor and founder, Papa's Grocery, a
> top-of-the-line store in South Central Los Angeles
> (*Business Week*, "Reinventing America," November 1992, p. 191)

"You and I are the same. We both screw people for money."

> RICHARD GERE, investment banker, to prostitute Julia Roberts in
> *Pretty Woman* (screenplay by J. F. Lawton)

"This is the way the world ends, not with a whim, but a banker."

> PAUL DESMOND, saxophonist, watching a former girlfriend on the arm of
> a banker (quoted in Rothschild, *Going for Broke*, p. 15)

"When Karl Marx
Found the phrase 'financial sharks'
He sang a Te Deum
In the British Museum."

> W. H. AUDEN, poet, clerihew

"A banker! A banker! I thought this business was just for furriers."

> Attributed to MARCUS LOEW, on hearing that Joseph Kennedy
> had bought into the film business, 1926

"Unscrupulous money changers."

> President FRANKLIN D. ROOSEVELT on bankers
> (First Inaugural Address, March 4, 1933)

BANKRUPTCY

"Capitalism without bankruptcy is like Christianity without hell."

> FRANK BORMAN, CEO, Eastern Airlines
> (*U.S. News and World Report*, April 21, 1986)

"How can they say I'm bankrupt? I owe a billion dollars."

> WILLIAM ZECKENDORF, SR., New York developer
> (Reich, *Financier: André Meyer*, 1982)

"Bankruptcy is not for bankrupts. If you want to use Chapter 11 to reorganize a business, you have to have a war chest. You've got to have some money available to you immediately."
                    HARVEY MILLER, bankruptcy lawyer (*Harper's*, March 1992)

"People say the city should be run like a business. If it were a business, it would have moved out. It would have gone south."
                    THOMAS J. WHITE, city alderman, Bridgeport, Conn.,
                    on the city's filing for bankruptcy (*New York Times*, June 10, 1991)

"We saved New York City from bankruptcy . . . by being ruthlessly realistic about the mess we were dealing with and by assuming, quite correctly, that when things look very bad, they usually turn out to be worse than they look."   FELIX ROHATYN, investment banker
                    (commencement address, Middlebury College, 1982)

"'How did you go bankrupt?' Bill asked.
'Two ways,' Mike said. 'Gradually and then suddenly.'"
                    ERNEST HEMINGWAY, writer (*The Sun Also Rises*, 1926)

"Bankruptcy in my opinion ever was and yet is considered as a crime, whatever tradesmen may now think of it. It was anciently punished with corporal punishment."
                    JUSTICE ABNEY (*Trive v. Webber*, 1744)

"It has been long my deliberate judgment that all bankrupts, of whatsoever denomination, civil or religious, ought to be hanged."
                    CHARLES LAMB, writer (letter to Bernard Barton, December 8, 1829)

"If the nation is living within its income its credit is good. If in some crisis it lives beyond its income for a year or two it can usually borrow temporarily on reasonable terms. But if, like the spendthrift, it throws discretion to the winds, is willing to make no sacrifice at all in spending, extends its taxing up to the limit of the people's power to pay, and continues to pile up deficits, it is on the road to bankruptcy."
                    President FRANKLIN D. ROOSEVELT (speech at Pittsburgh, October 19, 1932)

BANKS

"We rob banks."   WARREN BEATTY and FAYE DUNAWAY as *Bonnie and Clyde*
                    (screenplay by Daniel Newman and Robert Benton)

"Hey, I liked the '60s okay. But all my friends who were blowing up the Bank of America back then are now working there."

JAY LENO, comedian

"Banks are here to help the people who want to come up in the world."

DAVID ROCKEFELLER, investment banker (interview, 1977)

"The banks couldn't afford me. That's why I had to be in business for myself."

SAM GOLDWYN, film producer (Marx, *Goldwyn*, 1976)

BARGAIN

"This is the age of bargain hunters. If it had been this way in biblical times, we'd probably have been offered another Commandment free if we had accepted the first ten."

EARL WILSON, newspaper columnist (*Reader's Digest*, 1978)

"I'm being marked down? I've been kidnapped by K Mart!"

BETTE MIDLER to Helen Slater, bemoaning her reduced ransom in *Ruthless People* (screenplay by Dale Launer)

"My old father used to have a saying: If you make a bad bargain, hug it all the tighter."

ABRAHAM LINCOLN (letter to Joshua Speed, February 25, 1842)

BASEBALL

"The reason baseball calls itself a game, I believe, is that it is too screwed up to be a business."

JIM BOUTON, former major league pitcher (*Sports Illustrated*, January 4, 1993)

"Baseball fits America so well because it embodies the interplay of individual and group that we so love, and because it expresses our longing for the rule of law while licensing our resentment of law givers."

BARTLETT GIAMATTI, commissioner of baseball (*New York Times*, May 31, 1992)

BATTLE

"Not every battle is Armageddon."

WALTER WRISTON, former CEO and chairman, Citicorp (*Risk and Other Four-Letter Words*, p. 3)

"As Faulkner said, every so often the dog has to battle the bear just so he can call himself a dog again."
KEN KESEY, writer (New York Times, November 29, 1991)

BEAT

"We are not a womb-to-tomb outfit. We are not like big companies, although some of our new employees come to us and say, 'Let's do the things big companies do.' My answer to that is, 'Why should we copy the people we just beat?'"
WILLIAM G. MCGOWAN, founder and CEO, MCI Communications
(Henderson,Winners, p. 191)

"Why, if you listened to our guys, you'd think we were kicking the shit out of Philip Morris. It reminds me of the boxer who's getting beat up something awful and going back to his corner at the end of the round saying, 'He never laid a glove on me.' The trainer says, 'Well, keep an eye on the referee, because somebody's kicking the shit out of you.'"
ROSS JOHNSON, CEO, RJR Nabisco, telling his favorite story illustrating
RJR's misplaced confidence in its fight against rival Philip Morris
(Burrough and Helyar, Barbarians at the Gate, p. 73)

"A lot more people beat me now."
Former President DWIGHT D. EISENHOWER, on his golf game since leaving
the White House (recalled on his death, March 28, 1969)

"Walt never thought he was beaten at anything—ever."
LILLIAN DISNEY on husband Walt
(quoted in The Man Behind the Magic, p. 3)

"Listen, girl, I can count the great horses I ever saw on the fingers of one hand, and every one of 'em had a look in his eyes—like an eagle. You can't beat a horse with that look. You just can't beat him. And this colt's got it—the look of eagles!"
WALTER BRENNAN to Loretta Young in Kentucky
(screenplay by Lamar Trotti and John Taintor Foote)

BEAUTY

"For all the talk about its purity of shape and embodiment of the beauty inherent in function, the clipper ship was given its form by competition: it was capitalism made physical. Its success came not from the breaking down of production into individual processes, nor from the division of labor, but from a concentrated, plastic modeling of the form toward a single goal: Speed. Speed, to reach San Francisco or the Orient in record time. Speed, to hold off the attractions of steam packets for a few more years."

PHIL PATTON (*Made in USA*, p. 151)

"More art in a good shiny spark-plug than in all the fat Venus de Milos they ever turned out."

Sam Dodsworth's boss (to whom he had sold his car company) trying to discourage him from quitting the business and traveling to see the great works of Europe (Sinclair Lewis, *Dodsworth*, 1929)

"Beauty is the splendor of Truth.

ST. AUGUSTINE; a favorite saying of architect Ludwig Mies van der Rohe (*Chicago Daily News*, March 27, 1968)

BELIEVE

"We had a near maniacal belief that it would fly."

SCOTT ABBOTT, a former Montreal journalist who, with partner Chris Haney, made up the game Trivial Pursuit in 1980 (Henderson, *Winners*, p. 7)

"If you promise not to believe everything your child says happens at this school, I'll promise not to believe everything he says happens at home."

An English schoolmaster's note to parents (*Wall Street Journal*, January 4, 1985)

"We didn't exactly believe your story, Miss O'Shaughnessy. We believed your $200. You paid us more than if you'd been telling us the truth and enough more to make it all right."

HUMPHREY BOGART to Mary Astor in *The Maltese Falcon* (screenplay by John Huston)

"I believe that every right implies a responsibility; every opportunity an obligation; every possession a duty."

JOHN D. ROCKEFELLER, JR., financier (*Time*, July 21, 1941)

BEST

"The best ballplayer's the one who doesn't think he made good. He keeps trying to convince you."

CASEY STENGEL, baseball manager (*The Gospel According to Casey*, p. 152)

"Kurt Vonnegut said, 'The best of Bob and Ray is virtually indistinguishable from the worst.' I'm sure he meant that as a compliment."

BOB ELLIOTT, comedian, on his radio partnership
(*New York Times*, May 7, 1992)

"The best money could buy."

Governor HUEY LONG's description of the Louisiana legislature
(quoted in *Wall Street Journal*, November 1991)

"Please do not Shoot the Pianist
He is doing His Best."

Sign seen in a Leadville, Colorado, saloon by Oscar Wilde, writer
(*Personal Impressions of America*, 1883)

BETRAY

"The job of a writer is to betray . . . "

GRAHAM GREENE, English writer (quoted in Viertel, *Dangerous Friends: At Large with Huston and Hemingway in the Fifties*, frontispiece)

"It is harder for someone to screw you if they've had dinner at your house."

Attributed to SUE MENGERS, Hollywood agent

"I couldn't be fonder of you if you were my own son, but . . . "

SIDNEY GREENSTREET, in *The Maltese Falcon*
(screenplay by John Huston, quoted in Stone, *April Fools*, 1990)

"To betray, you must first belong. I never belonged."

KIM PHILBY, British subject who spied for the Soviet Union
(Winokur, *True Confessions*, p. 249)

"I'd rather have my hand cut off than betray the interests of a client."

Erle Stanley Gardner's PERRY MASON
(*The Case of the Singing Skirt*, 1959, p. 128)

BIG

"Stand back, honey. I don't know how big this is going to get."

Allegedly ADAM's first words to Eve, as quoted by Wall Street analysts
asked to predict how high a certain stock would rise
(Stone, *April Fools*, 1990, p. 72)

"Tall men come down to my height when I hit 'em in the body."

JACK DEMPSEY, heavyweight champion (Sherrin, *Cutting Edge*, p. 204)

"The Bell System is like a damn big dragon. You kick it in the tail, and two years later it feels it in its head."

FREDERICK R. KAPPEL, chairman, AT&T (*Look*, August 28, 1962)

"We're bigger than U.S. Steel."

HYMAN ROTH to Don Michael Corleone (Al Pacino) in *Godfather II*, on the combined power of the Jewish and Italian gangs (screenplay by Francis Ford Coppola and Mario Puzo)

"We're the little skiff slicing through the water, as the big ocean liners are throwing off furniture and bodies to stay afloat."

BARRY DILLER, CEO, Fox Television, on his fourth network versus the big three (quoted in Shawcross, *Murdoch*, p. 328)

"Whatever his weight in pounds, shillings and ounces, He always seems bigger because of his bounces."

A. A. MILNE, *The House at Pooh Corner* (quoted in Bower, *Maxwell, The Outsider*, on Robert Maxwell's characterization as "The Bouncing Czech")

"I am big. It's the *pictures* that got small."

GLORIA SWANSON rebuking William Holden in *Sunset Boulevard* (screenplay by Charles Brackett, Billy Wilder, and D. M. Marshman, Jr.)

"I never answer letters from large organizations."

JASON ROBARDS in *A Thousand Clowns* (screenplay by Herb Gardner)

"Why only twelve? Go out and get thousands."

SAM GOLDWYN, film producer, on restaging the Last Supper (Marx, *Goldwyn*, 1976)

"A ball player's got to be kept hungry to become a big leaguer. That's why no boy from a rich family ever made the big leagues."

JOE DIMAGGIO, New York Yankee outfielder (*New York Times*, April 30, 1961)

"He used to be a big shot."

GLADYS GEORGE weeping over the gunned-down James Cagney in the closing line of *The Roaring Twenties* (screenplay by Richard Macaulay, Jerry Wald, and Robert Rossen)

"One of the dangers of bigness is the smothering of the individual. This is not avoiding bigness. Few could have an automobile if we didn't have General Motors. We must find how an individual finds increased personal freedom and increased opportunity for achievement in a big society."

J. IRWIN MILLER, CEO, Cummins Engine (quoted in Moskin, *Morality in America*, p. 41)

"I like thinking big. I always have. To me, it's very simple; if you're going to be thinking anyway, you might as well think big."

DONALD TRUMP, developer
(*The Art of the Deal*, 1987)

BLAME

"Senator Goldwater confesses that he made some campaign mistakes in New Hampshire. He shouldn't blame himself, though. A man can't always get laryngitis when he needs it."

FLETCHER KNEBEL, journalist, on Senator Barry Goldwater's having
been called an extremist because of his speeches and remarks
(quoted in Hyman, *Washington Wind and Wisdom*, p. 102)

"It ain't the water cooler which is getting you out."

CASEY STENGEL, manager, New York Yankees, to Mickey Mantle
who kicked a water cooler after striking out
(*The Gospel According to Casey*, p. 102)

"I do not know the method of drawing up an indictment against a whole people."

EDMUND BURKE, British statesman, on the American Revolution
(*Second Speech on Conciliation with America.
The Thirteen Resolutions*, March 22, 1775)

BOARD OF DIRECTORS

"Pet rocks."

H. ROSS PEROT, founder, Electronic Data System, which he sold
to General Motors, on his fellow GM board members
(*Newsweek*, November 2, 1992)

"Après moi, le Board."

GEORGE BALLANCHINE, director, New York City Ballet,
predicting board dominance after his death
(*The New Yorker*, May 10, 1993)

BOASTING

"Boast is always a cry of despair except in the young, when it is a cry of hope."

BERNARD BERENSON, Renaissance art expert
(quoted in Morra, *Conversations with Berenson*, 1965)

BOOKS

"Americans like fat books and thin women."

RUSSELL BAKER, writer (*The Writer's Quotation Book*, p. 6)

"I wouldn't pay $50,000 for any damn book, any time."
JACK WARNER, turning down Gone With the Wind
(Wilk, The Wit and Wisdom of Hollywood, 1971)

"If my books had been any worse I would not have been invited to Hollywood, and if they had been any better I would not have come."
RAYMOND CHANDLER, writer (Winokur, True Confessions, p. 264)

BOOK PUBLISHING

"Too often book publishing takes its cue from Greek mythology: Expose the book on a hillside and hope some shepherd takes it home before it dies."
IVAN BERGER, novelist, on the lack of good marketing of most books
(New York Times, April 20, 1992)

"You know how it is in the kid's book world; it's just bunny eat bunny."
Anonymous

"Calvin Trillin once proposed that 'the advance for a book should be at least as much as the cost of the lunch at which it was discussed.' When he asked an editor what he thought of this formula, he was told that it was 'unrealistic.'"
WILLARD ESPY, writer (The Writer's Quotation Book, p. 63)

"The thing about being in publishing is that you must seem to be interested in art but imprisoned in a system that only values money. The superior *chic*, of course, is to appear interested only in money."
PETER RICE, a book editor in Paula Fox's novel
(The Widow's Children, p. 53)

BORE

"The secret of being a bore is to tell everything."
VOLTAIRE, as quoted by Slim Keith, celebrated and
much-married beauty, on holding some things back
(Slim: Memories of a Rich and Imperfect Life, p. 306)

"You cannot bore people into buying your product."
DAVID OGILVY, former chairman, Ogilvy and Mather
(Ogilvy on Advertising, p. 80)

"Boredom is the secret ailment of large-scale organization. Logan Pearsall Smith once said that boredom can rise to the level of mystical experience. I believe it, and I know some middle-level executives who rank with the great mystics of all time."

> JOHN W. GARDNER, chairman, Common Cause
> (speech to the Revson Foundation, June 10, 1992)

BORROW

"We at Chrysler borrow money the old-fashioned way. We pay it back."

> LEE IACOCCA, CEO, Chrysler Corp.
> (*Iacocca: An Autobiography*, p. 279)

"Neither a borrower nor a lender be;
For loan oft loses both itself and friend,
And borrowing dulls the edge of husbandry."

> Shakespeare (*Hamlet*, I, iii, 75)

BREAKTHROUGH IDEAS

"[The customers] had a tendency to stop shopping when the baskets became too full or too heavy."

> SYLVAN N. GOLDMAN, on why he designed
> the first grocery carts in the 1930s, recalled on his death
> (*New York Times*, November 27, 1984)

"I was the only non-Keynesian there."

> JOHN MAYNARD KEYNES, economist, after dining with
> Keynesian economists (interview, 1944)

"Why can't I see the picture right now?"

> EDWIN LAND's daughter to her father, the inventor of the
> Polaroid Land camera (Patton, *Made in USA*, p. 319)

"How about 'Mickey'?"

> LILLIAN DISNEY to husband Walt, who had created a character named
> Mortimer Mouse to stave off total disaster for his studio
> (*The Man Behind the Magic*, p. 5)

"'Kid, someday there'll be 50 hotels here and it'll be the entertainment capital of America.' And I thought at the time, 'There really is a reason why they call this guy Bugsy.'"

> ALAN KING, comedian, recalling his teenage encounter
> with gangster Ben Siegel in Las Vegas (*New York Times*, May 19, 1993)

"We are all Keynesians now."

MILTON FRIEDMAN, economist (Samuleson, *Economics*, 8th ed.)

BRIBE

"If you're going to bribe people, do it right:
• Never admit it's a bribe. Say you understand that you're presenting the official with unusual difficulties. Offer to pay an extra fee.
• Don't be afraid to haggle. I nearly always wound up paying less than was initially demanded.
• Never insult one of these uniformed extortionists. In Peru I nearly got arrested for calling a guard an idiot. It was fun but ultimately not worth the trouble.
• Ask for a receipt. On occasion it scares these people into taking their hands out of your pockets."

JIM ROGERS, former Wall Street investor, after travelling
through much of the world on a motorcycle
(*Fortune*, February 24, 1992)

"Never underestimate the effectiveness of a straight cash bribe."

CLAUD COCKBURN, Irish journalist and commentator
(*Time of Trouble*, 1956)

"There's a fine line between bribery and extortion."

IRVING KAHN, co-founder and chairman, Teleprompter, on his conviction
for bribing city officials in Johnstown, Pennsylvania
(*Fortune*, July 28, 1980)

"In politics in Louisiana, we'd call that bribery. I don't know what they call it in basketball circles. Free enterprise, I guess."

JACK DOLAND, former athletic director and president, McNeese State
University, on the six-figure consulting contracts
coaches have with shoe companies
(*Sports, Inc.*, February 8, 1988)

BROKE

"I've never been poor, only broke. Being poor is a frame of mind. Being broke is only a temporary situation."

MIKE TODD, producer (*All About Money*, p. 247)

"If he keeps going like that, he'll be broke in 250 years."

H. L. HUNT, oilman, on learning that his son Lamar was losing $1 million
a year owning the Kansas City Chiefs football team (*Harper's*, 1981)

"On a fine December day in 1924, as I walked down Hollywood Boulevard toward nowhere in particular, I was down to that essential starting place for actors. I was broke."
GARY COOPER, actor (Winokur, True Confessions, p. 135)

BROKER

"A broker is a man who takes your fortune and runs it into a shoestring."
ALEXANDER WOOLLCOTT, writer (Adams, Alexander Woollcott, chapter 15)

"I do not regard a broker as a member of the human race!"
BALZAC (quoted in Sharp, The Lore and Legends of Wall Street, p. 135)

BUDGETS

"The largest determining factor of the size and content of this year's budget is last year's budget."
AARON WILDAVSKY, political scientist
(The Politics of the Budgetary Process, 1964)

BUILD

"We need to find a way to make it more attractive for companies to get back in the business of doing the things they did historically to build their companies."
HUGH L. MCCOLL, JR., chairman and CEO, Nations Bank Corp.
(Business Week, "Reinventing America," November 1992, p. 22)

"Any jackass can kick down a barn, but it takes a good carpenter to build one."
SAM RAYBURN, chairman, House Ways and Means Committee

"You don't have to destroy the city before you can build a new Jerusalem."
LANE KIRKLAND, president, AFL-CIO
(Safire and Safir, Good Advice, p. 261)

BUREAUCRACY

"Bureaucracy, the rule of no one, has become the modern form of despotism."
MARY MCCARTHY, writer (The New Yorker, October 18, 1958)

"[The biggest risk of all] is that the lean, fast-acting management style that's made the company a winner will turn into a fat-assed

bureaucracy where managers spend all their time writing procedures, forming committees, attending meetings, decorating their offices, building empires, and protecting their tushes instead of making things happen."
WILLIAM G. McGowan, founder and CEO,
MCI Communications, on the risks of decentralizing
his fast-growing company (Henderson, *Winners*, pp. 190–91)

"If you're going to sin, sin against God, not the bureaucracy. God will forgive you but the bureaucracy won't."
Admiral HYMAN RICKOVER, after a Senate committee delayed his
confirmation as director of the Selective Service System
(*New York Times*, November 4, 1986)

"It is increasingly clear that the fate of the universe will come to depend more and more on individuals as the bungling of bureaucracy permeates every corner of our existence."
EDNA O'BRIEN, novelist (*New York Times Book Review*, February 14, 1993)

"I think we have more machinery of government than is necessary, too many parasites living on the labor of the industrious."
THOMAS JEFFERSON (letter to William Ludlow, 1824)

BUSINESS

"Business is war."
Japanese motto (Crichton, *Rising Sun*, frontispiece)

"My name is Sherlock Holmes. It is my business to know what other people don't know."
ARTHUR CONAN DOYLE ("The Adventure
of the Blue Carbuncle," *The Adventures of Sherlock Holmes*, 1891)

"It's like any other business, only here the blood shows."
KIRK DOUGLAS explaining boxing to his brother, Arthur Kennedy, in
Champion (screenplay by Carl Foreman)

"Business is a combination of war and sport."
ANDRÉ MAUROIS (*National Catholic Reporter*, October 27, 1991)

"Businesses can be misread: Witness the European reporter who, after being sent to this country to profile Andrew Carnegie, cabled his editor, "My God, you'll never believe the sort of money there is in running libraries.'"
WARREN BUFFETT, CEO, Berkshire Hathaway
(annual report, 1988)

"I am a sensitive writer, actor, and director. Talking business disgusts me. If you want to talk business, call my disgusting personal manager." SYLVESTER STALLONE, actor (Winokur, *True Confessions*, p. 21)

"If you break 100, watch your golf. If you break 80, watch your business." Attributed to columnist WALTER WINCHELL

"Business is a game, the greatest game in the world if you know how to play it." THOMAS J. WATSON, SR., chairman of IBM (Watson and Petre, *Father Son & Co.*, 1990)

"Business is taking a pile of cash, doing something with it, and winding up with a bigger pile of cash." LEONARD P. SHAYKIN, managing partner, Adler and Shaykin (*Fortune*, February 29, 1988)

"Business is like sex. When it's good, it's very, very good; when it's not so good, it's still good." GEORGE KATONA, director, University of Michigan Business Survey Research Bureau (*Wall Street Journal*, April 9, 1969)

"Kay, my father's way of doing things is over. It's finished. Even he knows that. I mean, in five years the Corleone family is going to be completely legitimate. Trust me—that's all I can tell you about my business." AL PACINO to Diane Keaton in *The Godfather* (screenplay by Mario Puzo and Francis Ford Coppola)

"The secret of business is to know something that nobody else knows." ARISTOTLE ONASSIS, Greek shipping magnate (*The Economist*, November 1991)

"'Why? Why should you carry other people's bags?'
'Well, that's my business, madame.'
'That's no business. That's social injustice.'
'That depends on the tip.'" GRETA GARBO, corrected by porter George Davis in *Ninotchka* (screenplay by Charles Brackett, Billy Wilder, and Walter Reisch)

"Perpetual devotion to what a man calls his business is only to be sustained by perpetual neglect of many other things." ROBERT LOUIS STEVENSON (*Virginibus Puerisque*, 1881)

"All business sagacity reduces itself in the last analysis to a judicious use of sabotage."

THORSTEIN VEBLEN (*The Nature of Peace*, 1919)

"You'll excuse me, gentlemen. Your business is politics. Mine is running a saloon."

HUMPHREY BOGART avoiding taking a stance in *Casablanca* (screenplay by Julius J. Epstein, Philip G. Epstein, and Howard Koch)

"The playthings of our elders are called business."

ST. AUGUSTINE

"When are you first in business, when you make your first tortilla? Or when you sell your first tortilla?"

ANNA HARTUNG, CEO, Maria and Riccardo's Tortilla Factory, responding to a question of how long the firm had been in business (to author, 1992)

"Years ago William Jennings Bryan once described big business as 'nothing but a collection of organized appetites.'"

DANIEL PATRICK MOYNIHAN, U.S. Senator (letter to constituents entitled *Special Report to New York*, 1986)

"To business that we love we rise betime,
And go to 't with delight."

Shakespeare (*Antony and Cleopatra*, Act IV, iv, 20)

"In former periods business was identified as secular, and service as sacred. In proportion as we have discerned that between secular and sacred no arbitrary line exists, public awareness has grown that the golden rule was meant for business as much as for other human relationships."

JAMES CASH PENNEY, founder, J. C. Penney Company (Tuleja, *Beyond the Bottom Line*, p. 3)

"Business is a . . . series of frauds, utilizing methods, both in its production and distribution, which are indistinguishable in spirit and effects from the practices of gangsterism."

J. B. MATTHEWS and R. E. SHALLCROSS (*Partners in Plunder*)

"Business is really more agreeable than pleasure; it interests the whole mind, the aggregate nature of man more continuously, and more deeply. But it does not look as if it did."

WALTER BAGEHOT (*The English Constitution*, 1867)

BUSINESS PEOPLE

"Our prototype for occupational fervor is the Catholic tailor who used his small savings to finance a pilgrimage to the Vatican. When he returned, his parish held a special meeting to get his first-hand account of the Pope. 'Tell us, just what sort of fellow is he?' Our hero wasted no words: 'He's a 44 medium.'"

> WARREN BUFFETT, CEO, Berkshire Hathaway
> (annual report, 1986)

"If only Mr. Ford was properly assembled! He has in him the makings of a great man but the parts are laying about him in disorder."

> SAMUEL MARQUIS, head of sociology department,
> Ford Motor Co., making his last comment before resigning
> (Collier and Horowitz, *The Fords: An American Epic*, p. 100)

"We're the only dinosaurs left who maintain that the myth of 'free trade' really exists."

> LEE IACOCCA, CEO, Chrysler Corp., and member,
> National Economic Commission (*Talking Straight*, 1988)

"People of the same trade seldom meet together but the conversation ends in a conspiracy against the public, or in some diversion to raise prices."

> ADAM SMITH, economist (*The Wealth of Nations*, 1776)

"I find it rather easy to portray a businessman. Being bland, rather cruel and incompetent comes naturally to me."

> JOHN CLEESE, British actor (*Newsweek*, June 15, 1987)

"You show me a successful businessman in Hollywood, and I'll show you a man who knows nothing about motion pictures."

> WILLIAM HOLDEN, actor (*People*, February 1988)

"Captains of Industry."

> THOMAS CARLYLE, British historian and essayist
> (*Past and Present*, 1843)

"Lieutenants of Industry."

> MIKE QUILL, head of New York City's Transport Workers Union, referring
> to the corporate leaders opposing his labor demands (interview, 1968)

"Everybody calls me a racketeer. I call myself a businessman."

> AL CAPONE, gangster
> (quoted by Claud Cockburn, *In Time of Trouble*, 1956)

"Few people do business well who do nothing else."
Lord CHESTERFIELD (letter to his son, August 7, 1749)

"Sotheby's are businessmen trying to be gentlemen, and
Christie's are gentlemen trying to be businessmen."
British saying (quoted in *New York Times*, November 15, 1991)

"In other countries, art and literature are left to a lot of shabby
bums living in attics and feeding on booze and spaghetti, but in
America the successful writer or picture-painter is
indistinguishable from any other decent businessman."
SINCLAIR LEWIS, novelist (*Babbitt*, 1922, chapter 14)

"[The businessman] is the only man above the hangman and the
scavenger who is forever apologizing for his occupation. He is
the only one who always seeks to make it appear, when he attains
the object of his labors, i.e., the making of a great deal of money,
that it was not the object of his labors."
H. L. MENCKEN, journalist (*Smart Set*, February 1921)

"In no country does one find so many men of eminent capacity
for business, shrewd, forcible, and daring, who are so
uninteresting, so intellectually barren, outside the sphere of their
business knowledge."
JAMES BRYCE (*The American Commonwealth*, 1888)

"Men of business must not break their word twice."
THOMAS FULLER (*Gnomologia*, 1732)

"There are geniuses in trade as well as in war, or the state, or
letters; and the reason why this or that man is fortunate is not to be
told. It lies in the man: that is all anybody can tell you about it."
RALPH WALDO EMERSON, essayist (*Character*, 1842)

BUSINESS AND PRESIDENTS

"My father always told me that all businessmen were sons-of-
bitches."
President JOHN F. KENNEDY, on the steel price rise
(to staff, April 11, 1962)

"I said sons of bitches, bastards, or pricks. I don't know which.
But I never said anything about *all* businessmen."
President JOHN F. KENNEDY, commenting on above (April 13, 1962)

"The President has great confidence in him because he has made his pile and knows all the tricks of the trade."

> ADOLPH BERLE, FDR advisor, speaking of Joseph P. Kennedy (1934)

"The business of America is business."

> President CALVIN COOLIDGE (speech before the Society of American Newspaper Editors, Washington, D.C., January 17, 1925)

"Business underlies everything in our national life, including our spiritual life. Witness the fact that in the Lord's Prayer, the first petition is for daily bread. No one can worship God or love his neighbor on an empty stomach."

> WOODROW WILSON (speech in New York, May 23, 1912)

"Merchants have no country. The mere spot they stand on does not constitute so strong an attachment as that from which they draw their gains."

> THOMAS JEFFERSON (letter to Horatio G. Spafford, March 17, 1814)

BUSINESS SCHOOL

"These kids are smart. But I'd as soon take a python to bed as hire one."

> NED DEWEY, Harvard Business School Class of '49
> (*Business Week*, March 24, 1986)

"The business schools have done more to insure the success of the Japanese and West German invasion of America than any one thing I can think of."

> H. EDWARD WRAPP, professor, University of Chicago School of Business (quoted in Peters and Waterman, *In Search of Excellence*, p. 35)

"He'd suck my brains, memorize my Rolodex and use my telephone to find some other guy who'd pay him twice the money."

> NED DEWEY, Harvard Business School Class of '49, on the newly graduated Harvard MBAs (*Business Week*, March 24, 1986)

BUSINESS WOMEN

"I love being a woman. I make money with women."

> DIANE VON FURSTENBERG, designer (*Metropolitan Home*, April 1985)

"The cosmetics business is the nastiest business in the world."

> ELIZABETH ARDEN, CEO of cosmetics firm
> (Lewis and Woodworth, *Miss Elizabeth Arden*, 1972)

"You're a girl. I guess you do it differently."

> DAN MELNICK, chairman, MGM, to Sherry Lansing, then a story editor
> who had insisted on letting her secretary call her by her first name
> (*People*, January 10, 1983)

"The advice I have for women in film is to toughen up and leave your sensitivities at the back door."

> JOAN MICKLIN SILVER, screenwriter and director
> (*Public Broadcast System*, "Tales," 1989)

"I tell my daughter, 'Always say yes, because nothing ever happens to girls who say no.' It's true in business and it's true in life. 'Will you stay late and work?' If you say no, nothing good is going to happen to you. 'Can you take this extra assignment?' If you say no, *nothing* is going to happen to you. You have to learn to say yes."

> LOIS WYSE, president of Wyse Advertising (interview, 1980)

BUY

"I buy when other people are selling."

> J. PAUL GETTY, oil magnate (quoted in Lenzner, *The Great Getty*, 1985)

"I just received the following wire from my generous Daddy. It says, 'Dear Jack: Don't buy a single vote more than is necessary. I'll be damned if I'm going to pay for a landslide.'"

> President JOHN F. KENNEDY (quoted in Cutler, *Honey Fitz*, p. 306)

"Buy for love and money: but first for love."

> JOHN L. MARION, chairman, Sotheby's, Inc. (*The Best of Everything: The
> Insider's Guide to Collecting—For Every Taste and Every Budget*, p. 19)

"The invitation says 'black tie.' How comes she opts for a dress kept lovingly wrapped in tissue paper, while you rent a been-to-the-dry-cleaners-more-times-than-Vicky-Carr's-sung-'It Must Be Him' dinner jacket? Be a grown-up and buy your own tuxedo."

> HAL RUBENSTEIN and JIM MULLEN, "Iron, John: How to Get Dressed
> Better" (*New York Times Magazine*: "Men's Fashions of the Times,"
> September 13, 1992)

CALIFORNIA

"Nothing wrong with Southern California that a rise in the ocean wouldn't cure."

> Ross Macdonald's LEW ARCHER (*The Drowning Pool*, 1950)

"The State of California has developed the most highly tuned, finely honed job-killing machine that this country has ever seen."
> PETER V. UEBERROTH, businessman and investor; chairman, Rebuild Los Angeles, a nonprofit group established after 1992's riots
> (*New York Times*, August 9, 1992)

"California is a tragic country—like Palestine, like every Promised Land."
> CHRISTOPHER ISHERWOOD, writer (*Exhumations*, 1966)

CANADA

"Canada was supposed to get British government, French culture, and American know-how. Instead, it got French government, American culture, and British know-how."
> LESTER PEARSON, the late prime minister (*The Economist*, July 27, 1991)

CAPITAL

"Capital isn't scarce; vision is."
> MICHAEL MILKEN, junk-bond creator and investment banker, Drexel Burnham Lambert (*The Nation*, December 16, 1991)

"Capital is that part of the wealth of a country which is employed in production, and consists of food, clothing, tools, raw materials, machinery, etc., necessary to give effect to labor."
> DAVID RICARDO, economist
> (*Principles of Political Economy, V*, 1817)

"In bourgeois society capital is independent and has individuality, while the living person is dependent and has no individuality."
> KARL MARX and FRIEDRICH ENGELS (*The Communist Manifesto*, 1848)

"Without the accumulation of capital the arts could not progress, and it is chiefly through their power that the civilized races have extended, and are now everywhere extending their range, so as to take the place of the lower races."
> CHARLES DARWIN, biologist (*The Descent of Man, V*, 1871)

"The number of useful and productive laborers is everywhere in proportion to the quantity of capital stock which is employed in setting them to work, and to the particular way in which it is so employed."
> ADAM SMITH, economist (*The Wealth of Nations, I*, 1776)

"Capital is dead labor that, vampire-like, lives only by sucking living labor, and lives the more, the more labor it sucks."

KARL MARX (*Das Kapital*, I, 1867)

"Labor is prior to, and independent of, capital. Capital is only the fruit of labor, and could never have existed if labor had not first existed. Labor is the superior of capital, and deserves much the higher consideration."

ABRAHAM LINCOLN (*Message to Congress*, December 3, 1861)

CAPITALISM

"It is now generally accepted that the Roosevelt revolution saved the traditional capitalist economic system in the U.S."

JOHN KENNETH GALBRAITH, economist (*Fortune*, May 18, 1992)

"You don't understand. In America, anyone can sell anything he wants, at any time. You're going to have to get that straight. That is just American capitalism."

THOMAS KEMPNER, board member, *New York* magazine, to
Byron Dobell, managing editor, who had yelled 'You don't have the right
to sell people' to the board that was selling *New York* to Rupert Murdoch
(quoted in Shawcross, *Murdoch*, p. 139)

"History suggests that capitalism is a necessary condition for political freedom. Clearly it is not a sufficient condition."

MILTON FRIEDMAN, economist (*Capitalism and Freedom*, 1962)

"I think that Capitalism, wisely managed, can probably be made more efficient for attaining economic ends than any alternative system yet in sight, but that in itself it is in many ways extremely objectionable."

JOHN MAYNARD KEYNES, economist
(*The End of Laissez-Faire*, 1962, part 4)

"Capitalist production is not merely the production of commodities; it is essentially the production of surplus value."

KARL MARX (*Das Kapital* I, 1867)

"Capitalism inevitably and by virtue of the very logic of its civilization creates, educates and subsidizes a vested interest in social unrest."

JOSEPH SCHUMPETER, economist
(*Capitalism, Socialism and Democracy*, 1942, chapter 1)

"As we see nowadays in Southeast Asia or the Caribbean, the misery of being exploited by capitalists is nothing compared to the misery of not being exploited at all."
> JOAN ROBINSON, economist (*Economic Philosophy*, 1962)

"Capitalism, it is said, is a system wherein man exploits man. And communism—is vice versa."
> DANIEL BELL, sociologist (*The End of Ideology*, 1960)

"I recall an advertising tycoon, Bruce Barton, saying in the late 1940s, when we were in a dither about the Russians: 'What we ought to do is to send up a flight of a thousand B-29s and drop a million Sears, Roebuck catalogs all over Russia.'"
> ALISTAIR COOKE, British journalist (*America*, 1973)

"History teaches us that capitalism is inherently unstable and from time to time needs to be rescued from itself. Inflation, financial panics, recessions, or depressions—all are intrinsic parts of capitalism. Capitalism is a phenomenal generator of goods and services, but like a finely tuned racing car, it often breaks down and needs a lot of regular repairs, service, and tune-ups."
> LESTER THUROW (*Head to Head*, p. 238)

CASH

"Cash is king."
> ROBERT MAXWELL, CEO, Maxwell Communications, who didn't heed his own warning and became mired in debt (*Business Week*, June 29, 1991)

"Cash is virtue."
> Lord BYRON, poet (letter to Douglas Kinnaird, December 6, 1822)

CAUSE

"I believe in Rhett Butler. He's the only cause I know. The rest doesn't mean much to me."
> CLARK GABLE disdaining Southern fervor in *Gone with the Wind* (screenplay by Sidney Howard)

CAUSE AND EFFECT

"The first and purest demand of society is for scientific knowledge, knowledge of the consequences of economic actions. . . . Whether one is a conservative or a radical, a protectionist or a free trader, a cosmopolitan or a nationalist, a churchman or a heathen, it is useful to know the causes and consequences of economic phenomena. . . . Such scientific information is value-free in the strictest sense; no matter what one seeks, he will achieve it more efficiently the better his knowledge of the relationship between action and consequences."

GEORGE STIGLER, economist, University of Chicago
(quoted in Wriston, *Risk and Other Four-Letter Words*, p. 120)

"Lighthouse, him no good for fog. Lighthouse, him whistle, him blow, him ring bell, him raise hell, but fog come in just the same."

Jamaican saying

"There's no reason to be the richest man in the cemetery. You can't do any business from there."

Colonel HARLAND SANDERS, founder, Kentucky Fried Chicken
(*All About Money*, p. 62)

CELEBRITY

"Fans don't boo nobodies."

REGGIE JACKSON, baseball player

"A boy must peddle his papers."

TRUMAN CAPOTE, writer, on cultivating his celebrity status
(*New Republic*, September 6, 1980)

"Everybody is somebody, so you don't have to introduce anybody."

VARTAN GREGORIAN, president, New York Public Library, at a Literary
Lions dinner honoring authors (*New York Times*, November 13, 1984)

"Hollywood is the only place in the world where an amicable divorce means each one gets 50 percent of the publicity."

LAUREN BACALL, actress (*People*, February 1988)

"I'm afraid of losing my obscurity. Genuineness only thrives in the dark."

ALDOUS HUXLEY, writer (Winokur, *True Confessions*, p. 121)

"Mankind is much more powerfully driven by the desire for recognition than by desires for a high standard of living. The mastery of nature owes more to the spirit of conquest than to economic calculation. A society, like our own, in which economic calculation holds sway is the byproduct of a history driven by the demand for recognition."

ALAN RYAN, writing about Francis Fukuyama's *The End of History and the Last of Man* (*New York Review of Books*, March 26, 1992)

CEO

"If we can't talk to the CEO, we're gone the next day. If the vision doesn't come from the top, forget it."

HARTMUT ESSLINGER, industrial designer and CEO, frogdesign, designer of the original MacIntoshes for Apple, the Sony Trinitron, frollerskates, the logo for Logitech, the nCube for NeXT, AT&T's 1337 answering machine (*Business Week*, December 3, 1990)

"Eventually, you're going to lose. Because the odds are always running against you in one of those jobs."

NED TANNEN, former president, Universal and Paramount Pictures, on the job of studio chief ("Naked Hollywood: Eighteen Months to Live," Channel 13, October 31, 1992)

"People think the president has to be the main organizer. No, the president is the main *dis*-organizer. Everybody 'manages' quite well; whenever anything goes wrong, they take immediate action to make sure nothing'll go wrong again. The problem is, nothing new will ever happen, either."

HARRY QUADRACCI, CEO, Quad/Graphics (Peters, *Liberation*, p. 9)

"Chief executives, who themselves own few shares of their companies, have no more feeling for the average stockholder than they do for baboons in Africa."

T. BOONE PICKENS, chairman, Mesa Petroleum Company (*Harvard Business Review*, May–June 1986)

"The day you get that job is the day the clock starts ticking. Soon you will not have that job anymore. It's a powerful job. It's a glamorous job. And you're doomed."

MEL BROOKS, producer, on the job of studio chief ("Naked Hollywood: Eighteen Months to Live," Channel 13, October 31, 1992)

"I see these CEOs wandering around with their blow-dried hair, their $3,000 suits, their 23-year-old trophy wives and I think, 'These are the stewards of millions of jobs.' I'd give anything if the old man in the White House would call them in and tell them:

'I'll support you, or I'll tear your head off. I'm tired of excuses. I want the jobs to stay here; I want the TV's made here. No excuses. Let's go back to basics.'"

H. Ross Perot, Chairman, Perot Systems Corp.
(*New York Times*, November 5, 1991)

CEO, CHARACTERISTICS

"Wherever I sit is the head of the table!"

Attributed to SAMUEL BRONFMAN, late CEO, Joseph E. Seagram and Co.,
reprimanding a young aide who asked him to move
from the middle of the table to the head

"Where are those butchers and scrap iron dealers and illiterate giants that ran the industry now that we need them? Would you believe that one would suddenly wake up in the morning with nostalgia for Louis B. Mayer? Give me a strong man. Give me somebody, but not a committee sitting up there deciding your fate."

BILLY WILDER, producer (*Movie Talk*, p. 217)

"The office of the Presidency requires the constitution of an athlete, the patience of a mother, and the endurance of an early Christian."

President WOODROW WILSON

"There's often a wounded prince or two who think they should have the job."

RYAL R. POPPA, new CEO, Storage Technology,
on being brought in from outside (*New York Times*, March 20, 1992)

"New executives usually bring in other new people, and if enough of this goes on, no one knows how the business runs. Things almost always slow down when there's a new executive on the job. The learning curve can last up to a year."

RICHARD GOULD, organizational psychologist (*Sacked*, 1986)

"Oh. I heard they hired a girl."

Gardener at the University of Wisconsin, to newly appointed
Chancellor Donna E. Shalala, who had introduced herself
(to author, 1990)

"Most CEOs got their jobs because their predecessors and the directors liked them. They slapped the right backs and laughed at the right jokes. It's reverse Darwinism: Once a backslapper gets the top job, he sure as hell isn't going to have somebody better than him as his heir apparent. So management gets worse and worse."

> CARL C. ICAHN, CEO, TWA, as well as raider and former arbitrageur, agreeing with Tom Watson, CEO, IBM, who said: "Give me the abrasive guys. They'll tell the truth and they're tough."
> (*Fortune*, February 29, 1988)

"For the actions of a new prince are much more closely scrutinized than those of an established one, and when they are seen to be intelligent and effective, they may win over more men and create stronger bonds of obligation than have been felt to the old line."

> MACHIAVELLI (*The Prince*, 1532)

CHAMPIONS

"Champions are pioneers, and pioneers get shot at. The companies that get the most from champions, therefore, are those that have rich support networks so their pioneers will flourish. This point is so important it's hard to overstress. No support systems, no champions. No champions, no innovations."

> THOMAS J. PETERS and ROBERT H. WATERMAN, JR.
> (*In Search of Excellence*, p. 211)

"I was a lousy football player, but I remember Chief Newman, our coach, saying that 'There's one thing about Nixon, he plays every scrimmage as though the championship were at stake.'"

> President RICHARD M. NIXON on his days at Whittier College
> (*Saturday Evening Post*, 1958)

"Play like a champion today."

> Sign over entrance to Notre Dame locker room

"Did I say killer? I meant champion. I get my boxing terms mixed."

> GEORGE SANDERS as the critic Addison Steele, commenting on Anne Baxter's character in *All About Eve* (screenplay by Joseph L. Mankiewicz)

CHANGE

"There is no way to make people like change. You can only make them feel less threatened by it."

> FREDERICK O'R. HAYES, former Director of the Budget, City of New York (interview, 1977)

"The urgent question of our time is whether we can make change our friend and not our enemy."

President BILL CLINTON (Inaugural Address, 1993)

"Companies have got to learn to eat change for breakfast."

TOM PETERS, on the combined effects of globalization and the information revolution (*Manhattan Inc.*, January 1990)

"'Battleship IBM' is trying to become a fleet of nimble 'destroyers.'"

New York Times, November 27, 1991

"If you recognize that there's a constant pressure to institutionalize rigidity, that there's a normal tendency to try and institutionalize the status quo, then what you have to do is institutionalize change, the exact opposite."

WILLIAM G. MCGOWAN, founder and CEO, MCI Communications (quoted in Peters, *Liberation*, p. 306)

CHAOS

"The business person who resists chaos will find in time his business will only grow brittle and irrelevant."

MEL ZIEGLER, founder, Banana Republic Company (*Fortune*, November 16, 1992)

"When the sea was calm
All ships alike
Showed mastership in floating."

SHAKESPEARE (*Coriolanus*, Act IV, i, 6–7)

"Chaos is a friend of mine."

BOB DYLAN, on his musical style in the 1960s (*Newsweek*, December 9, 1985)

CHARACTER

"The first thing is character. . . . A man I do not trust could not get money from me on all the bonds in Christendom."

J. P. MORGAN, banker, insisting that character and not money rule finance (House Committee on Banking and Currency, 1912)

"Mirrors in a room, water in a landscape, eyes in a face—these are what give character."

BROOKE ASTOR, foundation president (*Architectural Digest*, March 1982)

"I've told my wife, if I need surgery, get me the heart of an arb.
It's never been used."
CARL C. ICAHN, raider and former arbitrageur
(*Fortune*, February 29, 1988)

"Football doesn't build character. It eliminates the weak ones."
DARRELL ROYAL, coach, University of Texas (*Sports Illustrated*, 1973)

"What was he like under fire?"
Maj. Gen. JOHN H. RUSSELL, 16th Commandant of the U.S. Marine Corps,
whose daughter Brooke Astor says he assessed character by asking this
question (*New York Times Magazine*, November 17, 1991)

CHEAP

"It's nature's way of making water better; and it's dirt cheap
compared with Coke and Pepsi."
MORRIS J. SIEGEL, creator of Celestial Seasonings herbal teas,
on the company's big new product, herbal iced tea
(*New York Times*, August 6, 1991)

"Nothing is as cheap as a hit no matter how much it cost."
WALTER WANGER, producer (*Movie Talk*, p. 95)

"Don't ever do cheap songs."
FRANK SINATRA to Tony Bennett (*People*, October 26, 1992)

"The cheaper the crook, the gaudier the patter."
Dashiell Hammett's SAM SPADE (*The Maltese Falcon*, 1930)

"Nature laughs at a miser. He is like the squirrel who buries his
nuts and refrains from digging them up again."
HENRY GEORGE (*Progress and Poverty*, 1879)

"What we obtain too cheap, we esteem too lightly; 'tis dearness
only that gives everything its value."
THOMAS PAINE, American revolutionary and pamphleteer
(quoted in Kehrer, *Doing Business Boldly*, p. 85)

CHEAT

"I cheat my boys every chance I get. Makes 'em sharp."
JOHN D. ROCKEFELLER, SR.
(quoted by Jerry Goodman writing as
Adam Smith, *Esquire*, December 1983, p. 218)

CHOICE

"Even children learn in growing up that 'both' is not an admissible answer to a choice of 'Which one?'"

PAUL A. SAMUELSON (*Economics*, 8th ed.)

"We decided the best way to become the customer's restaurant of choice was to become the employer of choice. Our plan on this front was two-pronged: to work harder to develop the potential of the people we already had, and to move aggressively to attract and retain the best people we could find."

JAMES NEAR, chairman and CEO, Wendy's International
(*Wall Street Journal*, April 1992)

"When presented with freedom of choice, investors often behave in ways that reveal that what they really want is freedom *from* choice."

MEIR STATMAN, professor of finance
(quoted in Kehrer, *Doing Business Boldly*, p. 85)

"I do not choose to run."

A popular Lizzie Label—slogans painted on the Model T
in the mid-1920s (Patton, *Made in USA*, p. 177)

"People who are free to choose may choose wrongly. This is the age-old paradox. Sin is the other side of freedom's coin. A world without sin would be a world without choice."

CHARLES HANDY, chairman, Royal Arts Society (*Age of Unreason*, p. 259)

CIGARETTES

"You're dealing with a deep-grained anthropological habit."

GEORGE WEISSMAN, chairman, Philip Morris, dismissing the idea that the
tobacco industry was declining (*Forbes*, October 10, 1980)

"If what pleases some didn't make others miserable, you wouldn't have the world divided into Smoking and No Smoking."

GEORGE BURNS, comedian (*Wisdom of the 90s*, p. 65)

"The little white slavers."

LUCY PAGE GASTON, an anti-smoking activist who, in 1899, began fierce
legislative crusades that were fairly successful until her death, from
throat cancer, in 1924 (*Forbes*, October 10, 1980)

CITIES

"Hollywood is hype, New York is talk, Chicago is work."
MICHAEL DOUGLAS, film producer and actor
(*American Quotations*, p. 46)

"I was going to Chicago, that secret city. I drove across Indiana, and the city came up on me, almost too fast. I passed a sign that said, 'Welcome to Chicago, Richard J. Daley, Mayor.' Then I passed another, bigger sign that said, 'Welcome to the Tenth Ward, Edward R. Vrdolyak, Alderman.' I was in the country of the rank and file."
THOMAS GEOGHEGAN (*Which Side Are You On? Trying to Be for Labor When It's Flat on Its Back*, p. 61)

"You can't get to heaven without changing in Atlanta."
Southern saying, on Atlanta's being a hub for several airlines
(*The Economist*, January 4, 1992)

"I doubt if there is anything in the world uglier than a Midwestern city."
FRANK LLOYD WRIGHT, architect
(address in Evanston, Illinois, August 8, 1954)

"What is the city but the people?"   SHAKESPEARE (*Coriolanus*, Act III, i, 198)

CIVILIZATION

"Maybe civilization is coming to an end, but it still exists, and meanwhile we have our choice: We can either rain more blows on it, or try to redeem it."
SAUL BELLOW, novelist (quoted in Wriston, *Risk and Other Four-Letter Words*, p. 12)

"Civilization and profits go hand in hand."
President CALVIN COOLIDGE
(speech in New York City, November 27, 1920)

CLASS

"I am afraid in England we have too many artificial social barriers. We don't see as much as we should of the middle and lower classes."
Oscar Wilde's LADY HUNSTANTON
(*A Woman of No Importance*, 1893)

"I couldn't help where I was born. I just wanted to be near my mother at the time."

> President GEORGE BUSH, responding to criticism of his privileged background (Noonan,*What I Saw at the Revolution*, p. 56)

"I coulda been a contender! I coulda had class and been somebody! Instead of a bum which is what I am! Let's face it. It was you, Charlie."

> MARLON BRANDO to his brother, Rod Steiger, who made him throw a fight in *On the Waterfront* (screenplay by Budd Schulberg)

"In the 1990s, one billion middle-class people will be created in the world. And when people achieve middle class, they want to live like Americans."

> CLARK A. JOHNSON, CEO, Pier 1 Imports, on his company's expansion abroad (*New York Times*, January 14, 1993)

"The prettiest sight in this fine pretty world is the privileged class enjoying its privileges."

> JAMES STEWART to Katharine Hepburn in *The Philadelphia Story* (screenplay by Donald Ogden Stewart)

"While there is a lower class I am in it, while there is a criminal element I am of it, and while there is a soul in prison I am not free."

> EUGENE VICTOR DEBS, socialist and labor leader (during his trial at Canton, Ohio, June 16, 1913)

"The working class and the employing class have nothing in common. Between the two a struggle must go on until the workers of the world organize as a class, take possession of the earth and the machinery of production, and abolish the wage system."

> Preamble to the constitution of the Industrial Workers of the World (adopted at Chicago, June 1905)

"The most perfect political community is one in which the middle class is in control, and outnumbers both of the other classes."

> ARISTOTLE (*Politics*, IV)

"This is your neighbor speaking. I'm sure I speak for all of us when I say that something must be done about your garbage cans in the alley here. *It is definitely second-rate garbage*! Now, by next week, I want to see a better class of garbage. I want to see champagne bottles and caviar cans. I'm sure you're all behind me on this, so let's snap it up and get on the ball."

Jason Robards yelling out his window
in A Thousand Clowns (screenplay by Herb Gardner)

"The history of all hitherto existing society is the history of class struggles."   Karl Marx and Friedrich Engels (The Communist Manifesto, 1848)

CLEAN

"A clean, orderly workplace promotes quality. I can almost sense the extent of a plant's quality level just by walking through and observing their housekeeping. Ever see a plant after it's been straightened up for annual inventory? I used to take pictures which were then used as the 'acceptable standard' for the rest of the year."

Hammond Berry, furniture manufacturer
(Productivity: The American Advantage, p. 40)

"Mop Bucket Attitude says that all the business sophistication in the world pales before the 'wisdom' of a clean floor."

James W. Near, chairman and CEO, Wendy's International, summarizing
Wendy's MBA strategy (Wall Street Journal, April 27, 1992)

"'There won't be any revolution in America,' said Isadore. Nikitin agreed. 'The people are all too clean. They spend all their time changing their shirts and washing themselves. You can't feel fierce and revolutionary in a bathroom.'"

Eric Linklater (Juan in America, 1931, book 5, part 3)

CLIENT

"I remember seeing [my mother] kiss Rex Reed. He was her client and she treated him like a son. She treated me like a client."

Budd Schulberg, screenwriter (Winokur, True Confessions, p. 5)

"I'm a paid gladiator. I fight for my clients. Most clients aren't square shooters. That's why they're clients. They've got themselves into trouble. It's up to me to get them out. I have to shoot square with them. I can't always expect them to shoot square with me."

Earl Stanley Gardner's Perry Mason (The Case of the Velvet Claws, 1933)

CLOTHES

"Clothes don't make the man, but they go far towards making the businessman."

THOMAS J. WATSON, CEO, IBM (Patton, Made in USA, p. 85)

"It's a money-lending uniform. They're so well-designed, you'd never know it costs a pound of flesh to get them."

A Wendy Wasserstein character talking about
Turnbull and Asser shirts worn in The Sisters Rosensweig
(New York Times, December 6, 1992)

"His clothes were deliberately cheap, not only because he was poor but because he wanted to be able to forget them. He would work a suit into fitting him perfectly by the simple method of not taking it off much. In due time the cloth would mold itself to his frame. It did seem sometimes that wind, rain, work and mockery were his tailors."

WALKER EVANS, photographer, on James Agee
(Let Us Now Praise Famous Men, p. 303)

"Beware of all enterprises that require new clothes."

HENRY DAVID THOREAU, writer (Walden, 1854)

"I had a vision of what I wanted to be. . . . I saw a carriage stop, and out of it came a man dressed in a beautiful suit, with a homburg hat, and a cane and a pair of narrow shiny yellow boots, on top of which he wore spats, which I had never seen before. . . . I suddenly knew that my life would not be complete until I owned a similar pair. To get them I knew I would have to leave Kesckemet, and my family and my friends, and go out into the great world myself and become a success."

ALEXANDER KORDA, producer (quoted in Korda, Success, p. 68)

COMEBACKS

"At one point I could have stepped away undefeated, in boxing terms. But this is what I do. I'm a coach. You just can't spend the rest of your life going to banquets and hoping you'll be introduced."

BILL WALSH, coach, Stanford University Cardinals, former coach of the
San Francisco 49ers, one of the most winning teams in the
National Football League, on his return to coaching
(NBC-TV, Saturday, October 3, 1992)

"I've come down flat on my arse, but I'm going up again and this time I'm staying up." ROBERT MAXWELL, after his first bankruptcy
(Bower, *Maxwell, The Outsider*, p. 79)

COMMANDS

"Either lead, follow, or get out of the way."
TED TURNER, CEO, TNT Network, sign on his desk
(*Fortune*, January 5, 1987)

"Try again."
Newly elected Senator CAROL MOSELEY BRAUN to the Senate clerk who
gave her her new photo ID reading SPOUSE (*People*, December 28, 1992)

"If you really want to advise me, do it on Saturday afternoon between one and four o'clock. And you've got 25 seconds to do it, between plays. Not on Monday. I know the right thing to do on Monday." ALEX AGASE, assistant football coach, University of Michigan
(Peters and Austin, "A Passion for Excellence," *Fortune*, May 13, 1985)

"Go ahead and work something out. Get us off the hook, even if it means desegregating the stores."
IVAN ALLEN, JR., newly elected president, Atlanta Chamber of Commerce,
to fellow white business leaders, on resolving the SCLC's 1960 boycott
of Atlanta stores (Garrow, *Bearing the Cross*, p. 151)

"Me transmitte sursum, Caledoni!" ("Beam me up, Scotty!")
HENRY BEARD (*Latin for Even More Occasions*, p. 87)

"You know my methods. Apply them."
Arthur Conan Doyle's SHERLOCK HOLMES (*Sign of Four*, 1890, chapter 6)

"It's a damned good story. If you have any comments, write them on the back of a check."
ERLE STANLEY GARDNER's note on a manuscript submitted to recalcitrant
editors (quoted in Hughes, *Erle Stanley Gardner*, 1978)

COMMERCE

"Commerce cures destructive prejudices."
MONTESQUIEU (*The Spirit of the Laws*, 1748)

"Honour sinks where commerce long prevails."
OLIVER GOLDSMITH (*The Traveller*, 1764)

"As we were waiting for Fidel Castro to start speaking, I asked my guardian if he expected any changes at the Congress. 'You cannot have it done in a month or a year,' he said. 'We did it in Poland in one year,' I answered. 'But how do you avoid having all those *traficantes* [black marketeers]?' he asked. 'You simply change the law and they become businessmen,' I answered."

ANNE HUSARSKA, Polish journalist (*New Republic*, November 4, 1991)

"In democracies, nothing is greater or more brilliant than commerce. It attracts the attention of the public and fills the imagination of the multitude."

ALEXIS DE TOCQUEVILLE (*Democracy in America*, 1835)

COMMITTEES

"In 1486, King Ferdinand and Queen Isabella set up a committee, headed by Fray Hernanco de Talavera, to study Columbus's plan for reaching the Indies by sailing west. After four years' work the committee reported that such a voyage was impossible because: one, the western ocean is infinite and unnavigable; two, if Columbus reached the Antipodes he could not get back; and three, there are no Antipodes because the greater part of the globe is covered with water, as St. Augustine said much earlier."

WALTER WRISTON, former CEO and chairman, Citicorp
(*Risk and Other Four-Letter Words*, p. 54)

"Football combines two grim features of American life, violence and committee meetings [huddles]."

GEORGE F. WILL, columnist (*Newsweek* ad, 1985)

"Parkinson's Law applies to meetings as well as to organizations. Attendance at our meetings soon became a status symbol. Feelings had to be hurt, and were. . . . Proliferation of meetings . . . is an inevitable product of weak leadership and administration in the Department. When it is run by meetings, committees, or soviets, it isn't run at all."

DEAN ACHESON, former U.S. Secretary of State
(*Present at the Creation*, p. 129)

COMMUNICATIONS

"I am only a public entertainer who has understood his time."

Attributed to PABLO PICASSO, artist

"I told you 158 times I cannot stand little notes on my pillow. 'We are out of corn flakes, F. U.' It took me three hours to figure out F. U. was Felix Ungar. It's not your fault, Felix. It's a rotten combination, that's all."
WALTER MATTHAU to Jack Lemmon, *The Odd Couple*
(screenplay by Neil Simon)

"We could have told you it was a piece of junk."
Xerox employee to David Kearns, then-CEO, Xerox,
on the disastrous 1979 launch of a new copier
(*Prophets in the Dark*, 1992)

"Don't write anything you can phone, don't phone anything you can talk face to face, don't talk anything you can smile, don't smile anything you can wink, and don't wink anything you can nod."
Attributed to EARL LONG, Louisiana politician

"What we've got here is a failure to communicate."
Prison guard STROTHER MARTIN beating up Paul Newman in
Cool Hand Luke (screenplay by Donn Pearce and Frank Pierson)

"The fact of being reported multiplies the apparent extent of any deplorable development by five- to ten-fold."
BARBARA TUCHMAN, historian
(*A Distant Mirror*, 1978)

"This propensity of Americans to overstate and overkill is not new. The only difference today is that the technical scope and reach of our communications are much wider than ever before in history. One man saying that everything is wrong can command coast-to-coast attention in living color, a power not given to an absolute monarch a century ago."
WALTER WRISTON, former CEO and chairman, Citicorp
(*Risk and Other Four-Letter Words*, p. 9)

"Les plus speedy pizzas de Europe."
WILLIAM WEAVER, translator, quoting author Umberto Eco, saying this
sign in a Brussels pizza parlor shows the direction for all languages
today (speech, New York City, February 9, 1993)

"All the world's ills stem from the fact that a man cannot sit in a room alone."
PASCAL (quoted in Handy, *The Age of Unreason*, 1990,
on the effects of new technology that increasingly permits or
requires people to work alone)

COMMUNISM

"Communism is a virulent form of the messianic dream."

REINHOLD NIEBUHR, theologian
(quoted in Moskin, *Morality in America*, p. 26)

COMMUNITY

"The end is reconciliation; the end is redemption; the end is the creation of the beloved community."

MARTIN LUTHER KING, JR., civil rights leader, on the Montgomery,
Alabama, protest of 1955 (Garrow, *Bearing the Cross*, p. 81)

"Every state is a community of some kind, and every community is established with a view for some good, for men always act in order to obtain what they think good. But if all communities aim at some good, the state or political organization which is the highest of all and embraces all the others, aims, and in a greater degree than any other does, at the highest good."

ARISTOTLE (*Politics, 1*)

COMPENSATION

"The .350 hitter expects, and also deserves, a big payoff for his performance—even if he plays for a cellar-dwelling team. And the .150 hitter should get no reward—even if he plays for a pennant winner."

WARREN BUFFETT, CEO, Berkshire Hathaway,
on executive compensation practices (annual report, 1985)

"It's not the levels of compensation that will make or break the American corporation but rather the lack of any reliable link between what CEOs are paid and how well they perform."

HARVEY H. SEGAL, financial analyst (*Corporate Makeover:
The Reshaping of the American Economy*, 1991)

COMPETITION

"A competitor is the guy who goes in a revolving door behind you and comes out ahead of you."

GEORGE ROMNEY, former CEO, American Motors; former governor of
Michigan (*Productivity: The American Advantage*, p. 9)

"There's no resting place for an enterprise in a competitive economy."

ALFRED P. SLOAN, industrialist (*My Years with General Motors*, 1964)

"As a cub reporter for the old United Press, I learned the following rueful lesson: The competition kills you twice with a phony story—first with the exclusive and the next day with the news that it wasn't so."
JOHN L. HESS (*New York Observer*, October 19, 1992)

"Ignore, ridicule, attack, copy, steal."
ARTHUR JONES, inventor of Nautilus exercise equipment, on the reactions of competitors (Foster, *Innovation*, p. 137)

"Nothing focuses the mind better than the constant sight of a competitor who wants to wipe you off the map."
WAYNE CALLOWAY, CEO, Pepsico, which, despite record profits, continued to run second to Coca-Cola (*Fortune*, March 11, 1991)

"They remind me of a piranha around a chunk of meat. They're always making that water splash."
GRANT TEAFF, coach, Baylor University, on the Texas Longhorns (*Sports Illustrated*, 1983)

"There will be some substantial cannibalization. Either you eat your own children or someone else does."
RICHARD SWINGLE, director of new product development, Compaq, on the introduction of a low-priced line that would cannibalize sales of Compaq's traditional high-end products to corporate customers (*Wall Street Journal*, June 15, 1992)

"People are not dumb. They know that if their company is not competitive, there is no job security."
PERCY BARNEVIK, CEO, ABB Asea Brown Boveri, who, in his "Doom Speech," argued that two-thirds of Europe's giant companies will fail under European economic integration (*Fortune*, June 29, 1992)

"A man who, at 16, slashed his own father's tires while working for a competing paper in Sydney to prevent him getting an exclusive."
S. J. TAYLOR on Steve Dunleavy, former Metro editor of *New York Post* (*Shock! Horror! The Tabloids in Action*, 1991)

"Intelligence and industry ask only for fair play and an open field."
Attributed to DANIEL WEBSTER, American statesman

"Of all human powers operating on the affairs of mankind, none is greater than that of competition."
HENRY CLAY, American statesman (speech in the U.S. Senate, 1832)

"I don't meet competition; I crush it."
> CHARLES REVSON, founder, Revlon Inc. (*Time,* June 16, 1958)

"Competition, lauded as the foundation of America's strength and wealth, is a motherhood issue in theory but an abandoned child in practice."
> WALTER WRISTON, former CEO and chairman, Citicorp
> (*Risk and Other Four-Letter Words,* p. 73)

"The truckers are eating me for lunch."
> DAVID FINK, chairman, railroad unit, Guilford Transportation Industries
> Inc., on the fierce competition between the (mostly nonunion) truckers
> and the railroads (*Wall Street Journal,* May 1986)

COMPLAINTS

"I'm tired of being the poster boy for executive compensation."
> RAND ARASKOG, CEO, ITT Corp., after five months of publicity about his
> 1990 compensation of $11.4 million (*Wall Street Journal,* April 27, 1991)

"God damn it. Why is our morale so shitty?"
> BOB SMITH, president, American Express Bank, after an internal study
> suggested his bank executives suffered the worst morale in the entire
> American Express operation; when no one replied, Smith turned to one
> man cowering in a corner, "You, your morale is okay, isn't it?"
> (Burrough, *Vendetta,* p. 87)

"Whew! Have I got grievances!"
> Philip Roth's PORTNOY (*Portnoy's Complaint,* 1967)

"Your voice, it has no balls."
> Radio news director refusing to hire speechwriter Peggy Noonan
> (quoted in *What I Saw at the Revolution,* p. 23)

"One investment banker complained to me that he would go to a dinner party and sit next to a pretty girl who would ask him what he did. 'I'm a bond salesman.' She'd yawn and turn to the man on her other side. He said, 'What am I supposed to do? Wear a sign around my neck saying FINANCIAL GIANT?'"
> TOM WOLFE, writer (interviewed in Adelman, *Getting the Job Done,* p. 42)

"Nothing sickens me more than the closed door of a library."
> BARBARA TUCHMAN, historian (quoted in Brown, *Shoptalk,* p. 203)

"Ronald Reagan is going to free-market us to death."
> OSCAR WYATT, JR., oilman (quoted in *Molly Ivins Can't Say That,* p. 51)

"When Nelson buys a Picasso, he doesn't hire four housepainters to improve it."

> HENRY KISSINGER to Nelson Rockefeller aide Hugh Morrow, who had asked Rockefeller's speechwriting staff to edit Kissinger's draft of a foreign policy speech (quoted in Isaacson, *Kissinger: A Biography*, p. 125)

Modern mother to son: "You never call, you never write, you never fax. . . . "

> WILLIAM SAFIRE, political columnist ("On Language," *New York Times*, November 2, 1992)

"It was so hard on the daffodils."

> MARGARET THATCHER, on being hit with a bunch of them (*Esquire*, April 1992)

COMPUTERS

"If you work with numbers or words and you are not using a microcomputer, then you are working on borrowed time."

> ADAM OSBORNE, founder, Osborne Computer, which started in 1981, did $93 million in business its first fiscal year, and declared bankruptcy in 1983 (Henderson, *Winners*, p. 164)

"Computers don't really erase. They just take the label off and throw the file away, and if we try we'll probably retrieve large portions, which is how, by the way, they got Ollie."

> CARLOS BONILLA, computer expert, reassuring the author that he could retrieve erased files on her book while explaining the source of Oliver North's troubles (quoted in Noonan, *What I Saw at the Revolution*, p. viii)

"The computer and the human have fused."

> LARRY SMARR, director, National Center for Supercomputing Applications, University of Illinois, on virtual reality (*Fortune*, June 3, 1991)

"All I need is a personal computer to track any of the 1.2 million containers we have in our computer system. I can do that just as well from my house, or a hotel suite in Hong Kong, as I can from a high-rise office overlooking the docks. Who needs to be near the ships?"

> Executive, Sea-Land Service, an ocean shipper owned by CSX Corp., which moved from its urban Edison, New Jersey, headquarters to more rural Liberty Corner, New Jersey (*Forbes*, November 23, 1992)

"A computer doesn't charge for overtime and doesn't get health care benefits."

> ADAM SMITH (GEORGE J. W. GOODMAN) (*New York Times Book Review*, April 11, 1993)

CONFIDENCE

"You've got to take the initiative and play *your* game. In a decisive set, confidence is the difference."

CHRIS EVERT, tennis player (Safire, *Wit and Wisdom*, p. 66)

"I lack athletic confidence, which is why I sank to journalism."

GEORGE F. WILL, columnist (Winokur, *True Confessions*, p. 223)

CONFLICT OF INTEREST

"Without conflict there is no interest."

FRANK IRWIN, president, Board of Regents, University of Texas, to Dean John Silber who had accused Irwin of conflict of interest (told to author, 1993)

"It's not a conflict. It's a tradition."

RICHARD AVEDON, photographer, on shooting a 10-page Gianni Versace ad that appeared in the same magazine as his editorial work (*New York Times*, February 14, 1993)

CONFRONTATION

"I am looking forward to talking with you balls to balls."

Attributed to ANDREI GROMYKO, Soviet foreign minister, garbling an allusion to Dean Rusk's "eyeball-to-eyeball" comment during the Cuban missile crisis

"First, all means to conciliate; failing that, all means to crush."

CARDINAL RICHELIEU

CONSCIENCE

"The New England conscience . . . does not stop you from doing what you shouldn't—it just stops you from enjoying it."

CLEVELAND AMORY (*Who Killed Society?*, 1960)

"If cooks genuinely love a product and it's the best one for the recipe, they should be able to mention it. It's a matter of conscience. But . . . conscience is a frail thing."

JUDITH JONES, cookbook editor, on the practice of prominent chefs and food writers promoting commercial products (*Newsweek*, June 15, 1992)

"Every team needs a mad bomber with the conscience of a rattlesnake."

JOHNNY BACH, defensive coach, Chicago Bulls (*New York Times*, June 16, 1993)

CONSERVATIVE

"There is always a certain meanness in the argument of conservatism, joined with a certain superiority in its facts."

RALPH WALDO EMERSON, essayist (*The Conservative*, 1842)

"The most radical revolutionary will become a conservative the day after the revolution." HANNAH ARENDT (*The New Yorker*, October 12, 1970)

"You feel like a housefly in a bowl of buttermilk."

WALTER WILLIAMS, conservative, on often being the only black at conservative gatherings (quoted in *What I Saw at the Revolution*, p. 264)

CONSULTING

"I left McKinsey, to a substantial degree, because consulting is not my thing. It seemed no matter how clever the strategy, companies couldn't get the damn thing done."

TOM PETERS, consultant (*Manhattan, Inc*, January 1990)

"You hire me a consulting firm, and I'll prove whatever you want." LAWRENCE J. KORB, former assistant secretary of defense; currently, senior fellow, Brookings Institution, on whether proposed cuts in Pentagon spending are too big or too small (*Fortune*, March 9, 1992)

"For young MBAs, being a consultant means big money. In middle age it means you're unemployed. At our age, it means you're retired." JOHN SHAD, former chairman, Drexel Burnham (speech at the 40th reunion of the Harvard Business School's class of 1949)

CONSUMER

"When I was 12 years old my mother asked me to go to the store and buy some apples and warned me to pick good ones. But back then they came in baskets, not clear plastic containers. So I picked the best ones I could, brought them home and said, 'Mom, look at these great apples.' But only the ones on top were good; the rest were rotten. Thus was born a consumer advocate."

RALPH NADER (Winokur, *True Confessions*, p. 223)

"The boycott is a splendid example of consumer democracy at its best." ANTHONY J. F. O'REILLY, CEO, H. J. Heinz Co.
(*Washington Post*, April 17, 1990)

"Wal-Mart's eventually going to have to change its mix. And that's why the consumer doesn't bother looking too far down the road. We're a *now* society. We have confidence in the market. We know that if Wal-Mart puts somebody out of business, somebody else will come along and put Wal-Mart out."

> JAKE FOSTER, retail entrepreneur and Wal-Mart competitor
> (*Atlantic*, June 1992)

CONSUMPTION

"The product Coca-Cola had been losing market share for over 25 years. It was a product much admired and much revered, like a religious icon, but not *consumed* very much."

> ROBERTO C. GOIZUETA, CEO, Coca-Cola, on why he pushed a new formula
> (quoted in Kehrer, *Doing Business Boldly*, p. 23)

"You in the West think of [consumer electronics] products as consumer *durables*, things which last. For you consumption is an act which you undertake in bursts, periodically. Japanese consumption is a continuous cycle of new products replacing old products, everything is in a process of change, nothing endures. We do not seek permanence."

> MASATOSHI NAITO, Chief of Design,
> Matshushita (*Financial Times*, September 3, 1991)

CONTRACTS

"A verbal contract isn't worth the paper it's written on."

> SAM GOLDWYN, film producer
> (Johnston, *The Great Goldwyn*, 1937, chapter 1)

"When Dame Edith Evans was introduced to Billy Graham he told her, 'We in the ministry could learn a good deal from you about how to put our message across.' 'You in the ministry have an advantage over us,' replied Edith. 'You have long-term contracts.'"

> BRYAN FORBES, writer, *Ned's Girl*
> (*Harper Religious and Inspirational Quotation Companion*, p. 91)

"If I promise, I promise on paper."

> Attributed to SAM GOLDWYN, film producer

"Let's not linger over it."

> BETTE DAVIS to John Loder breaking their engagement in *Now, Voyager*
> (screenplay by Casey Robinson)

CONTRIBUTION

"Always remember the distinction between contribution and commitment. Take the matter of bacon and eggs. The chicken makes a contribution. The pig makes a commitment."

> JOHN MACK CARTER, editor, *Good Housekeeping*
> (Safire, *Wit and Wisdom*, p. 59)

"Nobody's trying to buy social prominence with a big, sudden donation. But, of course, I would love to see Bill Gates take half a day's earnings and give the arts community $100 million."

> PETER DONNELLY, president, Corporate Council for the Arts, on Bill Gates,
> founder of Microsoft, whose net worth based on stock appreciation goes
> up some days by more than $100 million (*New York Times*, June 28, 1992)

"You give some small environmental group a few thousand dollars and you make yourself 50 new customers."

> YVON CHOUINARD, founder and CEO, Patagonia
> (*M*, September 1991)

"Always remember, fund-raising is a contact sport."

> RAHM EMANUEL, fund raiser for then-Governor Clinton, on being found
> in his office at midnight phoning California for donations to the
> presidential campaign (*Wall Street Journal*, June 18, 1993)

CONTROL

"Don't waste your time trying to control the uncontrollable, or trying to solve the unsolvable, or thinking about what could have been. Instead, think about what *can be* if you wisely control what you *can* control and solve the problems you *can* solve with the wisdom you have gained from both your victories and your defeats in the past."

> DAVID MAHONEY, chairman, Norton Simon, Inc.
> (*Confessions of a Street-Smart Manager*, p. 49)

"Of all men's miseries the bitterest is this, to know so much and to have control over nothing."

> HERODOTUS, historian (*Histories*, c. 455 B.C.)

CORPORATION

"Corporation. n. An ingenious device for obtaining individual profit without individual responsibility."

> AMBROSE BIERCE (*The Devil's Dictionary*, 1906)

"Humans must breathe, but corporations must make money."

ALICE EMBREE (quoted in Morgan, *Sister Is Powerful*, 1970)

CORRECTIONS

"Mr. Hitchcock did not say actors are cattle. He said they should be treated like cattle."

JAMES STEWART, actor (Corey, *Man in Lincoln's Nose*, p. 86)

"That's not a knife; *this* is a knife."

PAUL HOGAN, pulling his knife, on some New York muggers in *Crocodile Dundee* (screenplay by Paul Hogan, Ken Shadie, and John Cornell)

CORRUPTION

"There's something on everybody. Man is conceived in sin and born in corruption."

BRODERICK CRAWFORD in *All the King's Men* (screenplay by Robert Rossen)

"Corrupt influence, which is itself the perennial spring of all prodigality, and of all disorder; which loads us, more than millions of debt; which takes away vigor from our arms, wisdom from our councils, and every shadow of authority and credit from the most venerable parts of our constitution."

EDMUND BURKE, British statesman
(speech on the Economical Reform, 1780)

COST

"Ivan breaks out in a serious rash if he puts anything that costs less than $250 next to his skin."

Attorney HARVEY PITT joking about the reluctance of his client, Ivan Boesky, to wear an undershirt offered by an SEC investigator who did not want to tape the SEC's microphone to Boesky's skin (quoted in Stewart, *Den*, p. 287)

"If you have to ask how much it costs, you can't afford it."

Attributed to J. P. MORGAN, financier

COURAGE

"It is stupidity rather than courage to refuse to recognize danger when it is close upon you."

Arthur Conan Doyle's SHERLOCK HOLMES to Watson ("The Adventure of the Final Problem" in *The Memoirs of Sherlock Holmes*, 1894)

"It's no good. I've got to go back. They're making me run. I've never run from anyone before."

> GARY COOPER telling bride Grace Kelly that he can't leave until he meets the high noon showdown with his enemies in *High Noon* (screenplay by Carl Foreman); on showing the film after the 1992 election, President-elect Clinton said it was his 19th viewing (*New York Times*, December 10, 1992)

"Exactly what do you mean by 'guts'? 'I mean,' Ernest Hemingway said, 'Grace under pressure.'"

> ERNEST HEMINGWAY, writer, interviewed by Dorothy Parker (*The New Yorker*, November 30, 1929)

"I stick my neck out for nobody."

> HUMPHREY BOGART in *Casablanca* (screenplay by Julius J. and Philip G. Epstein and Howard Koch)

COWARDICE

"Cowardice, as distinguished from panic, is almost always simply a lack of ability to suspend the functioning of the imagination."

> ERNEST HEMINGWAY, writer (*Men at War*, 1942)

"You miserable, cowardly, wretched little caterpillar! Don't you ever want to become a butterfly? Don't you want to spread your wings and flap your way to glory?"

> ZERO MOSTEL trying to talk accountant Gene Wilder into going into business with him in *The Producers* (screenplay by Mel Brooks)

"The hero and the coward both feel the same thing, but the hero uses his fear, projects it onto his opponent, while the coward runs. It's the same thing, fear, but it's what you do with it that matters."

> Trainer CUS D'AMATO to heavyweight boxer Mike Tyson (Winokur, *Friendly Advice*, p. 216)

"Those who won our independence were not cowards. They did not fear political change. They did not exalt order at the cost of liberty."

> Justice LOUIS BRANDEIS (quoted in Wriston, *Risk and Other Four-Letter Words*, p. 50)

CREATIVE

"Creative people are like a wet towel. You wring them out and pick up another one."

> Attributed to CHARLES REVSON, founder, Revlon Inc.

"Creative geniuses are a slap-happy lot. Treat them with respect."

JAMES MICHENER, novelist (*The Novel*, p. 53)

"Americans have always believed that—within the law—all kinds of people should be allowed to take the initiative in all kinds of activities. And out of that pluralism has come virtually all of our creativity. Freedom is real only to the extent that there are diverse alternatives."

JOHN W. GARDNER, founder, Common Cause
("Preserving the Independent Sector,"
speech to the Council on Foundations, May 16, 1979)

"Creativity is the sudden cessation of stupidity."

Attributed to EDWIN H. LAND, CEO, Polaroid

"We were not the victims of ancestor worship. We had the benefits of a fresh start."

MATHEW MILLER, on why his firm, General Instruments,
led the field in digital HDTV (*New York Times*, July 12, 1992)

"If it doesn't sell, it isn't creative."

A Benton and Bowles advertising principle
(*Ogilvy on Advertising*, p. 24)

"Creation is a drug I can't do without."

CECIL B. DE MILLE, producer (Winokur, *True Confessions*, p. 113)

CREDIT

"It's amazing what can be accomplished when no one cares who gets the credit."

Sign in Boston College locker room put there by Coach Tom Coughlin

"Now comes credits. This turns out to be a learning experience, for though we get the same height as Zanuck/Brown, we neglect to negotiate for the same width of the letters of our name. It is agreed that the credit bloc will read A Zanuck/Brown Presentation of a Bill/Phillips Production of a George Roy Hill Film, Tony Bill and Michael and Julia Phillips, Producers. When the picture comes out, everyone's name is in thick black letters but ours, which are willow thin."

JULIA PHILLIPS, director
(*You'll Never Eat Lunch in This Town Again*, p. 130)

"I don't want my name on the screen because credit is something that should be given to others. If you are in a position to give credit to yourself, then you do not need it."

> MONROE STAHR, the character based on Hollywood producer
> Irving Thalberg (Fitzgerald, *The Last Tycoon*, 1941)

CREDO

"The world belongs to the discontented."

> ROBERT WINSHIP WOODRUFF, CEO, Coca-Cola, who molded the company
> (quoted in Kehrer, *Doing Business Boldly*, p. 28)

"My motto has always been, 'Attack, attack, attack.' There ain't no mercy out there."

> GLENN R. JONES, chairman, Jones Intercable (Henderson, *Winners*, p. 109)

"Man does not live by GNP alone."

> PAUL A. SAMUELSON, economist (speech, Chicago 1973)

"*Citius, Altius, Fortius!*" ("Faster, higher, stronger!")

> LESLIE MILLER, winning contestant on "Jeopardy," wrote this motto on the
> front of her study book (*Wall Street Journal*, October 14, 1992)

"Sell cheap and tell the truth."

> ROSE BLUMKIN, CEO, Nebraska Furniture Mart
> (Berkshire Hathaway annual report, 1988)

"There's an old Vulcan proverb: Only Nixon could go to China."

> SPOCK, urging reconciliation with the Klignons, in *Star Trek V*
> (screenplay by Jim Statner, Harvey Bennett, and David Longhery)

"Form follows emotion."

> HARTMUT ESSLINGER, industrial designer and CEO, frogdesign; when
> Dieter Rams, Braun designer, said that frogdesign's work was only
> possible because of his own distinctive, minimalist look that showed the
> way, Esslinger replied: "Who wants to be clean and quiet? My designs
> are screaming with emotions." (*Business Week*, December 3, 1990)

"Ars in pecunia."

> Movie studio motto in *Silent Movie* (screenplay by Mel Brooks)

"I made my millions from maxims, chief of which was the one my father favored, which went: 'Any man can earn a dollar, but it takes a wise man to keep it!'"

> RUSSELL SAGE, investor and speculator
> (quoted in Sharp, *The Lore and Legends of Wall Street*, p. 156)

"Pecunia non olet." ("Money never stinks.")

> VESPASIANUS, Roman emperor, who gave this answer
> to those who objected to his taxing public urinals
> (quoted in Salvadori, *Why Buildings Stand Up*, p. 169)

"To avoid war and taxes, to disbelieve governments and stability, to trust only in money and himself."

> ANDREW SINCLAIR, critic, on film producer Sam Spiegel's beliefs
> (*New York Review of Books*, March 17, 1988)

"Thank you for smoking."

> Sign on many executive desks at Philip Morris

"One soweth, and another reapeth."

> JOHN IV, 37

CRITICS

"Never answer a critic, unless he's right."

> BERNARD M. BARUCH, financier (Grant, *Bernard Baruch*, 1983)

"I love every bone in their heads."

> EUGENE O'NEILL, playwright, on critics (quoted by Brooks Atkinson on
> accepting a medal from the Theater Committee for Eugene O'Neill,
> *New York Times*, December 1, 1980)

"It is a very easy, simple matter to dissociate one's self from a policy. It is not quite so easy to assert what an alternative policy might have been. I concede that it is easier to be critical than to be correct."

> Senator Arthur Vandenberg to the U.S. Senate
> (Acheson, *Present at the Creation*, p. 304)

"The whole stadium wasn't booing me. Not more than a third to forty-five percent were booing me."

> GEORGE STEINBRENNER, owner, New York Yankees
> (Coffey, *The Wit & Wisdom of George Steinbrenner*, p. 57)

CULTURE

"A cultural Chernobyl."

> ARLENE MNOUCHKINE, French theater director,
> on Euro Disneyland (*New York Times*, April 1992)

"The culture of the bank is criminal."

> ROBIN LEIGH-PEMBERTON, Governor of the Bank of England, on why
> regulators seized the Bank of Credit and Commerce International
> (*New York Times*, December 31, 1991)

"Don't forget: I'm at Skadden, Arps now. We pride ourselves on being a-holes. It's part of the firm culture."

SUSAN GETZENDANNER, former federal judge, on her move
to the powerful New York corporate law firm
(*Newsweek*, November 18, 1991)

CURRENCY

"With a good electronic system, the [Visa] card can be made acceptable anywhere. It transcends language, currency, law, custom. It's the closest thing to a universal currency there is. And getting closer."

DEE WARD HOCK, founder, Visa International (*Fortune*, March 11, 1991)

"Lenin was right. There is no subtler, no surer means of overturning the existing basis of society than to debauch the currency. The process engages all the hidden forces of economic law on the side of destruction, and does it in a manner which not one man in a million is able to diagnose."

JOHN MAYNARD KEYNES, economist
(*The Economic Consequences of the Peace*, 1919, chapter 6)

"I will not be a party to debasing the currency."

JOHN MAYNARD KEYNES, a notorious cheapskate,
responding to a friend who urged him to give more money
to the boys polishing his shoes, whom he had underpaid
(quoted in Sharp, *The Lore and Legends of Wall Street*, p. 187)

CUSTOMER

"We figured out that a customer base with a salary was better than a customer base with an allowance."

MICHAEL A. WEISS, president, Express, a trendy, profitable women's
clothing store owned by the Limited (*Fortune*, May 18, 1992)

"In the United States, you say the customer is always right. In Japan, we say the customer is God. There is a big difference."

JAMES MORGAN, CEO, Applied Materials, and Jeffrey Morgan, who runs a
small software firm, quoting a long-time Japanese friend
(*Cracking the Japanese Market*, p. 53)

"We play with our customers."

STEVE RICHARDSON, founder, Stave Puzzles of Norwich, Vermont, which
profitably makes hand-cut jigsaw puzzles that sell for between
$95 and $3,000 (*The Economist*, November 14, 1992)

CYCLE

"When you're green, you're growing; when you're ripe, you rot."
RAY A. KROC, Chairman, McDonald's
(Boas and Chain, *Big Mac*, p. 63)

"The chump-to-champ-to-chump cycle used to be three generations. Now it's about five years."
WILLIAM G. McGOWAN, founder and CEO, MCI Communications, on the life cycle of companies (Peters, *Liberation*, p. 18)

DATA

"If you torture the data long enough, they will confess."
MIT T-shirt

"It is a capital mistake to theorise before one has data. Insensibly one begins to twist facts to suit theories, instead of theories to suit facts."
Arthur Conan Doyle's SHERLOCK HOLMES to Watson
(*Study in Scarlet*, chapter 3, 1888)

DEALS

"If I were a girl, I'd be pregnant all the time. When someone comes in with a good deal, I can't say no."
HARRY B. HELMSLEY, developer (*New York Daily News*, June 1, 1980)

"Normal is overrated. Wackos make the best deal men."
JEFF BECK, investment banker, Donaldson, Lufkin and Jenrette, on his fellows (Bianco, *Rainmaker*, p. 115)

"Spielberg was Disney with technie razzmatazz. Of course, everyone in the business was aware of the hard side. The public might think of him as Peter Pan, but anyone who had ever negotiated with him knew Peter Pan dictated a mean deal memo. He was said to believe in the 99–1 split: he took 99 percent and his partners took 1."
JULIE SALAMON, author, on director Steven Spielberg
(*The Devil's Candy*, p. 253)

"Somebody better coach him on the difference between a gross deal and a net deal—that's all I can say."
ROBERT REDFORD, actor and director, on Mikhail Gorbachev's meeting with Hollywood celebrities such as Warren Beatty, Annette Bening, and Sean Penn (*Newsweek*, May 18, 1992)

"The deal, that's all this business is about. . . . Who's available, when you can get him, start date, stop date, percentages—the deal, it's the only thing that matters. Listen, if Paul Newman comes in and says he wants to play Gertrude Lawrence in *Star!*, you do it, that's the nature of the business."

JOHN GREGORY DUNNE, screenwriter (*The Studio*, 1969)

DEATH

"After all, the three major sources of apartments are death, divorce, and transfer."

CORNELIUS GALLAGHER, realtor, on the practice of reading obituaries to obtain a Manhattan apartment (*New York Times*, May 2, 1985)

"I get sick and it isn't my thing to challenge death."

RONALD TOOMER, president, Aero Dynamics, Inc., and designer of the Drachen Fire roller coaster—which turns its riders upside down 15 stories above the ground before hurtling 60 miles an hour over woods— which he refuses to ride (*Wall Street Journal*, May 28, 1992)

"If UA [United Artists] hears . . . they'll make me finish the movie with what I've got, and I don't have the movie. If Marty dies, I want to hear Marty's OK until I say Marty's dead."

FRANCIS FORD COPPOLA, director, talking about the heart attack of Martin Sheen, the star of his film, *Apocalypse Now*, in a documentary, *Hearts of Darkness: A Filmmaker's Apocalypse* (screenplay by Fax Bahr and George Hickenlooper)

"We voted to die with dignity."

Reporter, Buffalo's *Courier Express*, whose unions had refused to accept the scale of cuts Rupert Murdoch demanded to buy the paper; the paper shut down when he walked away from the deal (quoted in Shawcross, *Murdoch*, p. 202)

"I am become death, the destroyer of worlds."

BHAGAVAD GITA's words remembered by Robert Oppenheimer, director of the atomic energy project at Los Alamos from 1942 to 1945, as he witnessed the power of the first atomic explosion on July 16, 1945 (Giovanitti and Freed, *The Decision to Drop the Bomb*, 1965)

"They wanted to make sure he was dead."

SAM GOLDWYN, film producer, on why so many people showed up at the funeral of Louis B. Mayer (Marx, *Goldwyn*, p. 30)

"He's dead."

Rabbi EDGAR MAGNIN's response on being asked to say something good about the recently deceased Harry Cohn (Dunne, *Crooning*, p. 210)

"I believe in mortality but not in inflicting it on myself."
SAM SPIEGEL, film producer (*New York Review of Books*, March 17, 1988)

"Biography lends to death a new terror."
OSCAR WILDE, writer

". . . and when I get knocked off in a dark alley sometime, if it happens, as it could to anyone in my business, and to plenty of people in any business or in no business at all these days, nobody will feel that the bottom has dropped out of his or her life."
Raymond Chandler's PHILIP MARLOWE (*The Long Goodbye*, 1953)

"If a guy's a cocksucker in his life, when he dies he don't become a saint."
MORRIS LEVY, president, Roulette Records (*Hit Men*, p. ii)

"A single death is a tragedy, a million deaths is a statistic."
Attributed to JOSEF STALIN, communist dictator

"I have worked. I have schemed and dreamed to make us the greatest architects in the world. I have made him see it and kept him at it—and now he dies—damn! damn! damn!"
Attributed to DANIEL BURNHAM, on the death
of his architectural partner, John Wellborn Root

DEBT

"Willy, I made the final payment on the mortgage today. We're free and clear . . . we're free . . . we're free."
LINDA speaking at the grave of Willy Loman who had
driven himself to his death (Miller, *Death of a Salesman*, 1949)

"A small debt makes a man your debtor, a large one makes him your enemy."
SENECA (*Ad Lucilium* XIX)

"If a man ever pays you what he owes you,
You're greatly beholden to him."
TERENCE (*Phormio I*)

"At the end of every seven years thou shalt make a release. Of a foreigner thou mayest exact it again."
Book of Deuteronomy, quoted ironically by BENJAMIN WEINER, president
of Probe International, the economic consulting firm, in arguing that
Third World debt should be forgiven by the United States
(*New York Times*, May 18, 1986)

"Countries import capital in order to speed their economic development. The capital inflow permits a higher level of domestic investment and more economic growth than would have occurred without it. It adds to the countries' capacity to repay at the same time that it increases their external debt. This is the regular situation of a successful private firm—and of a successful developing country. It is an accurate description of the United States of America from colonial days up to about 1915. It is a hallmark of progress. The caveat is that the imported capital must be used to create new domestic economic activity sufficient to at least cover the carrying charge on the debt."

WALTER WRISTON, former CEO and chairman, Citicorp
(*Risk and Other Four-Letter Words*, p. 145)

"People don't commit murder on credit."

RAY MILLAND in *Dial M for Murder* (screenplay by Frederick Knott)

"[MCI's balance sheet] looked like Rome after the Visigoths had finished with it. We had a $90-million negative net worth, and we owed the bank $100 million, which was so much that they couldn't call the loan without destroying the company."

WILLIAM G. McGOWAN, founder and CEO, MCI Communications,
who had introduced cut-rate long-distance telephone service
in defiance of the Federal Communications Commission's order
to cease competing with AT&T; MCI then became the
second-largest long-distance telecommunications network
(Henderson, *Winners*, p. 187)

"Debt is the slavery of the free."

PUBLIUS SYRUS (*Maxims*)

"As kids, we all worked for the company in one way or another. I got to work behind the candy counter or run the popcorn stand when I was five years old. The business was part of life, and it was always included in the dinner conversation. We heard a lot about the debt it took to open new stores, and I worried about it. I remember confiding to my girlfriend one time—crying—and saying, 'I don't know what we're going to do. My daddy owes so much money, and he won't quit opening stores.'"

ALICE WALTON, on father, Sam (*Sam Walton*, p. 67)

"Creditors have better memories than debtors."

JAMES HOWELL (*Proverbs*)

DECISION-MAKING

"I gather his spleen has the deciding vote."

> MARK RUSSELL, comedian, on New York Governor Mario Cuomo's
> comment that while his heart told him to run for the presidency he was
> still working on his head (*Greensboro News & Record*, November 17, 1991)

"I have just made my first top-level decision. I have decided not to throw up."

> ARTHUR OCHS (Punch) SULZBERGER, to his sister Judy,
> on being made publisher of the *New York Times*
> (quoted in Robertson, *The Girls in the Balcony*, p. 5)

"He was trying to get everyone on board in an office where the best decisions are often the loneliest ones."

> DAVID HALBERSTAM, writer, on President Lyndon B. Johnson
> (*The Best and the Brightest*, 1969)

DEFEAT

"Don't cut my throat. I may want to do that later myself."

> CASEY STENGEL, baseball manager, to his barber after his Brooklyn
> Dodgers lost a doubleheader (*The Gospel According to Casey*, p. 13)

"They laid into us and there was nothing we could do about it. That's when I said that 100 million Chinese wouldn't know that this thing was played. The next day I got two wires from China: 'What happened?'"

> JOHN McCAY, football coach, University of Southern California, on his
> team's 51–0 defeat by the University of Notre Dame in 1985
> (NBC-TV, "Halftime Report," November 28, 1992)

"A man can be destroyed but not defeated."

> ERNEST HEMINGWAY, writer (*The Old Man and the Sea*, 1952)

DEFENSE

"There's got to be some way of stopping the word of mouth on this picture."

> SAM GOLDWYN, film producer, after a disastrous sneak preview of one of
> his films (Randall and Mindlin, *Which Reminds Me*, p. 48)

"Tackling is more natural than blocking. If a man is running down the street with everything you own, you won't let him get away. That's tackling."

> Attributed to VINCE LOMBARDI, coach, Green Bay Packers

"Good pitching will always stop good hitting and vice-versa."
CASEY STENGEL, baseball manager (*The Gospel According to Casey*, p. 13)

"Washington is like a self-sealing tank on a military aircraft.
When a bullet passes through it closes up."
DEAN ACHESON, former U.S. Secretary of State
(quoted in Isaacson and Thomas, *The Wise Men*, 1986)

"I don't like them fellas who drive in two runs and let in three."
CASEY STENGEL, who as manager of the New York Yankees emphasized
fielding as much as hitting (*The Gospel According to Casey*, p. 62)

"Appear at points which the enemy must hasten to defend, march
swiftly to places where you are not expected."
SUN TZU, Chinese military thinker (*The Art of War*, 490 B.C.)

"Good defense always beats good offense."
Attributed to VINCE LOMBARDI, coach, Green Bay Packers

DELEGATION

"The importance of devolving initiative and responsibility was
never more clearly expressed than it was by Alfred Sloan, the
man who built General Motors. He once said to me, 'I just want
my man in Denver to stay awake and be thinking about the
future of the company, and the only way I can do that is to push
some decisions in his direction.'"
JOHN W. GARDNER, founder, Common Cause
(speech to the Revson Foundation, June 10, 1992)

DEMAND

"When I find me a white boy who can sing black, I'll make me a
fortune."
Attributed to Colonel TOM PARKER,
Elvis Presley's discoverer and manager

"Through habit and the requirements of the economic order, what
people think they 'need' for a minimally satisfactory life is set at an
extremely high level. What a poor society might consider optimal
(plentiful meat, spacious dwellings, refrigerators, and television
sets, for instance), Western technological societies consider
imperative. That many people, both in and out of government,
could seriously contemplate going to war as a means of combating

a fuel crisis which somewhat lowered our standard of living (but posed no possible threat to survival) is as good an indicator as any of the terms in which 'need' is defined, at least in the United States."

DANIEL CALLAHAN, director and cofounder,
The Hastings Institute (What Kind of Life?, 1990)

"Chinese deco rugs are a little like radicchio. It's been around for years. When it was in a two-buck salad, no one paid attention. Now that it costs $6, everybody wants it."

DORIS LESLIE BLAU, Manhattan rug dealer,
on supply and demand (Metropolitan Home, September 1986)

DEMAND (CONSUMER)

"If you have a lot of what people want and can't get, then you can supply the demand and shovel in the dough."

Attributed to MEYER LANSKY, gangster,
on what became known as "Lansky's Law"

"There's a tremendous difference between what the public wants and what the critics want."

ALAN STILLMAN, New York City restauranteur
(New York Times, May 23, 1993)

"The number of people who will not go to a show they do not want to see is unlimited."

OSCAR HAMMERSTEIN, lyricist (New York Times, March 7, 1991)

"To found a great empire for the sole purpose of raising up a people of customers may at first sight appear a project fit only for a nation of shopkeepers. It is, however, a project altogether unfit for a nation of shopkeepers; but extremely fit for a nation whose Government is influenced by shopkeepers."

ADAM SMITH (The Wealth of Nations, 1776); "A nation of shopkeepers" was
subsequently used derisively by Napoleon in speaking of the English

"A customer can have a car painted any color he wants so long as it's black."

HENRY FORD, founder, Ford Motor Company, refusing to bend to the
market (Collier and Horowitz, The Fords, p. 58)

DEMOCRACY

"Our democracy rests upon the assumption that set free, the common man can manage his own fate; that errors will cancel each other by open discussion; that the interest of each, even when unguided from above, will not diverge too radically from the interests of all."

Justice LEARNED HAND
(quoted in Wriston, *Risk and Other Four-Letter Words*, p. 40)

DEPRECIATE

"Once he bought something, it depreciated in his value scale. The way André looked at it, if you don't own something, it must be good. When you do, it must be bad, because what are you doing with something that's good?"

PETER LEWIS, investment banker, Lazard Frères, on his boss André Meyer
(Reich, *Financier: André Meyer*, p. 151)

DESCRIPTIONS

"He's not your typical great man. His greatness—if you could call it that—sort of sneaks up on you."

WHITNEY YOUNG, civil rights leader, National Urban League,
on Henry Ford (Collier and Horowitz, *The Fords*, p. 193)

"He looks like a man who has just swallowed an entire human being."

TRUMAN CAPOTE, writer, describing William Paley
(quoted in Smith, *In All His Glory*, p. 15)

"If I were a woman, I'd marry Herbert. He's handsome, he's wealthy, he's fun, he loves dogs, and he loves children."

RAY STARK, producer, on Herbert Allen, investment banker and chairman,
Allen and Co. Inc. (*Esquire*, June 1991)

"An economic samurai."

An unnamed colleague, on Michael Ovitz of the Creative Arts Agency,
for brokering the acquisition of MCA by Matsushita (quoted in Bruck,
"The World of Business," *The New Yorker*, October 9, 1991)

"He had a second-rate mind but a first-rate intuition about people. I have a first-rate mind but a third-rate intuition about people."

HENRY KISSINGER, diplomat, on Nelson Rockefeller
(quoted in Isaacson, *Kissinger: A Biography*, p. 91)

"I'm kind of drawing him as a cross between a bad-hair-day Elvis and Jack Kennedy on anabolic steroids."

JACK OHMAN, cartoonist, Portland Oregonian, on CNN's *Crossfire*, on
President Clinton (*Wall Street Journal*, January 20, 1993)

"He carves you up but leaves the skin around the body."

> Ford Motor Co. executive on Philip Caldwell, president of
> international operations (*New York Times*, March 13, 1977)

"Lacking the established corporate connections of a Goldman, Sachs or a First Boston, Jay Lyman had driven Gould, Axeworth to the top ranks of the deal makers by being aggressive to the point of shamelessness, and attentive to the point of obsession. He worried each deal as if it were a fetus threatened with miscarriage, and when he gave birth, he sank into a slough of depression."

> DAVID AARON's description of his fictional hero, based on Jeff Beck,
> investment banker (*Agent of Influence*, 1989)
> (Beck's complaint of the not always flattering portrayal:
> "I can't believe this. Aaron stole all my best lines.")

"He had a big serve but no ground game."

> Donald Trump's doubles partner, Fordham University tennis team
> (Barrett, *Trump*, p. 7)

"With President, no complete sentences. Talks funny. Getting funnier. Could go back to speech lessons. Media consultants. Hand gestures coach. Not going to do it. Wouldn't be prudent at this juncture. Not going to get into that overexposure thing."

> MAUREEN DOWD, reporter, *New York Times*, on President George Bush
> (*New York Observer*, July 27, 1992)

"A pale-faced, absent-minded accountant who dresses like an Easter egg."

> Friend describing Phil Knight, founder and CEO, Nike
> (*People*, May 4, 1992)

"A loose cannon on a rolling deck."

> President GEORGE BUSH, on Atlanta Mayor Andrew Young

"Jon Peters was raised by wolves. That's why, when people complain about him—it's like having a wolf in your house. It's not his fault. He's a wild thing."

> ANDREW SMITH, screenwriter, on the CEO of
> Columbia Pictures and partner, Guber-Peters
> Entertainment Company (*Premiere*, March 1990)

"He has the sacred fire."

> MADAME ROUSANE SARKISSIAN, ballet teacher, on Rudolph Nureyev,
> dancer (quoted in Colcacello, "The Last Days of Nureyev,"
> *Vanity Fair*, March 1993)

"Piggy, piggy, piggy."

> EDWARD I. KOCH, mayor, New York City, on Donald Trump during negotiations to keep NBC in New York (Barrett, *Trump*, p. 397)

"He's contentious, he's contrarian, I could see how he could be a real pain in the butt at a department store."

> SALLY FRAME KASAKS, president, Ann Taylor, on former boss, Mickey Drexler, CEO, The Gap, Inc. (*Business Week*, March 9, 1992)

"The guy was four feet, 10 inches, 90 pounds soaking wet, a pit bull, tenacious as hell. He was there when you opened the door in the morning and the last to leave at night. Jeffrey was also a bit of a fire buff and slept with a fire radio by his bed. The fire deputy, responding to an alarm, would pick him on up on the way. Jeffrey saw himself as a player . . . even at a young age. He didn't have to be center stage. He just wanted to be at the middle of everything."

> SID DAVIDOFF, New York lobbyist, on Jeffrey Katzenburg as a very young aide to Mayor John Lindsay (*The Prince of the Magic Kingdom*, p. 73)

"He'll charm the birds off the trees and then shoot them."

> BILL KEYES, English trade unionist, predicting Robert Maxwell's behavior with the unions at the *New York Daily News*, which Maxwell was buying (Bower, *Maxwell, The Outsider*, p. 433)

"Dennis the Menace as Attila the Hun."

> IRVING AZOFF, CEO, MCA Records, on Walter Yetnikoff, president, CBS Records (*Hit Men*, p. 138)

"You don't hear of [Clark] Clifford running around nights. You don't hear of Clifford stealing. You don't read about Clifford in *Confidential* magazine. That's what I like about Clifford. He never gets caught."

> BOB HOPE, comedian (speech at 1961 Alfalfa Club annual dinner)

"It will take a hundred years to tell whether he helped us or hurt us, but he certainly didn't leave us where he found us."

> WILL ROGERS, comedian, on Henry Ford, founder, Ford Motor Co. (Collier and Horowitz, *The Fords*, p. 13)

"The man's charm is *lethal*. One minute he's swimming along with a smile, then *snap*! There's blood in the water. Your head's gone."

> JOHN BARRY, journalist with the London *Sunday Times*, on Rupert Murdoch, who was acquiring the paper (Shawcross, *Murdoch*, p. 173)

"Once a peacock, now a feather duster."

> SAMUEL J. LEFRAK, chairman, Lefrak Organization,
> on a fellow developer (interview, 1989)

"The Acne and the Ecstasy."

> On Walter Annenberg's *Seventeen*, a magazine for teenage girls
> (quoted in Shawcross, *Murdoch*, p. 311)

"An IBM machine with legs."

> Senator BARRY GOLDWATER,
> on Robert McNamara, Secretary of Defense and former president,
> Ford Motor Co. (quoted in Shapley, *Promise and Power*, p. 102)

"He was one of the only writers I ever saw who seemed to write the copy first in his head; all we saw was the typing. He'd sit there heaving, tie askew and white shirt wilting, chain-smoking unfiltered cigarettes, nodding to himself. He looked like a factory foreman running behind in stock. Hours later, combed, powdered, and wearing a fresh blue shirt, he'd lean into the camera cool and unflappable, perfectly urbane. TV is such a liar."

> PEGGY NOONAN, speechwriter, on Charles Kuralt,
> CBS Morning News (*What I Saw at the Revolution*, p. 23)

"He spoke like a poor man and walked like a king."

> DICK GREGORY, comedian and social commentator, on Malcolm X
> (Goldman, *The Death and Life of Malcolm X*, 1973)

"The eyes of Caligula and the mouth of Marilyn Monroe."

> French President FRANÇOIS MITTERRAND, on British Prime Minister
> Margaret Thatcher (*Atlantic Monthly*, April 1990)

"Here come Arsenic and Old Luce."

> Attributed to DOROTHY PARKER, writer,
> describing Clare Boothe and Henry Luce

"Pretty, pretty, and deadly as an asp. . . . "

> HOWARD TEICHMANN, writer, on Dorothy Parker, writer,
> (*George S. Kaufman: An Intimate Portrait*, 1972)

"In defeat unbeatable; in victory unbearable."

> WINSTON CHURCHILL on Viscount Montgomery
> (Marsh, *Ambrosia and Small Beer*, 1964, chapter 5)

"Like Knute Rockne without a football team to coach."

> DAVID O. SELZNICK, director, on Louis B. Mayer
> after Mayer was fired from MGM (interview, 1960)

"Oh, yes, I studied dramatics under him for twelve years."
President DWIGHT D. EISENHOWER, on
Douglas MacArthur, General of the U.S. Army
(Reynolds, *By Quentin Reynolds,* 1964)

". . . the glaring meteor, abominable in his lusts, and flagrant in his violation of public decency . . . "
HENRY WARD BEECHER, preacher and orator,
on James Fisk, Jr., financier
(Josephson, *The Robber Barons,* 1934)

"The shyster in the backroom of illusion, diluting his witch's brew with tap water."
JOHN CIARDI's description of Walt Disney after the creation of Disneyland
(*The Prince of the Magic Kingdom,* p. 18)

"America's greatest nineteenth-century architect."
PHILIP JOHNSON, architect, on Frank Lloyd Wright
(Secrest, *Frank Lloyd Wright,* p. 392)

"He's the bee with the pollen."
LUCY FISHER on producer Peter Guber
(Salamon, *The Devil's Candy,* p. 38)

"Acheson found it difficult to conceal his contempt for the contemptible."
DOUGLAS SOUTHALL FREEMAN, historian, on Secretary of State
Dean Acheson (quoted in Miller, *Plain Speaking:*
An Oral Biography of Harry S Truman, p. 372)

"His touch is death!"
DANIEL DREW, nineteenth-century speculator,
on his protégé Jay Gould, who ruined him
(quoted in Sharp, *The Lore and Legends of Wall Street,* p. 126)

DESIGN

"I hold you marketing people responsible for the downfall of American enterprise."
MASSIMO VIGNELLI, New York designer, to Philip Kotler, professor of
marketing, arguing that marketers obstruct good design because they
rely on overly statistical research (*Fortune,* March 11, 1991)

"Good design is good business."
THOMAS WATSON, JR., CEO, IBM, after hiring Eero Saarinen in 1966
to design IBM headquarters in Armonk, New York
(recalled when National Design Museum conferred
its Honor award on IBM, *New York Times,* May 13, 1990)

"Bland. Just a shame. It's not representing what its company should be. IBM's logo is classy, and it demonstrates what its products could be, but the design has no advantage over any clone." HARTMUT ESSLINGER, industrial designer and CEO, frogdesign, designer of the original MacIntoshes for Apple, the Sony Trinitron, frollerskates, the logo for Logitech, the nCube for NeXT, AT&T's 1337 answering machine, on IBM personal computers (*Business Week*, December 3, 1990)

DESTINY

"You gotta play the hand that's dealt you. There may be pain in that hand, but you play it. And I've played it." JAMES BRADY, President Reagan's press secretary, shot during an assassination attempt against the president

"Biology is destiny." Attributed to SIGMUND FREUD, psychoanalyst

"Each of them seems marked out by the will of heaven to sway the destinies of half the globe." ALEXIS DE TOCQUEVILLE, on the United States and Russia (*Democracy in America*, 1835)

"Character is destiny." HERACLITUS, Greek historian (Diogenes Laertius, *Lives of Eminent Philosophers*, c. 150 B.C.)

DETERMINATION

"You've got to take the bull by the teeth." SAM GOLDWYN, film producer (Marx, *Goldwyn*, p. 187)

"Whatever I engage in, I must push inordinately; therefore should I be careful to choose that life which will be the most elevating in its character." ANDREW CARNEGIE, industrialist and philanthropist, in his diary (quoted in Josephson, *The Robber Barons*, 1934)

"Elephants have a hard time adapting. Cockroaches outlive everything." PETER DRUCKER, management consultant (*Forbes*, August 19, 1991)

"It's not whether you get knocked down. It's whether you get up again." VINCE LOMBARDI, coach, Green Bay Packers (*Run to Daylight*, 1963)

"We will either find a way, or make one."   HANNIBAL

"Hard pounding this, gentlemen. Let's see who will pound
longest."   WELLINGTON at Waterloo

DIFFICULT

"In difficult economic times, this is a classless product. If you
used to have a Mercedes and can't afford it anymore, you can have
an Explorer and people won't think you've run out of money."

ALLAN GILMOUR, executive vice president, Ford Motor Co.,
on why the Ford Explorer is the best-selling consumer product
costing more than $20,000 (*Fortune*, September 21, 1992)

"First-hand knowledge about the difficulties business people
experience every day would have made me a better senator and a
more understanding presidential contender."

GEORGE McGOVERN, on the government regulations that contributed to
the bankruptcy of his Stratford (Connecticut) Inn (*Fortune*, June 29, 1992)

"Nothing, unless it is difficult, is worthwhile."   Ovid (*Ars Amatoria*, c. 10)

"I've watched so much Olympics that when Barbara asked me to
move a piece of furniture, I asked her, 'What's the degree of
difficulty?'"   President GEORGE BUSH (*Sports Illustrated*, January 4, 1993)

DIPLOMACY

"Man does not live by words alone, despite the fact that
sometimes he has to eat them."

ADLAI STEVENSON, statesman (*Eat*, frontispiece)

"Not the least of the arts of diplomacy is to grant graciously what
one no longer has the power to withhold."

EDMUND BURKE, British statesman
(quoted in Acheson, *Present at the Creation*, p. 335)

"History teaches us that men and nations behave wisely once
they have exhausted all other alternatives."

ABBA EBAN, Foreign Minister of Israel
(speech in London, December 16, 1970)

"As a matter of fact, they [reporters] were ahead of the diplomats. After all, Mr. Secretary, diplomats are only badly trained reporters." ANNE O'HARE McCORMICK, *New York Times* reporter, to British foreign secretary Anthony Eden, who had commented testily that reporters had *also* realized the menace from fascism and Nazism (Robertson, *The Girls in the Balcony*, p. 39)

DIRECTIVES

"You've got to jump when I say jump, sleep when I say sleep. Otherwise you're wasting my time."
Attributed to trainer JACK BLACKBURN to the young boxer Joe Louis

"Disperse with the objections."
GIB LEWIS, Speaker of the Texas House, who, according to Molly Ivins, is so well known for his malapropisms that his speech is called Gibberish (*New York Times*, October 17, 1989)

"Vote for the man who promises least; he'll be the least disappointing."
BERNARD M. BARUCH, financier (quoted in *Meyer Berger's New York*, 1960)

DISCRIMINATION (RACE AND ETHNICITY)

"The food was better at the Jewish club."
WARREN BUFFETT, CEO, Berkshire Hathaway, on becoming the first non-Jewish member of an all-Jewish country club in Omaha

"Discrimination is a hellhound that gnaws at Negroes in every waking moment of their lives to remind them that the lie of their inferiority is accepted as truth in the society dominating them."
MARTIN LUTHER KING, JR. (speech to Southern Christian Leadership Conference, Atlanta, August 16, 1967)

"The huddle is colorblind."
JOHN MACKEY, black former Baltimore Colt tight end (*Newsweek*, August 17, 1992)

"If anybody had said that in the future, there will be an Irish Catholic who would head not just General Motors but any of the leading companies of the time, I would have said, 'You are out of your mind. The Irish are not going to get there, nor the Catholics.'"
THOMAS AQUINAS MURPHY, president, General Motors, on the company that he joined in 1944 (interview, 1974)

"I don't see a great deal of movement for blacks off the playing field in baseball. We still can't even get a black coach on third base. I've seen maybe two black third-base coaches in my 37 years in baseball. I don't understand why. Do people really think a black man can't give signals like a white man, or be able to tell a runner to score or hold up? We do in the field, don't we?"

> HANK AARON, after a 23-year career with the Braves and the Brewers, farm director and vice president of the Atlanta Braves, one of the few blacks in baseball to have an important front office job
> (*New York Times*, February 24, 1991)

DISCRIMINATION (SEX)

"Women have gone about as far as they ought to go now."

> JIMMY CARTER, at the First Baptist Church Bible Class
> (quoted in McLellan, *Ear on Washington*, 1982)

"The corporation seems to seek an arrangement which is surely an anomaly in human society, that of homosexual reproduction."

> WILBERT MOORE, arguing that male managers reproduce themselves in their own image
> (*The Conduct of the Corporation*, 1962)

"Men associate their wives and daughters with *spending* money, not making it."

> ADELA CEPEDA, Harvard-educated investment banker who, on leaving a Wall Street firm where she failed to make managing partner, had trouble finding financing for her new firm, Abacus Financial Group, which soon had $40 million in assets and outperformed the bond-index average
> (*Newsweek*, August 24, 1992)

"In a marriage, where one is so willing to take on responsibility, and the other so willing to keep the bathrooms clean . . . that's the way you get treated."

> BARBARA BUSH, first lady (*Esquire*, June 1991)

"I have a brain and a uterus and I use both."

> Congresswoman PATRICIA SCHROEDER, on being an elected official and a mother (*New York Times*, May 6, 1977)

"Women get hit with a double whammy. If they're attractive, they're presumed to have slept their way to the top. If they're unattractive, they are presumed to have chosen a profession because they could not get a man."

> GLORIA STEINEM, editor, *Ms.* magazine (interview, 1979)

"As a woman, she is more motherly."

> Senator HOWELL HEFLIN, a former Alabama justice, explaining why he
> approved of appointing Sandra Day O'Connor to the Supreme Court
> (McLellan, *Ear on Washington*, p. 81)

"Women are not perceived as having a small business; we're
perceived as having a *little* business. It's as though we're doing it
for pin money."

> ROXANNE GIVENS, president, Legacy Management of Edina, Minnesota,
> who repeatedly had to send her brother to secure financing from banks
> (*Newsweek*, August 24, 1992)

"I've been sexually harassed every day I've spent on a trading
floor. That's life in this business. That's life. Period."

> SHARON KALIN, founder, Kalin Associates, an institutional stock
> brokerage boutique (*Wall Street Journal*, October 10, 1991)

"I feel like the beheaded queen."

> LYNDA EMON, sales representative, *Billboard* magazine, on the effects her
> divorce from powerful record producer Walter Yetnikoff had on her
> business connections (*Hit Men*, p. 307)

DO

"Don't just do something—stand there."

> GEORGE SHULTZ, former Secretary of State, on government interference
> (Safire and Safir, *Good Advice*, p. 117)

"Don't just stand there—undo something."

> MURRAY WEIDENBAUM, economist, on government regulation
> (Safire and Safir, *Good Advice*, p. 117)

"Let's do it."

> GARY GILMORE after being asked by the warden if he had anything to say
> before electrocution (Mailer, *The Executioner's Song*, 1979)

"A man's gotta do what a man's gotta do."

> ALAN LADD in *Shane* (screenplay by A.B. Guthrie, Jr., and Jack Sher)

DOUBT

"Rocco started brooding about the possible trial: reasonable
doubt can be a real ass-kicker sometimes."

> RICHARD PRICE (*Clockers*, p. 123)

"When in doubt, punt, any way, anywhere."

> Attributed to JOHN WILLIAM HEISMAN, football player

DREAM

"Lift up your eyes upon
This day breaking for you.
Give birth again
To the dream."

MAYA ANGELOU, poet
(poem read at President Clinton's 1993 inaugural)

"It's the stuff that dreams are made of."   HUMPHREY BOGART to Ward Bond,
last line of The Maltese Falcon (screenplay by John Huston)

"The great thing about being an architect is you can walk into
your dreams."   HAROLD E. WAGONER, quoted by Episcopal priest
Edward Chinn in tribute to Wagoner's restoration of
All Saints' Church in Philadelphia (Episcopalian, October 1986)

"World domination, eh? Same old dream."
Sean Connery's JAMES BOND in Dr. No (screenplay by Richard Maibaum,
Johanna Harwood, and Berkley Mather)

"What happens to a dream deferred?
Does it dry up?
like a raisin in the sun?
Or fester like a sore—
And then run?
Does it stink like rotten meat?
Or crust and sugar over—
like a syrupy sweet?
Maybe it just sags
like a heavy load.
Or does it explode?"

LANGSTON HUGHES, poet (Harlem, 1951)

DUTY

"The ship's company will remember that I am your captain, your
judge and your jury. You do your duty, and we may get along.
Whatever happens, you do your duty."

CHARLES LAUGHTON in Mutiny on the Bounty
(screenplay by Talbot Jennings, Jules Furthman, and Carey Wilson)

"I consider it my patriotic duty to keep Elvis in the 90 percent tax
bracket."   TOM PARKER, Elvis Presley's manager (Quain, *The Elvis Reader*, p. 52)

"I do my duty. Other things do not trouble me."

MARCUS AURELIUS, *Meditations*, which came to new prominence when President Clinton said he admired the writings of the second-century Roman emperor (*Wall Street Journal*, January 20, 1993)

ECONOMIC

"Call a thing immoral or ugly, soul-destroying or a degradation of man, a peril to the peace of the world or to the well-being of future generations: as long as you have not shown it to be 'uneconomic' you have not really questioned its right to exist, grow, and prosper."

E. F. SCHUMACHER, economist (*Small Is Beautiful*, 1973, part 1, chapter 3)

"In the wave of economy that studios generally have when they get desperate, they drop a few hundred-dollar-a-week employees and then hire a four-thousand-a-week executive."

JOSEPH M. SCHENCK (*Movie Talk*, p. 118)

ECONOMICS

"Few aspects of bumblebee life, or human life, can escape the pervasive influence of economics. Economics can be defined as the study of the acquisition or production, distribution, and consumption of goods and services. But what makes economics so compelling and important a science is not just its breadth but its urgency: resources, or goods and services, seldom, if ever, exceed or even keep up with needs and wants."

BERND HEINRICH, entomologist (*Bumblebee Economics*, p. 2)

ECONOMISTS

"If the nation's economists were laid end to end, they would point in all directions."

Anonymous

"Let us remember the unfortunate econometrician who, in one of the major functions of his system, had to use a proxy for risk and a dummy for sex."

FRITZ MACHLUP (*Journal of Political Economy*, 1974)

"An economist is a person who has one foot in the oven and the other in the freezer and says, 'Things aren't half bad.'"

Anonymous

"Another difference between Milton [Friedman] and myself is that everything reminds Milton of the money supply; well, everything reminds me of sex, but I try to keep it out of my papers."
ROBERT SOLOW, Nobel Prize economist (interview, 1983)

"The age of chivalry is gone; that of sophisters, economists and calculators has succeeded."
EDMUND BURKE, British statesman
(*Reflections on the Revolution in France*, 1790)

"The ideas of economics and political philosophers, both when they are right and when they are wrong, are more powerful than is commonly understood. Indeed, the world is ruled by little else. Practical men, who believe themselves exempt from any intellectual influences, are usually the slaves of some defunct economist. Madmen in authority, who hear voices in the air, are distilling their frenzy from some academic scribbler of a few years back."
JOHN MAYNARD KEYNES, economist
(*The General Theory of Employment, Interest, and Money*, 1936, chapter 24)

"Economists do it on demand."
University of Chicago T-shirt

"Professors of the Dismal Science, I perceive that the length of your tether is now pretty well run; and that I must request you talk a little lower in future."
Thomas Carlyle, British historian and essayist
(*Latter Day Pamphlets*, 1850)

ECONOMY

"The paradox of a free economy of the American type is that people should want to make money, and at the same time the system can work only when you teach people to respect legality. This paradox is fundamental in American society. There has always been in America an underworld of illegality."
RAYMOND ARON, French political writer and historian
(quoted in Moskin, *Morality in America*, p. 128)

"No President can be all things to all people. But in America we believe that no matter what difficulties you face, no matter what obstacles are in your path, anything is possible if you've got the media eating out of your hand. My Administration's first priority will be economic growth. I have a plan for growth. I'm going to apply the principles of government to business and industry because government grows no matter what. Likewise with the environment. Endangered species will be eligible for Federal entitlement grants. We should see an almost immediate increase in the number of ivory-billed woodpeckers, black-footed ferrets and desert pupfish."

> P. J. O'ROURKE, "All My Priorities," in the *New York Times Book Review* (January 17, 1993), which had asked him to write a pithy inaugural speech for President-elect Clinton

"A great danger facing modern democracy is the difficulty of allocating sacrifice fairly. But a growing economy allows even an arthritic system to apportion some of that growth to all elements of society, something that cannot happen in a stagnating economy. Where sacrifice has to be apportioned, single-interest groups take savage retribution on any politician reckless enough to challenge them. Whether the issue be Social Security, defense installations or gasoline prices, enough contrary votes can always be mobilized to exercise veto power."

> FELIX ROHATYN, investment banker (commencement address, Middlebury College, 1982)

EDUCATION

"A place that would turn the likes of us into the likes of them."

> Father of Calvin Trillin, writer, on sending his son to Yale in the 1940s (*Mirabella*, March 1993)

"I can say that anyone who, like me, has been educated in English public schools and served in the ranks of the British Army is quite at home in a Third World prison."

> ROGER COOPER, British businessman, on being released after five years in an Iranian prison (*Newsweek*, April 15, 1991)

"It's not just a school, it's a job."

> Fuqua School of Business, Duke University, T-shirt

"I was never too happy with that punchy-punchy stuff. But he worked hard at it, and now he's the champion, but he'd better get some education, so he can keep it."

> PEGGY HAYES, heavyweight champion Riddick Bowe's godmother (*New York Times*, November 24, 1992)

"An ignorant nation is a weak nation. That is why I propose to start an anti-illiteracy campaign, considering illiteracy an enemy as dangerous as foreign aggression and famine."

> Ho Chi Minh, Vietnam communist leader, 1945
> (quoted in *The Economist*, March 1992)

"Education makes a people easy to lead, but difficult to drive; easy to govern, but impossible to enslave."

> Henry Peter Brougham, Scottish statesman
> (speech to the House of Commons, 1828)

"The myth is that learning can be guaranteed if instruction is delivered systematically, one small piece at a time, with frequent tests to ensure that students and teachers stay on the track. . . . Nobody learns anything, or teaches anything, by being submitted to such a regimen of disjointed, purposeless, confusing, tedious activities. Teachers burn out, pupils fall by the wayside, and parents and administrators worry about the lack of . . . progress . . . or interest."

> Frank Smith (*Insult to Intelligence:
> The Bureaucratic Invasion of Our Classrooms*, p. ix)

"Human history becomes more and more a race between education and catastrophe."

> H. G. Wells, writer (*The Outline of History*, XV)

"The aim of totalitarian education has never been to instill convictions but to destroy the capacity to form any."

> Hannah Arendt (*Origins of Totalitarianism*, 1973)

"A good education is usually harmful to a dancer. A good calf is better than a good head."

> Agnes de Mille, choreographer (Winokur, *Friendly Advice*, p. 208)

"[There are times when] we need education in the obvious more than investigation of the obscure."

> Justice Oliver Wendell Holmes, Jr.
> (quoted in Acheson, *Present at the Creation*, p. 628)

EMPLOYEE PARTICIPATION

"Everybody wants to get inta the act!"

> Jimmy Durante in *Good Night, Mrs. Calabash* (screenplay
> by S. J. Perelman); a favorite phrase at a corporation
> facing an Employee Stock Ownership Plan (ESOP)

"You just don't keep them on because they own the company or there's not going to be any company to own."

> HARRY E. LESTER, official, United Steelworkers, on the fired employee-owners at the McLouth Steel Products Corp. in Trenton, Michigan, which laid off 600 of 2,200 workers, who own 87 percent of the company
> (*Business Week*, October 9, 1991)

"I'm not going to have the monkeys running the zoo."

> FRANK BORMAN, former CEO, Eastern Airlines, on worker participation (interview, 1986)

"The lunatics have taken charge of the asylym."

> RICHARD ROWLAND, New York wit, on hearing that Mary Pickford, Douglas Fairbanks, Charlie Chaplin, and D. W. Griffith had formed their own company, United Artists (Bach, *Final Cut*, p. 29)

"It doesn't rewrite the laws of capitalism. The bottom line is the bottom line—not guaranteed jobs."

> J. MICHAEL KEELING, president, ESOP Assn., a Washington trade group, on the fired employee-owners at Weirton Steel Corp., which had been bought through an employee-stock ownership plan in 1984
> (*Business Week*, October 9, 1991)

EMPLOYMENT

"Every man has a right to be employed."

> RALPH WALDO EMERSON, essayist

"If we face a recession, we should not lay off employees; the company should sacrifice a profit. It's management's risk and management's responsibility. Employees are not guilty; why should they suffer?"

> AKIO MORITA, chairman, Sony (interview, 1983)

"I'm adamant. I will not have an officer from my battalion working as a coolie."

> ALEX GUINNESS, insisting that only enlisted men do physical labor in *The Bridge on the River Kwai* (screenplay by Carl Foreman and Michael Wilson)

"If we have too many people, we consider it a management problem, not an employee problem."

> LOWELL MAYONE, vice president, Hallmark (interview, 1987)

"When more and more people are thrown out of work, unemployment results."

> Attributed to President CALVIN COOLIDGE

"Every man has the inalienable right to work."
EUGENE DEBS, labor organizer (speech, 1914)

"I will undoubtedly have to seek what is happily known as gainful employment, which I am glad to say does not describe holding public office."
DEAN ACHESON, on leaving his job
as U.S. Secretary of State (*Time*, December 22, 1952)

"I believe in the dignity of labor, whether with head or hand; that the world owes no man a living but that it owes every man an opportunity to make a living."
JOHN D. ROCKEFELLER, JR., financier ("Credo," *Time*, July 21, 1941)

ENDORSEMENT

"Carnation milk is the best in the land;
        Here I sit with my can in my hand—
No tits to pull, no hay to pitch,
        You just punch a hole in the son-of-a-bitch."
DAVID OGILVY, former chairman, Ogilvy and Mather, says this was
written by an anonymous dairy farmer (*Ogilvy on Advertising*, p. 81)

"For a while we had an alligator with a little shirt on him, but nobody got the point, he outgrew it, he ate neighbors. Finally had to get rid of him. Then, alligator shirts became so un-chic that the alligator shirt people started leaving the alligators off. And my kids started insisting on polo shirts. No one in my family, for generations, has played polo. We are not of that crowd. We are more of the alligator-keeping crowd, if it weren't for all the headaches. So I was glad to receive four No-Polo shirts. My son took one and said it was neat. My daughter took one and said it was neat. It's a good thing we don't still have the alligator, he'd want one and that would leave me with just one, which I would hate to sweat in. As it is, I have two, one of which I sweat in, and one of which I save in case we ever have neighbors again and they come to call, and both of which I say are neat."
ROY BLOUNT, JR., author, endorsing
Banana Republic's No-Polo shirt (*Banana Republic Catalog*, 1990)

"Sure I eat what I advertise. Sure I eat Wheaties for breakfast. A good bowl of Wheaties with bourbon can't be beat."
DIZZY DEAN, baseball player and announcer
(Sherrin, *Cutting Edge*, p. 211)

ENEMIES

"I bring out the worst in my enemies and that's how I get them to defeat themselves."

> Roy Cohn, counsel to Senator Joseph McCarthy and highly successful
> New York lawyer (Winokur, *True Confessions*, p. 61)

"People let you wander around in mediocrity as long as you want. But at the top of the hill, enemies await."

> Sam Wyche, Cincinnati Bengals coach (*Sports Illustrated*, 1989)

"He can run, but he can't hide."

> Joe Louis before his heavyweight title fight with Billy Conn
> (*New York Herald Tribune*, June 9, 1946)

"With so many new enemies out there, old enemies have a way of looking like new friends."

> Eugene Keilin, investment banker, Keilin and Bloom
> (to author, 1985)

"Show me somebody who can't tell his friends from his enemies and I'll show you somebody who's going to end up with no friends."

> Oklahoma politician quoted by Jim Lehrer, newscaster
> (*A Bus of My Own*, 1991)

"Talleyrand treats all his enemies as if they were one day to become his friends; and friends as if they were to become his enemies."

> Napoleon (*Maxims*)

"The enmity of this community is not a matter to invite lightly."

> Theodore White, writer, to Ray Kroc, chairman, McDonald's,
> which was planning to open on Manhattan's East Side in 1974
> (Boas and Chain, *Big Mac*, p. 62)

"About one-fifth of the people are against everything all the time."

> Robert F. Kennedy (speech at University of Pennsylvania, May 6, 1984)

"He could not live without adversaries, no more than a tree can live without soil; like mangrove trees, which make their own soil, he could create enemies from within himself."

> Peter Evans, writer, on Aristotle Onassis (*Ari*, 1986)

"A man cannot be too careful in the choice of his enemies."
OSCAR WILDE, writer (*The Picture of Dorian Gray*, 1981)

"Because I'd rather have him inside the tent pissing out than outside the tent pissing in."
President LYNDON B. JOHNSON, on why he would not force his old enemy, J. Edgar Hoover, to retire at age 65 from the FBI, 1963 (Tom Wicker, *Esquire*, December 1983, p. 151)

"My friends call me Mr. Crandall. My enemies call me Fang."
ROBERT L. CRANDALL, CEO, American Airlines (*New York Times Magazine*, September 23, 1990)

"He is his own worst enemy."
CICERO, said of Julius Caesar; this was similarly said of a man disliked by Winston Churchill who responded, "Not while I live."

"Take heed of a reconciled enemy."
ROBERT BURTON, English clergyman (*Anatomy of Melancholy*, 1621–57)

"There is no little enemy." BENJAMIN FRANKLIN (*Poor Richard's Almanack*, 1733)

ENTREPRENEURS

"If you want to understand entrepreneurs, you have to study the psychology of the juvenile delinquent. They don't have the same anxiety triggers that we have."
ABRAHAM ZALEZNIK, psychoanalyst and Matsushita Professor of Leadership, Harvard Business School (*U.S. News & World Report*, October 5, 1992)

"Entrepreneurs have an obsessive concern with doing things faster, cheaper, better."
LYLE SPENCER, president, McBer and Co. of Boston, business consultants (*U.S. News & World Report*, October 5, 1992)

"An entrepreneur tends to bite off a little more than he can chew hoping he'll quickly learn how to chew it."
ROY ASH, CEO, AM International (interview, 1984)

"In line with [our] owner-orientation, our directors are major shareholders of Berkshire Hathaway. . . . We eat our own cooking. We will only do with your money what we would do with our own."
WARREN BUFFETT, CEO, Berkshire Hathaway (annual report, 1989)

"We're not building a business. We're collecting entrepreneurs."
> DICK DOTTS, president, Pedus International, a janitorial services company
> (Henderson,*Winners*, p. 11)

"Entrepreneurs have a contempt for power."
> LYLE SPENCER, president, McBer and Co. of Boston, business consultants
> (*U.S. News and World Report*, October 5, 1992)

ENVIRONMENT

"You spill it, we bill it."
> JUDITH YASKIN, commissioner, New Jersey Department of
> Environmental Protection (*Fortune*, February 26, 1990)

"Poverty is as much a destroyer of the rain forest as greed. These people don't want to live in Stone Age zoos."
> JASON CLAY, anthropologist and founder of Cultural Survival Enterprises,
> which helps natives form cooperatives to harvest and sell
> rain forest products (interview, 1989)

"The ocean is closed."
> Sign posted by the management of a Miami Beach hotel
> (quoted by Lewis H. Lapham, *Harper's*, October 1991)

"We abuse land because we regard it as a commodity belonging to us. When we see land as a community to which we belong we may begin to use it with love and respect."
> ALDO LEOPOLD, ecologist (*A Sand Country Almanac*, 1949)

"The recycling process has worked smoothly to date—the real process of adjustment less so. Let us not delude ourselves: financial flows cannot fill indefinitely a gap that must be covered by conservation, production, and new forms of energy. Our past success in recycling—and the role it can play today—must not lead us to stretch that process to the breaking point."
> PAUL A. VOLCKER, chairman, board of governors, Federal Reserve System
> (quoted in Wriston, *Risk and Other Four-Letter Words*, p. 156)

"I wish I could have advice from a one-armed scientist, who won't tell me something and then say 'on the other hand.'"
> ERIC ASHBY quoting an American senator
> (*Reconciling Man with the Environment*, p. 37)

"That which is everybody's business is nobody's business."
> IZAAK WALTON (*The Compleat Angler*, 1653)

"In wilderness is the preservation of the world."
HENRY DAVID THOREAU, essayist (Atlantic Monthly, June 1862)

EPHEMERAL

"With the advent of fast personal computers, digital television and high bandwidth cable and radio-frequency networks, so-called post-industrial societies stand ready for a yet deeper voyage into the 'permanently ephemeral.'"
MICHAEL BENEDIKT, futurist (Cyberspace, p. 11)

"I like the word 'ephemeral' almost as much as 'fashion' or 'fickle.' In fact, I'm fond of speaking of 'the four ephemerals': ephemeral 'organizations' . . . joined in ephemeral combinations . . . producing ephemeral products . . . for ephemeral markets . . . FAST."
TOM PETERS, business consultant (Liberation, p. 18)

"The fabric of this business is ephemeral. There is no fabric. It isn't just get rich quick. It's get everything quick. There is no building of anything."
PAT ROTHSTEIN, trader, Merrill Lynch (Salamon, The Devil's Candy, p. 67)

EQUAL

"God created all men but Sam Colt made them equal."
Bumper sticker in the West (Made in USA, p. 50)

"Inequality is as dear to the American heart as liberty."
WILLIAM DEAN HOWELLS, author and editor

"The New York Times is an equal opportunity oppressor."
City room joke after the Times was forced by the court
to produce its personnel records by race and gender
(Robertson, The Girls in the Balcony, 1991)

ERROR

"When all else fails, immortality can always be achieved through spectacular error.
JOHN KENNETH GALBRAITH, economist

"To err is human but to really foul things up requires a computer."
Farmers Almanac, 1978

"Ignorance is preferable to error; and he is less remote from the truth who believes nothing, than he who believes what is wrong."

THOMAS JEFFERSON (*Notes on the State of Virginia Query 6*, 1781–1785)

ESTABLISHMENT

"I always knew there was an Establishment. I just used to think I was part of it."   SAUL STEINBERG, CEO, Leasco, and CEO, Reliance Insurance Corp., on the savage reception his attempted takeover of Chemical Bank received on Wall Street (*New York Times*, June 19, 1969)

"We saw that the British Establishment were snobs and they thought Maxwell was a wog. We felt nothing against him because they condemned him as a noisy upstart—in fact we felt the opposite."   ROBERT HODES, lawyer, to Saul Steinberg's Leasco, on Robert Maxwell, who sold Leasco a grossly overvalued company, Pergamon (Bower, *Maxwell, The Outsider*, p. 185)

"There is a big contradiction in my makeup that I don't completely understand to this day. In many of my core values— things like church and family and civic leadership and even politics—I'm a pretty conservative guy. But for some reason in business, I have always been driven to buck the system, to innovate, to take things beyond where they've been. On the one hand, in the community, I really am an establishment kind of guy; on the other hand, in the marketplace, I have always been a maverick who enjoys shaking things up and creating a little anarchy."   SAM WALTON, founder and CEO, Wal-Mart stores (*Sam Walton*, p. 48)

ETHICS

"We've fabricated a society of wolves and coyotes. Why does anybody think that we are better than we were in robber baron days?"   LOUIS AUCHINCLOSS, novelist and lawyer (*Honorable Men*, 1985)

"It is not easy in any given case—indeed, it is at times impossible until the courts have spoken—to say whether it is an instance of praiseworthy salesmanship or a penitentiary offense."

THORSTEIN VEBLEN, economist
(*Absentee Ownership and Business Enterprise in Recent Times*, 1923)

"Avoid clients whose ethos is incompatible with yours. I refused
Charles Revson of Revlon and Lew Rosentiel of Schenley."

DAVID OGILVY, former chairman, Ogilvy and Mather
(*Ogilvy on Advertising*, p. 61)

"Business people don't want to talk about ethics. They have
decisions to make."

JOHN FONTANA, Crossroads Center for Faith and Work,
Old St. Patrick's, Chicago (*National Catholic Reporter*, December 28, 1990)

"An organized money-market has many advantages. But it is not
a school of social ethics or of political responsibility."

R. H. TAWNEY, British historian (*The Acquisitive Society*, 1920)

EVIL

"Let us not paralyze our capacity for good by brooding on man's
capacity for evil."

DAVID SARNOFF, founder and chairman, RCA
(*Wisdom of Sarnoff*, 1968)

"I and the public know
What all schoolchildren learn,
Those to whom evil is done
Do evil in return."

W. H. AUDEN, poet ("September 1, 1939," *Another Time*)

"The law of retaliation is the law of the multiplication of evil."

Rev. GLENN E. SMILEY, a white official of Montgomery, Alabama's
Fellowship of Reconciliation, summarizing the principles of Mahatma
Gandhi for Martin Luther King, Jr.
(Garrow, *Bearing the Cross*, p. 69)

"Whenever I'm caught between two evils, I take the one I never
tried before."

MAE WEST in *Klondike Annie* (screenplay by Mae West)

EXCELLENCE

"The society which scorns excellence in plumbing because
plumbing is a humble activity, and tolerates shoddiness in
philosophy because philosophy is an exalted activity, will have
neither good plumbing nor good philosophy. Neither its pipes
nor its theories will hold water."

JOHN W. GARDNER, then president,
The Carnegie Corporation (*Saturday Evening Post*, December 1, 1963)

"Supreme excellence consists in breaking the enemy's resistance without fighting." Sun Tzu, Chinese army commander and military thinker
(*The Art of War*, 490 B.C.)

EXPERIENCE

"It is sad to remember that, when anyone has fairly mastered the art of command, the necessity for that art usually expires—either through the termination of the war or through the advanced age of the commander." General George S. Patton, Jr. (*War As I Knew It*, 1947)

"I don't have any experience in running up a $4 trillion debt." H. Ross Perot, after President Bush's stress on experience in the 1992
presidential election debates (*Newsweek*, October 19, 1992)

"Experience is a hard teacher because she gives the test first, the lesson afterward." Vernon Law, Pittsburgh Pirates pitcher
("How to Be a Winner," *This Week*, August 14, 1960)

"Men who experience a great deal of accountability make accurate decisions." Karlene Roberts, industrial psychologist
(quoted in Peters, *Liberation*, p. 460)

"A triumph of optimism over experience." Attributed to Henry VIII, on deciding to take a fourth wife

EXPERT

"Make three correct guesses consecutively and you will establish a reputation as an expert." Laurence J. Peter (*The Peter Principle*, 1969)

"An expert is one who knows more and more about less and less." Nicholas Murray Butler, president, Columbia University
(commencement address, 1931)

EXPORT

"It makes no difference whether the United States exports potato chips or silicon chips." Michael Boskin, chairman, Council of Economic Advisers
(*Wall Street Journal*, October 26, 1992)

"I think we should keep the grain and export the farmers."
President RONALD REAGAN (Washington Gridiron Club, March 23, 1985)

EXTERMINATE

"We fall back into the biological category of the potato bug which exterminated the potato, and thereby exterminated itself."
ALDO LEOPOLD, on humanity's destruction of the Amazon rain forest
(*The River of the Mother of God and Other Essays*, 1991)

FACTORY

"We have our factory, which is called a stage. We make a product, color it, we title it and we ship it out in cans."
CARY GRANT, actor, on the film industry (*Newsweek*, January 3, 1969)

"In the factory we make cosmetics; in the drugstore we sell hope."
Attributed to CHARLES REVSON, founder, Revlon Inc.

FACTS

"Does your mother say she loves you? Check it out."
Chicago newspaper maxim (*Nieman Reports*, Winter 1989)

"Facts do not cease to exist because they are ignored."
ALDOUS HUXLEY, writer ("A Note on Dogma," *Proper Studies*, 1917)

"It is of the highest importance in the art of detection to be able to recognize out of a number of facts which are incidental and which vital. Otherwise your energy and attention must be dissipated instead of being concentrated."
Arthur Conan Doyle's SHERLOCK HOLMES ("The Adventures of the
Reigate Squires" in *The Memoirs of Sherlock Holmes*, 1894)

"Never confuse wishes with facts." Edward J. FLYNN, Bronx political leader
(quoted in McCullough, *Truman*, 1992, p. 639)

"Facts are stubborn things."
EBENEZER ELLIOTT, English Chartist leader (*Field Husbandry*)

"Comments are free, but facts are expensive."
A former editor of the *Manchester Guardian* quoted by CHARLES W. BAILEY,
managing editor (*Nieman Reports*, Winter 1990)

"'Our Congressman just came back from a fact-finding trip to Las Vegas, Honolulu, Paris, and Monte Carlo.' Said a political observer: 'Boy, those facts sure know where to hide.'"

BOB ORBEN, comic
(quoted in Hyman, *Washington Wind and Wisdom*, p. 96)

"There is nothing more deceptive than an obvious fact."

Arthur Conan Doyle's SHERLOCK HOLMES
to Watson ("The Bascombe Valley Mystery" in
The Adventures of Sherlock Holmes, 1892)

FAILURE

"Fear of failure must never be a reason not to try something."

FREDERICK SMITH, founder and CEO, Federal Express
(*Federal Express Manager's Guide*)

"I think it's important to have a good hard failure when you're young."

WALT DISNEY (*The Man Behind the Magic*, p. 37)

"Failure is a highly contagious disease."

PAUL NEWMAN explaining his bad luck to Shirley Knight in
Sweet Bird of Youth (screenplay by Richard Brooks)

"A novel can probably stand 20 bad pages. But an hour and 50 minute movie can't stand 20 bad minutes. I'll never forget opening night of *92 in the Shade*. I was sitting in a crowded theater and I remember a great big lady staggering out of her seat, screaming 'I want my money back.' It's unforgettable. So when you go back to writing fiction, you're not as congenial to your own writing leisure; you take a tighter, more critical look at how time is passing because that lady rises up on the pages and wants her money back."

THOMAS McGUANE, novelist and screenwriter
(*New York Times*, April 25, 1982)

"You can fall down, but you can't climb down."

KEITH RICHARDS, guitarist, Rolling Stones
(quoted in Appleyard, *Vanity Fair*, December 1992, p. 272)

"Everyone should fail in a big way at least once before reaching 40."

AL NEUHARTH, former chairman, Gannett Company
(*Confessions of an S.O.B.*, 1989)

"We fail forward to success."
> MARY KAY ASH, founder and CEO, Mary Kay Cosmetics
> (Henderson,*Winners*, p. 106)

"One of the things we do best is to plan for failure. We assume every well we're going to drill is a dry hole, so we drill the cheapest dry holes out there."
> JOE B. FOSTER, founder, Newfield Exploration, an independent oil
> company started in 1988, about the time sliding prices and rising costs
> devastated oil and gas exploration in the Gulf of Mexico
> (*Wall Street Journal*, September 30, 1992)

"They have no fear of failure. It's not part of their makeup."
> ABRAHAM ZALEZNIK, psychoanalyst and Matsushita Professor of
> Leadership, Harvard Business School, on entrepreneurs
> (*U.S. News and World Report*, October 5, 1992)

"I was subject to mixed emotions. It was something like watching my mother-in-law go over a cliff in my Cadillac."
> LOU GOLDSTEIN, owner of Grossinger's, after the resort closed, 1985
> (recalled in *New York Times*, December 1, 1991)

"Failure is the condiment that gives success its flavor."
> TRUMAN CAPOTE (*The Dogs Bark*, 1973)

"I ain't in no slump. I just ain't hitting."
> YOGI BERRA (Berra, *It Ain't Over*, 1989)

"Bloom, look at me. Look at me, Bloom. Bloom. I'm drowning. Other men have sailed through life. Bialystock has struck a reef. Bloom. I'm going under. I'm being sunk by a society that demands success when all I can offer is failure. Bloom, I'm reaching out to you."
> ZERO MOSTEL pleading with Gene Wilder
> in *The Producers* (screenplay by Mel Brooks)

"One of the great American liberties is the right to fail economically."
> TOM DONOHUE, president, American Trucking Association,
> whose industry has a failure rate of 150 per 10,000 companies
> (*New York Times*, December 1, 1991)

"I always turn to the sports page first. The sports page records people's accomplishments; the front page nothing but man's failure."
> Chief Justice EARL WARREN (Winokur, *True Confessions*, p. 148)

"I started at the top and worked my way down."
Attributed to ORSON WELLES, actor and director

"Satire is what closes on Saturday night."
GEORGE S. KAUFMAN, playwright
(Teichmann, *George S. Kaufman*, 1972)

"There is the greatest practical benefit in making a few failures early in life."
T. H. HUXLEY, English writer (*On Medical Education*, 1870)

"The play was a success but the audience was a failure."
OSCAR WILDE, playwright, on a play of his that had opened
to an audience that hated it

"Failures are like skinned knees—painful but superficial."
H. ROSS PEROT, founder and chairman,
Electronic Data Systems (*Look*, March 24, 1970)

FAIR

"At the end of the card game one of the boys looked across the table and said: 'Now, Reuben, play the cards fair. I know what I dealt you.'"
President LYNDON B. JOHNSON (Steinberg, *Sam Johnson's Boy*, 1968)

"It's far better to buy a wonderful company at a fair price than a fair company at a wonderful price."
WARREN BUFFETT, CEO, Berkshire Hathaway (annual report, 1989)

FAKE

"Fake it! Fake it!"
DIANA VREELAND's cry to assistants and photographers
doing layouts for *Vogue* magazine (*D.V.*, 1984)

"A bad forgery's the ultimate insult."
Jonathan Gash's English antique dealer, LOVEJOY (*The Vatican Rip*, 1981)

"If horses don't eat it, I don't want to play on it."
Attributed to RICHIE ALLEN, baseball infielder, about artificial turf

FAMILY BUSINESS

"A man's enemies are the men of his own house."
MICAH 7:6

"Small business is a large family: no shop steward or punch clerk or quick firing. You put up with erratic habits as you'd put up with your barmy old aunt, because she is irreplaceable. . . . So, for these men I write the parole board and break up fights and loan cash that, we all know, can never be repaid. In return, they've enabled us to operate in our eccentric and self-indulgent way."

> D. KEITH MANO, novelist and fourth-generation owner of a cement powder manufacturing plant in Long Island City, New York
> (*Business World, New York Times Magazine,* June 6, 1986)

"One does tend to get involved in the family business, doesn't one?"

> PRINCESS ANNE, to Shari Lewis after the puppeteer explained that she had learned ventriloquism from her father (*People,* April 13, 1992)

"We're not a family, we're a firm."

> Attributed to GEORGE VI

FAMOUS

"Famous isn't good, Ben. For Clark Gable, it's good. For Joe DiMaggio, it's good. For you, it isn't good, Ben."

> MEYER LANSKY warning Warren Beatty's Bugsy Siegel that the fame he's developed in Hollywood is dangerous in *Bugsy*
> (screenplay by James Toback)

"I'll make the name Disney famous around the world."

> WALT DISNEY to his father, 1923 (*The Man Behind the Magic,* p. 44)

"I do not believe they are right who say that the defects of famous men should be ignored. I think it is better that we should know them. Then, though we are conscious of having faults as glaring as theirs, we can believe that that is no hindrance to our achieving also something of their virtues."

> SOMERSET MAUGHAM, English novelist (Morgan, *Maugham,* 1980)

"Fame, like a drunkard, consumes the house of the soul."

> MALCOLM LOWRY, English author

FARMING

"Tillage and pasturage are the two breasts of France."

> Duc DE SULLY, chief minister to Henry IV, on farming
> (quoted in *The Economist,* September 19, 1992)

"Those who labor in the earth are the chosen people of God, if ever He had a chosen people, whose breasts He has made His peculiar deposit for substantial and genuine virtue."

THOMAS JEFFERSON (*Notes on the State of Virginia Query 6*, 1781–1785)

"The Unexpected stalks a farm in big boots like a vagrant bent on havoc. Not every farmer is an inventor, but the good ones have the seeds of invention within them. Economy and efficiency move their relentless tinkering and yet the real motive often seems to be aesthetic. The mind that first designed a cutter bar is not far different from the mind that can take the intractable steel of an outsized sickle blade and make it hum in the end. The question is how to reduce the simplicity that constitutes a problem ('It's simple; it's broke.') to the greater simplicity that constitutes a solution."

VERNE KLINKENBORG, author (*Making Hay*, p. 33)

FASHION

"This book is animated by a single word: fashion. Life cycles of computers and microprocessors have shrunk from years to months. Some 300 new grocery and drugstore products grace the shelves of American retailers each *week*. Even the materials and chemicals and pharmaceutical industries have gone high-fashion—with a rash of 'products' spewing forth, each aimed at customers' ever-shifting, ever narrower-gauge needs."

TOM PETERS, business consultant (*Liberation*, p. xxxii)

"Fashion magazines are the mother of invention. May the best mother win."

RICHARD AVEDON, photographer, on the war among *Vogue*, *Harper's Bazaar*, and *Elle* (*New York*, March 27, 1992)

"It's a bit expensive to eat here at McDonald's. But I guess for a high-fashion restaurant like this, the prices are O.K."

ZHANG WEI, customer at McDonald's in Beijing, on her breakfast of a hamburger, french fries, chocolate sundae, and Coke (*New York Times*, April 24, 1992)

"Fashion is never made by designers. Fashion is made by fashionable people. If Mrs. William Paley wears my hat, it becomes fashion. If it hangs in my stockroom, it's nothing."

HALSTON, designer (*Simply Halston*, p. 83)

"The fashion industry is no more able to preserve a style that men and women have decided to abandon than to introduce one they do not choose to accept. In America, for instance, huge advertising budgets and the wholehearted cooperation of magazines such as *Vogue* and *Esquire* have not been able to save the hat, which for centuries was an essential part of everyone's outdoor (and often of their indoor) costume. It survives now mainly as a utilitarian protection against weather, as part of ritual dress (at formal weddings, for example) or as a sign of age or individual eccentricity."   ALISON LURIE, author (*The Language of Clothes*, 1983)

FEAR

"If you're not scared, you're too stupid to work here."
LEE IACOCCA, CEO, Chrysler Corp. (senior management meeting, 1990)

"Am I afraid of high notes? Of course I am afraid! What sane man is not?"   Attributed to LUCIANO PAVAROTTI, tenor

"*Oderint dum metuant*." ("Let them hate us so long as they fear us.")
Roman saying

"Never let the fear of striking out get in your way."
Attributed to GEORGE HERMAN (Babe) RUTH

"Bite on the bullet, old man, and don't let them think you're afraid."   RUDYARD KIPLING, writer (*The Light That Failed*, 1890)

"Nothing in life is to be feared. It is only to be understood."
Attributed to MARIE CURIE, co-discoverer of radium

FIGHT

"Jesus had guts! He wasn't afraid of the whole Roman army. Think that quarterback's hot stuff? Well, let me tell you, Jesus would have made the best little All-American quarterback in the history of football. Jesus was a real fighter—the best little scrapper, pound for pound, that you ever saw. And why, gentlemen? Love! Jesus had love in both fists."
BURT LANCASTER preaching in *Elmer Gantry*
(screenplay by Richard Brooks)

"Bullfight critics ranked in rows
Crowd the enormous Plaza full;
But he's the only one who knows—
And he's the one who fights the bull."

> Attributed to DOMINGO ORTEGA, Spanish poet and bullfighter;
> often quoted by President Kennedy

"He could get into a fight in an empty elevator."

> JOE GARAGIOLA about Billy Martin (quoted in Stone, *April Fools*, 1990,
> as the preferred personality at Drexel Burnham)

"A draft-dodger in the fight against the federal deficit."

> Senator MARK O. HATFIELD on Secretary of Defense
> Caspar W. Weinberger (*New York Times*, January 31, 1985)

"The world is a fine place and worth fighting for."

> ERNEST HEMINGWAY, writer (*For Whom the Bell Tolls*, 1940, p. 43)

"In all fighting the direct method may be used for joining battle,
but indirect methods will be needed in order to secure victory."

> SUN TZU, Chinese commander and military thinker
> (*The Art of War*, 490 B.C.)

"Whoever fights monsters should see to it that in the process he
does not become a monster."

> NIETZSCHE, German philosopher (*The Portable Nietzsche*, 1954)

"Don't fight the problem, gentlemen. Solve it!"

> General GEORGE MARSHALL (Acheson, *Present at the Creation*, p. 216)

FIRINGS

"Studio executives are intelligent, brutally overworked men and
women who share one thing in common with baseball managers:
They wake up every morning of the world with the knowledge
that sooner or later they're going to get fired."

> WILLIAM GOLDMAN, screenwriter (*Adventures in the Screen Trade*, p. 39)

"In the language of football, 'resign' is a code word meaning 'he
was given the choice of quitting, being fired, or having the fans
blow up his house.'"

> GENE KLEIN, former owner of the San Diego Chargers
> (*First Down and a Billion*, 1987)

"80 percent of us have been fired and only 22 percent of the time was it a complete surprise."

> ROBERT HALF, employment consultant *(Robert Half on Hiring*, 1985)

"I thought my job was to run the company and try to get along with Mr. Geneen. I found out that I was supposed to get along with Geneen and try to run the company."

> LYMAN C. HAMILTON, after being fired as ITT's CEO (interview, 1979)

"I'll never make the mistake of being 70 again."

> CASEY STENGEL, on being fired by the Yankees, who said it was part of a youth movement *(The Gospel According to Casey*, p. 13)

"I fired him because he wouldn't respect the authority of the President. That's the answer to that. I didn't fire him because he was a dumb son-of-a-bitch, although he was, but that's not against the law for generals. If it was, half to three-quarters of them would be in jail."

> President HARRY S TRUMAN, on General Douglas MacArthur (Miller, *Plain Speaking*, p. 287)

"Well, sometimes you just don't like somebody."

> HENRY FORD, II, CEO, Ford Motor Company, to Lee Iacocca, who had pressed for an explanation on being fired from the Ford presidency (Collier and Horowitz, *The Fords*, p. 411)

When Lincoln fired a cabinet member, some senators pressed him to dismiss the whole cabinet. That reminded the president of a farmer who confronted seven skunks. "I took aim," the farmer said, ""blazed away, killed one, and he raised such a fearful smell that I concluded it was best to let the other six go."

> President ABRAHAM LINCOLN ("The Furrows of His Face," *U.S. News & World Report*, October 5, 1992)

"Sure we're speaking, Jedediah. You're fired."

> ORSON WELLES firing Joseph Cotten in *Citizen Kane* (screenplay by Herman J. Mankiewicz and Orson Welles)

FIX

"Rodeoing is about the only sport you can't fix. You'd have to talk to the bulls and horses and they wouldn't understand."

> BILL LINDEMAN, cowboy (Sherrin, *Cutting Edge*, p. 212)

"Everything goes wrong every minute. What you do is fix it."

Lt. Gen. Gus Pagonis, chief of logistics for
General H. Norman Schwarzkopf in Persian Gulf War,
on moving 200,000 allied troops 300 miles west for "Hail Mary"
maneuver against Iraq (*Newsweek*, March 19, 1991)

FLEXIBILITY

"Dad always said you've got to stay flexible. We never went on a
family trip nor have we ever heard of a business trip in which the
schedule wasn't changed at least once after the trip was
underway. Later, we all snickered at some writers who viewed
Dad as a grand strategist who intuitively developed complex
plans and implemented them with precision. Dad thrived on
change, and no decision was ever sacred."

Jim Walton, on his father, Sam (*Sam Walton*, p. 70)

"In flood time you can see how some trees bend, and because
they bend, even their twigs are safe, while stubborn trees are torn
up, roots and all."

Sophocles (Antigone)

FOOD

"A hosiery queen masquerading as a food company."

Anthony J. F. O'Reilly, CEO, Heinz, on Sara Lee food company, the world's
largest maker of women's hose (*The Economist*, November 14, 1992)

"WASPs are the only ones who don't have cockroaches, because
there's no food in the house."

Jackie Mason, comedian (interview, 1988)

"By and by
God caught his eye."

David McCord's "Epitaph for a Waiter" (Sherrin, *Cutting Edge*, p. 34)

"Restaurants now make more foreign currency for France than
arms sales abroad."

Paul Bocuse, owner of a three-star restaurant near Lyon
(*U.S. News & World Report*, February 8, 1993)

"I've run more risk eating my way across the country than in all
my driving."

Duncan Hines, founder and CEO of the food company bearing his name
(Calder, *Eat These Words*, p. 46)

"Manhattan is a narrow island off the coast of New Jersey devoted to the pursuit of lunch."

RAYMOND SOKOLOV, restaurant critic (*Wall Street Journal*, June 20, 1984)

"You can't eat well and keep fit if you don't shop well."

ADELLE DAVIS, food writer who, in the 1960s, successfully promoted nutritional cooking and eating (*Let's Eat Right to Keep Fit*, 1954)

FOOTBALL

"Football is much like chess. Match-ups. Harassments. Lines and rules and squares and decisions. Sucker him in and whack him."

MIKE HOLOVAK, football player
(*Violence Every Sunday—The Story of a Professional Football Coach*, 1967)

"In the East college football is a cultural exercise. On the West Coast it is a tourist attraction. In the Midwest it is cannibalism. But in the Deep South it is religion, and Saturday is the holy day."

MARION CASEM, long-time coach, Alcorn State University
(quoted in Morris, "The South, " in *Game Day USA
NCAA College Football*, p. 68)

"Football is rules and discipline and I happen to think that's what life is all about."

DAVID BROWNING, Texas Tech offensive tackle (*Sports Illustrated*, 1971)

"He's gonna have to find a way to take his biting and maiming skills and put them to use in the private sector."

DAUBER, assistant football coach, talking about a friend retiring from the pros ("Coach," ABC-TV, June 23, 1993)

FORGET

"In politics, the worst insult is to be forgotten."

ABRAHAM BEAME, mayor, New York City
(interview, 1981)

"Dear, never forget one little point: It's my business. You just work here."

ELIZABETH ARDEN, founder of cosmetics firm, to her husband
(Lewis and Woodsworth, *Miss Elizabeth Arden*, 1972)

"Forget the damned motor car and build the cities for lovers and friends."

LEWIS MUMFORD (*My Work and Days*, 1979)

"If you can't peel it, cook it, or boil it, forget it."

Peace Corps advice about eating abroad

FORGIVE

"Forgive your enemies, but never forget their names."

Attributed to President JOHN F. KENNEDY

"I believe in redeemable sin."

SYDNEY GRUSON, vice chairman, The New York Times Co., on his
willingness to negotiate with convicted felon Irving Kahn (the co-
founder of Teleprompter had spent 20 months in federal prison) to buy
two cable-television stations (<i>Fortune</i>, July 28, 1980)</div>

"Why, of course, he will forgive me; that's his business."

HEINRICH HEINE (on his deathbed, 1856, responding to a priest
who had told him God would forgive his sins)

FORTUNE

"The Fortune 500 is over."

PETER DRUCKER, management consultant (Fortune, April 20, 1992)

"There is no great secret to fortune making. All you have to do is buy cheap and sell dear, act with thrift and shrewdness and be persistent."

HETTY GREEN, nineteenth-century speculator and investor known
as the Witch of Wall Street (quoted in Sharp,
The Lore and Legends of Wall Street, p. 150)

"One number is as good as another. When you get that high, what difference does it make?"

JAMES SQUIRES, spokesman for H. Ross Perot, on conflicting reports that
Perot's fortune is $2.2 or $3.3 billion (<i>Newsweek</i>, June 1, 1992)</div>

FRANCHISE

"If you're going to own the Travelers Insurance Company, you need brilliant management, because Travelers is no different from Aetna or Reliance; it's almost a commodity. But if you own the only newspaper in town, if you own Walt Disney, if you own Coca-Cola, it's a franchise, it's not a commodity. You can't replace them easily."

SAUL STEINBERG, on why he went after Disney even as he was being
described as the takeover banker who would engulf and devour
Mickey Mouse (<i>The Prince of the Magic Kingdom</i>, p. 110)</div>

"When you buy a franchise, you're starting a business from zero and you gotta work at that business, building it up. You gotta do everything. Clean the floors, put the light bulbs in, run the books, hire the personnel, train 'em—everything. In the normal franchise business you're not going to make any money the first year. You're going to break even, if you're lucky. But then you start making money. Since 1950 franchising has created more millionaires than anything else."

ANDREW KOSTECKA, U.S. Department of Commerce
(quoted in Henderson, *Winners*, p. 39); Henderson adds
that the word *franchise* comes from the French *franchir*,
meaning "to be free from servitude"

"In business for yourself, not by yourself."

RAY A. KROC, Chairman, McDonald's
(Love, *McDonald's: Behind the Arches*, 1986)

FREE

"I'm going to build my own park because I like the free enterprise system."

WALTER O'MALLEY, owner, Brooklyn Dodgers,
on moving to Los Angeles (interview, 1957)

"There are overwhelming reasons for kinship, instead of hostility, between the free market for intellectual life and the free market for economic life."

WALTER WRISTON, former CEO and chairman, Citicorp
(*Risk and Other Four-Letter Words*, p. 31)

"Those in the free seats hiss first."

Chinese proverb quoted by Erica Jong in arguing against the publishing
industry's practice of sending out free copies of books (interview, 1991)

FRIENDS

"It is good to be on such cordial and increasingly relaxed terms with so remarkable a man in the art of inquisitiveness."

DAVID LILIENTHAL, former chairman, Atomic Energy Commission,
on his business relationship with André Meyer
(Reich: *Financier: André Meyer*, p. 65)

"It was a friendship founded on business, which is a good deal better than a business founded on friendship."

JOHN D. ROCKEFELLER, SR., financier
(Harr and Johnson, *The Rockefeller Century*, 1988)

"Only my friends call me 'wop.'"
FRANK SINATRA to Ernest Borgnine in
From Here to Eternity (screenplay by Daniel Taradash)

"When you get through a hole, don't run out there like a mule in the 20-acre pasture. Look for *friends*."
Attributed to JACK CURTICE,
Stanford University football coach, on using blockers

FUTURE

"Gone today, here tomorrow."
Attributed to ALFRED A. KNOPF, among others,
on the book industry's willingness to let stores return unsold books

"Those who are going to be in business tomorrow are those who understand that the future, as always, belongs to the brave."
WILLIAM BERNBACH, Doyle Dane Bernbach credo

"Give them back their future."
JOHN W. GARDNER, founder, Common Cause, advice to a political
candidate asked the most important thing a leader could do for the
American people (speech to the Revson Foundation, June 10, 1992)

"To many people the past seems inevitable and the future impossible. History is seen to have arisen not from unpredictable flows of genius and heroism, but more or less inevitably, from preordained patterns of natural resources and population."
GEORGE GILDER, writer
(quoted in Wriston, *Risk and Other Four-Letter Words*, p. 52)

"President Reagan remembers the future and imagines the past."
Senator EUGENE MCCARTHY, quoted by Thomas Winship
(*Nieman Reports*, XLIV, 4, Winter 1990)

"We *forecast*. Magicians and fortune-tellers *predict*."
ROBERT H. SMITH, CEO, The Futures Group (*Manhattan, Inc.*, January 1990)

"What's the use of worrying? It's silly to worry, isn't it? You're gone today and here tomorrow."
GROUCHO MARX in *The Cocoanuts*
(screenplay by Morrie Ryskind)

"It is easy to conquer posterity; the hard job for an original mind is to make any dent on its contemporaries."
LEWIS MUMFORD, planner and writer (Secrest, *Frank Lloyd Wright*, p. 483)

"I recalled an old epigram which had often comforted me, that the future comes one day at a time."

> DEAN ACHESON, former U.S. Secretary of State
> (*Present at the Creation,* p. 628)

"In human affairs, nothing is predetermined until after it has occurred."

> CARL BECKER, historian
> (quoted in Wriston, *Risk and Other Four-Letter Words,* p. 58)

"We are not managing this company for the next quarter. We are building it for the next generation."

> SAMUEL C. JOHNSON, chairman, S. C. Johnson and Son, Inc.,
> started by his great-grandfather in 1886 (Henderson, *Winners,* p. 209)

"I bet I'm the only guy here who don't know how the thing comes out."

> Attributed to TOOTS SHOR, restauranteur,
> to friends who had taken him to see *Hamlet*

"We often tend to be marching backward into the future."

> PAUL VALERY, French poet
> (quoted by Wriston, *Risk and Other Four-Letter Words,* p. 8)

"You cannot fight against the future. Time is on our side."

> WILLIAM GLADSTONE, proposing that the franchise be open
> to working men (quoted in *The Economist,* February 1992)

"I am captivated more by dreams of the future than by the history of the past."

> Attributed to THOMAS JEFFERSON

GAMBLE

"People are saying, 'Oh, this was Prince's big gamble.' What gamble? I made a $7 million movie with somebody else's money."

> PRINCE, rock star, on his film *Graffiti Bridge,*
> which flopped at the box office (*Newsweek,* December 24, 1990)

"The urge to gamble is so universal and its practice so pleasurable that I assume it must be evil."

> HEYWOOD BROUN, newspaper reporter
> (*All About Money,* p. 93)

"A lottery is a tax on imbeciles."

> Italian expression

GENEROSITY

"Generous people are rarely mentally ill people."
                    Attributed to Dr. KARL MENNINGER, co-founder, Menninger Clinic

"We'd all like a reputation for generosity and we'd all like to buy it cheap."
                    MIGNON MCLAUGHLIN (*The Neurotic's Notebook*, 1966)

"[John D. Rockefeller III] had not waited to become rich before he became generous."
                    ALLAN NEVINS (*Business Week*, August 22, 1988)

GENIUS

"Do you know what makes a man a genius? The ability to see the obvious."
                    CHARLES MCCARRY (*The Last Supper*, 1983)

"It takes a lot of time being a genius—you have to sit around so much doing nothing."
                    GERTRUDE STEIN, author (Souhami, *Gertrude and Alice*, 1992)

"True genius lies not in doing extraordinary things but in doing ordinary things extraordinarily well."
                    Maj. Gen. LOUIS H. WILSON, later Commandant,
                    U.S. Marine Corps (March 30, 1970)

"I'm an alcoholic. I'm a drug addict. I'm a homosexual. I'm a genius."
                    TRUMAN CAPOTE, writer (Winokur, *True Confessions*, p. 92)

GOD

"Deep down inside I wanted to say it the way I was thinking it: 'So . . . help me, God!'"
                    BILL CLINTON, on delivering the Presidential
                    oath of office (*Newsweek*, February 15, 1993)

"I believe in God, family, and McDonald's and in the office, that order is reversed."
                    RAY A. KROC, Chairman, McDonald's
                    (Love, *McDonald's: Behind the Arches*, 1986)

"It's the only business I know where you get to play God."
                    SAMUEL J. LEFRAK, chairman, Lefrak Organization,
                    discussing what drives developers (*Fortune*, May 1988)

"The Lord God is subtle, but malicious he is not."

ALBERT EINSTEIN (inscription in Fine Hall, Princeton University)

"*George:* 'God will never let this pilot be made. He'll never let
    me be successful. He'll kill me first.'

"*Psychiatrist:* 'I thought you didn't believe in God.'

"*George:* 'I do for the bad things.'"

LARRY DAVID ("The Jerry Seinfeld Show, " NBC-TV, May 1993)

"The Lord is on my side but He has a lot of getting even to do for
me."

General GEORGE S. PATTON, JR., on his 60th birthday
(Farago, *The Last Days of Patton*, p. 30)

"Our ambition is not business, but to love God. To love God,
one must live. To live, one must balance one's budget."

Dom SEBASTIAN, abbot, Notre Dame des Dombes monastery, on why the
monks make *muscaline*, a high-protein food for mountaineers
(*Fortune*, April 9, 1990)

"God is not dead but alive and well and working on a much less
ambitious project."

Graffiti (cited in *The Guardian*, November 26, 1975)

"Not only is there no God, but try getting a plumber on
weekends."

WOODY ALLEN, writer
("My Philosophy, " *The New Yorker*, December 27, 1969)

"Now I know why God has kept me alive for the last 25 years."

JOHN NORTHROP, aging and exiled deep in the Pentagon, on being shown
the new Stealth bomber, the offspring of his dream flying-wing bomber,
whose cancellation by President Truman had ruined his company
(Patton, *Made in USA*, p. 229)

"This is what God could have done if He'd had money."

GEORGE S. KAUFMAN, playwright, on Moss Hart's having planted fully
grown maples around his country home
(Goldstein, *George S. Kaufman*, 1979)

"Our senior partner is the Lord."

Company maxim at National Liberty Life Insurance

"I don't know how God managed. I'm having a terrible time."

JOHN HUSTON, producer, while making *The Bible*
(Grobel, *The Hustons*, 1989)

"There are two kinds of people: those who say to God, 'Thy will be done, ' and those to whom God says, 'All right, then, have it your way.'"   C. S. Lewis, writer (recalled on his death, November 22, 1963)

"Gods do not answer letters."   John Updike, writer, on Ted Williams' refusal to respond to critical letters

"Maybe God can do something about such a play; man cannot."   Casey Stengel, baseball manager, on Pittsburgh Pirate Bill Virdon's 8th-inning hit in the 7th game of the 1960 World Series, which Pittsburgh went on to win 10–9 (Carruth and Ehrlich, *American Quotations*, p. 94)

"I am a religious man. I pray for Milky Way, I pray for Snickers . . ."   Forrest Mars, CEO, Mars Inc., to executives in his newly expanded company (*Fortune*, July 3, 1989)

"I am prepared to meet my Maker. Whether my Maker is prepared for the great ordeal of meeting me is another matter."   Winston Churchill (news conference in Washington, D.C., 1954)

"God gave me my money."   John D. Rockefeller, Sr., financier (Flynn, *God's Gold: The Story of Rockefeller and His Times*, 1932)

"Mammon, the god of the world's leading religion. His chief temple is the holy city of New York."   Ambrose Bierce (*The Devil's Dictionary*, 1887)

"God don't make no mistakes. That's how he got to be God."   Archie Bunker, TV character (*Newsweek*, May 20, 1991)

"[Nothing upsets us more than to be told] our purposes differ from those of the Almighty."   Abraham Lincoln (quoted in Wriston, *Risk and Other Four-Letter Words*, p. 185)

"If there be a God, the Cardinal de Richelieu will have much to answer for. If there be none, why he lived a successful life."   Attributed to Pope Urban VIII, on learning of Richelieu's death

"Avoid, as you would the plague, a clergyman who is also a man of business."   St. Jerome (Letters, no. 52)

GOLD

"Gold don't carry any curse with it. It all depends on whether or not the guy who finds it is the right guy. The way I see it, gold can be as much of a blessing as a curse."

> HUMPHREY BOGART as Fred C. Dobbs trying to assure himself things are OK in *The Treasure of the Sierra Madre* (screenplay by John Huston)

"Saint-seducing gold."

> Shakespeare (*Romeo and Juliet*, Act I, i, l. 220)

"Those with the gold make the rules."

> SAMUEL J. LEFRAK, New York developer (*Business Week*, October 1992)

"I could have made $20 million in gold last year, but I chose to make maybe $8 million. That's what my father always taught me: take the sure thing."

> EDMOND SAFRA, CEO, Republic Bank, to *Forbes* magazine (Burrough, *Vendetta*, p. 51)

"I know what gold does to men's souls."

> WALTER HUSTON in *The Treasure of the Sierra Madre* (screenplay by John Huston)

"You shall not crucify mankind upon a cross of gold."

> WILLIAM JENNINGS BRYAN, presidential candidate, supporting greenback borrowers against the hard-money gold lenders (speech at Democratic National Convention, 1896)

GOOD

"There is nothing wrong with doing well from doing good."

> JOHN BRYANT, entrepreneur and founder of Operation Hope to rebuild South Central Los Angeles after the 1992 riots (*Wall Street Journal*, July 10, 1992)

"The Salvation Army was founded by an extraordinary person who asked the question, 'Why should the devil have all the good songs?'"

> WALTER WRISTON, former CEO and chairman, Citicorp, on why the advocates of bigger government and more regulation should be so lightly opposed in the battle of ideas (*Risk and Other Four-Letter Words*, p. ix)

"You have to hang on in periods when your style isn't popular, because if it's good, it'll come back, and you'll be a recognized beauty once again."

> ANDY WARHOL, artist (Winokur, *Friendly Advice*, p. 42)

"Every good and excellent thing stands moment by moment on the razor's edge of danger and must be fought for."

THORTON WILDER, playwright
(quoted in Kehrer, *Doing Business Boldly*, p. 91)

"No good deed goes unpunished."

Attributed to CLARE BOOTHE LUCE, author

"Goodness had nothing to do with it."

MAE WEST, responding to a hatcheck girl's comment,
"Goodness, what beautiful diamonds, " in *Night After Night*
(screenplay by Vincent Lawrence and Mae West)

"I can't stand it, I'm so good."

TED WILLIAMS, baseball player
(quoted in George F. Will, *New York Times Book Review*, April 7, 1991)

"When I'm good I'm very good, but when I'm bad I'm better."

MAE WEST in *I'm No Angel* (screenplay by Mae West)

"It used to be a good hotel, but that proves nothing—I used to be a good boy, for that matter."

MARK TWAIN (*The Innocents Abroad*, 1869)

"You can't make a man good by passing a law that he must be good. It's against human nature."

TOM PENDERGAST, head of Kansas City's Pendergast machine
(McCullough, *Truman*, p. 155)

"The offices men create live after them, the good is oft interred with their purpose."

DEAN ACHESON, former U.S. Secretary of State
(*Present at the Creation*, p. 186)

"I have never known much good to be done by those who affected to trade for the public good. It is an affectation, indeed, not very common among merchants, and very few words need be employed in dissuading them from it."

ADAM SMITH (*The Wealth of Nations*); George Stigler, economist, University
of Chicago, commented that "unfortunately, in a rare display of
reticence, Adam Smith failed to tell us what those few words are"
(quoted in Wriston, *Risk and Other Four-Letter Words*, p. 95)

"The only thing necessary for the triumph of evil is for good men to do nothing."

EDMUND BURKE, British statesman (*Thoughts and Details on Scarcity*, 1800)

"How long is it good?"

Attributed to NICHOLAS SCHENCK,
on being asked how long a film should be

"I do not want to be interesting. I want to be good."

LUDWIG MIES VAN DER ROHE, architect (*Chicago Daily News*, August 23, 1969)

GOSSIP

"Office gossip can work for you if you keep your mouth shut and ears open. Volunteer nothing, but listen to everything. If you accumulate enough gossip, it becomes information, and enough information can reveal truth."

ROBERT L. GENVA (*Managing Your Mouth:
An Owners Manual for Your Most Important Business Asset*, 1993)

GOVERNMENT

"One way to make sure crime doesn't pay would be to let the government run it."

President RONALD REAGAN (interview, 1967)

"Too bad all the people who know how to run the country are busy driving taxi cabs and cutting hair."

GEORGE BURNS, comedian (*Life*, December 1979)

"He'll sit right here, and he'll say, 'Do this! Do that!' And nothing will happen. Poor Ike—it won't be a bit like the army. He'll find it very frustrating."

President HARRY S TRUMAN, predicting problems
for his successor (quoted in McCullough, *Truman*, p. 914)

"This bill, if passed, will derail the ship of state."

STANLEY STEINGUT, former Speaker of the New York Assembly
(*New York Times*, October 17, 1989)

"This is the essential fact: The government did not know what it was doing."

Senator DANIEL P. MOYNIHAN, on urban poverty programs
as a whole (interview, 1978)

"What is this oozing behemoth, this fibrous tumor, this monster of power and expense hatched from the simply human desire for civic order? How did an allegedly free people spawn a vast, rampant cuttlefish of dominion with its tentacles in every orifice of the body politic?"

P. J. O'ROURKE, writer (*Parliament of Whores*, 1991)

"Experience should teach us to be most on our guard to protect liberty when the government's purposes are beneficent. . . . The greatest dangers to liberty lurk in insidious encroachment by men of zeal, well-meaning but without understanding."

Justice LOUIS BRANDEIS
(quoted in Wriston, *Risk and Other Four-Letter Words*, p. 92)

"The nine most terrifying words in the English language are, 'I'm from the government and I'm here to help.'"

President RONALD REAGAN on assistance to farmers
(press conference in Chicago, August 2, 1986)

"Unlike the corporate governance systems in other major industrialized countries—including those in Germany, France, Japan, and to a lesser degree Britain—the American system of governance has never relied on a stable set of close relationships between large financial institutions and major corporations. Rather, it has relied upon no one and everyone—upon the actions of uncounted numbers of individual, corporate, and institutional investors, operating within a deep, liquid, and anonymous securities market."

JOHN POUND, professor, Harvard School of Business
(*Journal of Applied Corporate Finance*, Fall 1992)

"The history of liberty is a history of limitations of governmental power, not the increase of it."

WOODROW WILSON
(quoted in Wriston, *Risk and Other Four-Letter Words*, p. 32)

"Low-weight babies, preschool nutrition, drugs, and family disintegration are economic problems. If you don't address them, they end up in your cost base anyway, and we all carry the competitive burden. That makes you look at government in a different way."

FRANK P. DOYLE, executive vice-president, General Electric Co.
(*Business Week*, "Reinventing America," November 1992, p. 78)

"[Adam] Smith's desire to keep government's hands off business had nothing to do with protecting business from government. On the contrary, it was his knowledge that whenever business and government walk hand in hand, the inevitable result is to afford some businessmen the opportunity to keep others out of the marketplace."

WALTER WRISTON, former CEO, Citicorp
(*Risk and Other Four-Letter Words*, p. 96)

"Government is the biggest enemy of moral values. Why did we see things we saw in General Electric and other companies— price-fixing? What does high taxation do? The little businessman starts to connive, cutting corners in order to get along. Moral values decline as government grows. We have a powerful government that bears on the daily lives of every American. This shouldn't be."

> Senator BARRY GOLDWATER (quoted in Moskin, *Morality in America*, p. 120)

"If men were angels, no government would be necessary."

> ALEXANDER HAMILTON, Secretary of the Treasury (*The Federalist*, 1787)

"No man is a warmer advocate for proper restraints and wholesome checks in every department of government than I am; but I have never yet been able to discover the propriety of placing it absolutely out of the power of men to render essential services, because a possibility remains of their doing ill."

> GEORGE WASHINGTON (letter to Bushrod Washington, November 10, 1787)

GOVERNMENT APPOINTMENTS

"Three presidents—Harding, Coolidge, and Hoover—served under Secretary of the Treasury Andrew Mellon."

> Washington adage

"Every time I fill a vacant office, I make ten malcontents and one ingrate."

> Attributed to King LOUIS XIV of France

GOVERNMENT REGULATION

"The creeping notion that additives are badditives."

> CHARLES G. MORTIMER, president, General Foods Corporation
> (*Wall Street Journal*, December 29, 1960)

"You can get a lot more done with a kind word and a gun, than with a kind word alone."

> AL CAPONE, gangster (quoted by economist Walter Heller,
> on wage and price controls in Safire and Safir, *Good Advice*, p. 118)

"Somehow a bunch of sanctimonious wackos have managed to legalize torture."

> Airline passenger about the smoking ban on U.S. domestic flights
> (*Life*, 1989)

"Those who would substitute the judgment of the bureaucrat for the judgment of the consumer inevitably forget that the free market for goods and the free market for ideas stem from the same root—freedom." WALTER WRISTON, former CEO and chairman, Citicorp
(*Risk and Other Four-Letter Words*, p. 30)

"The government doesn't have to give us a thing. All they have to do is get out of our way." FREDERICK C. SMITH, founder, Federal Express,
on the Civil Aeronautics Board's refusal to let Fed Ex fly
bigger, more fuel-efficient jets (Henderson, *Winners*, p. 173)

"I'm going to introduce a resolution to have the postmaster general stop reading dirty books and deliver the mail."
GALE W. MCGEE, U.S. Senator (*Quote*, October 11, 1959)

"All over this land today Americans under no instructions from government—scientists, businessmen, engineers, teachers, artists, nurses, labor leaders, you name it—are solving problems, starting organizations, devising new technologies, helping their neighbors, combating injustice, pioneering new fields of science, creating jobs, and enriching the lives of others. We love that torrential flow of human initiative, and we intend to hold on to it. Perhaps we'd feel less strongly about it had our history as a nation been different, had we been fenced in early; but now we're too used to the open range."
JOHN W. GARDNER, founder, Common Cause
(speech to the Council on Foundations, May 16, 1979)

"Whatever is not compulsory is forbidden."
MILTON FRIEDMAN's summation
of a world regulated by government rather than markets
(quoted in Wriston, *Risk and Other Four-Letter Words*, p. 97)

"All purchases must be made in France, rather than in foreign countries, even if the goods should be a little poorer and a little more expensive, because if the money does not go out of the realm, the advantage to the state is double."
COLBERT, finance minister to Louis XIV
(quoted in Wriston, *Risk and Other Four-Letter Words*, p. 188)

GRAFFITI

"Is there life before death?"
Graffiti in a Dublin slum

"I don't talk to no truck."

> Graffiti scrawled on a New York City Consolidated Edison repair truck
> whose side had been painted with the slogan:
> "Ask me how you can save on your electric bills."

"If this lady was a car she'd run you down."

> Graffiti on a Fiat billboard that read,
> "If it were a lady, it would get its bottom pinched."

"Every day at Armonk you could see him arrive
In a big fancy car that a chauffeur would drive
Kind of big in the wallet and narrow in the mind
And every V P knew how to kiss the behind
Of Big John."

> Corporate graffiti, to be sung to the tune of Big John, about IBM CEO John
> Akers, circulated on IBM's internal electronic network after a proxy
> statement disclosed that Akers and his management team had received
> raises of 36% and up while laying off thousands of employees
> (*Wall Street Journal*, December 13, 1991)

"Make it first, make it fast. Make it accurate." Alongside this
official Murdoch slogan was written: "Then go and make it up."

> Motivational slogans at newspaper printing plant
> (quoted in Shawcross, *Murdoch*, p. 320)

GRASP

"As someone pointed out recently, if you can keep your head
when all about you are losing theirs, it's just possible you haven't
grasped the situation."

> JEAN KERR, writer (*Please Don't Eat the Daisies*, 1957, introduction)

"Ah, but a man's reach should exceed his grasp,
Or what's a heaven for?"

> ROBERT BROWNING, poet (*Andrea del Sarto*, 1855)

GRATITUDE

"Gratitude, like love, is never a dependable international
emotion."

> JOSEPH ALSOP, columnist (*Observer*, November 30, 1952)

"If you pick up a starving dog and make him prosperous he will
not bite you. This is the principal difference between a dog and a
man."

> MARK TWAIN (*What Is Man?*, 1906)

GREAT

"I never wanted to be famous; I only wanted to be great."
RAY CHARLES, jazz singer and pianist (Winokur, *True Confessions*, p. 248)

"Few great men could pass Personnel."
Attributed to PAUL GOODMAN, commentator

"You were great out there today—now go out and be great again tomorrow." Pittsburgh relief pitcher DAVE GIUSTI defining a professional athlete
(quoted in Angell, *The New Yorker*, October 7, 1992)

"Great men are almost always bad men."
Lord ACTON, British statesman (1887)

GREED

"Greed is right! Greed works! Greed will save the USA!"
MICHAEL DOUGLAS as a Wall Street raider in *Wall Street*
(screenplay by Oliver Stone)

"You might as well go out on me. Get out. The business is for the needy, not the greedy." RAY KROC, chairman, McDonald's,
to an early stockholder planning to sell (Boas and Chain, *Big Mac*, p. 46)

"The reason that writers get submerged in the film business is simply a result of ordinary human greed. There's nothing literary about it—it's just greed. Why should I blame Warner Brothers for my own greed? Faulkner always presented himself as this martyr to Hollywood. Well, bullshit. His family evolved such a high nut that he had to keep doing it, because he was supporting 17 people— his brother's children, retainers, aunts, uncles, an alcoholic wife— and whether old Billy wanted to go to L.A. or not they stuck that sucker on the train and shot him out there to make some more money." JIM HARRISON, screenwriter (Plimpton, *The Writer's Chapbook*, p. 251)

"One man's greed is another man's incentive."
REGINALD F. LEWIS, CEO, TLC Beatrice (interview, 1989)

"Avaritia bona est." ("Greed is good.")
HENRY BEARD (*Latin for More Occasions*, p. 14)

"Greed really turns me off." HENRY K. KRAVIS, investment banker
(interview in *Fortune*, January 29, 1989)

"I think greed is healthy. You can be greedy and still feel good
about yourself." IVAN BOESKY, arbitrageur (commencement speech,
School of Business, University of California, Berkeley, 1986)

"The covetous man is ever in want." HORACE, Roman poet (*Odes*, 23 B.C.)

"Whoever has the most toys when he dies wins."
DANNY DE VITO in *Other People's Money* (screenplay by Alvin Sargent)

"It is better to *live* rich than to *die* rich."
SAMUEL JOHNSON (*Boswell's Life of Johnson*, 1778)

"Collecting is the only socially commendable form of greed."
EUGENE SCHWARTZ, high-profile New York art collector

"All pigs are equal.
But some pigs are more equal than others."
GEORGE ORWELL, writer (*Animal Farm*, 1945, ch. 10)

"A mere madness, to live like a wretch, and die rich."
ROBERT BURTON, English clergyman (*Anatomy of Melancholy*, 1621-51)

"Greedy of filthy lucre." I Timothy 3:3

"The greatest crimes are caused by surfeit, not by want. Men do
not become tyrants in order that they may not suffer cold."
ARISTOTLE (*Politics*)

"They are greedy dogs which can never have enough." ISAIAH 16:2

"Selling my merchandise is easy because it sells itself. Dreams of
glory always sell themselves. Men and women lie, cheat, steal, kill
and commit suicide over my merchandise. It makes them
miserable and it makes them joyous; it makes everything possible
and everything impossible. I'm a stockbroker and my game is
greed." BRUTUS (*Confessions of a Stockbroker*, 1971)

GUILTY

"We find the defendants incredibly guilty."

The foreman returning the verdict on Zero Mostel and Gene Wilder
in The Producers (screenplay by Mel Brooks)

"Saints should always be judged guilty until they are proved to be innocent."

GEORGE ORWELL (Reflections on Gandhi)

HARD WORK

"If hard work were such a wonderful thing, surely the rich would have kept it all to themselves."

Attributed to LANE KIRKLAND, union leader

"Go to the ant, thou sluggard; consider her ways, and be wise."

Proverbs 6:6

HATRED

"I am the product of hatred and love."

Justice CLARENCE THOMAS, explaining during Congressional hearings that
he is a conservative because he had to rely on himself when growing up
in the segregated South (Newsweek, July 15, 1991)

"I forgave the DAR many years ago. You lose a lot of time hating people."

MARIAN ANDERSON, singer, announcing her retirement almost 25 years
after the DAR refused her concert space in Washington's
Constitution Hall (New York Times, December 13, 1963)

"Detestation of the high is the involuntary homage of the low."

Charles Dickens (A Tale of Two Cities, 1, 1859)

HEALTH

"You have to wonder about a marriage in which the husband encourages the wife to take on health care policy and the wife keeps a cat even though he's allergic."

MAUREEN DOWD, reporter, New York Times, on President and Mrs. Clinton
(speech, New York City, February 10, 1993)

"Thousands upon thousands of persons have studied disease. Almost no one has studied health."

ADELLE DAVIS, food writer (Let's Eat Right to Keep Fit, 1954)

"We have to act now to make sure you don't have to be a
Rockefeller to afford decent health care in this country."

> Senator JAY ROCKEFELLER, urging national health coverage
> (*Life*, November 1991)

"What we would have is a combination of the compassion of the
IRS and the efficiency of the post office."

> LOUIS SULLIVAN, Secretary of Health and Human Services, on how health
> care would work if it were nationalized (*Newsweek*, February 1992)

HEART

"Their hearts are in it. Shortly their heads will be in it."

> PAT RILEY, coach, New York Knicks, on his team's valiant but losing play
> against the champion Chicago Bulls in the 1992 playoffs
> (*New York Times*, May 10, 1992)

"I aimed at the public's heart and by accident hit it in the
stomach."

> UPTON SINCLAIR, talking on his *Jungle* (1906), whose coverage of the
> Chicago stockyards so provoked the public that President Theodore
> Roosevelt ordered an investigation and Congress passed the Pure Food
> and Drug Act. Sinclair had hoped that his story of immigrant
> Lithuanians would win sympathy for the working class.
> (*Wall Street Journal*, Centennial Edition, 1989)

HELL

"Hell is truth seen too late."

> THOMAS HOBBES, English philosopher
> (quoted in Wriston, *Risk and Other Four-Letter Words*, p. 141)

HEROES

"The Americans are certainly hero-worshippers, and always take
their heroes from the criminal classes."

> OSCAR WILDE, writer (letter to Norman Forbes-Robertson, April 19, 1882)

"Show me a hero and I will write you a tragedy."

> F. SCOTT FITZGERALD, writer (*Notebooks*, 1978)

HIRE

"If he's got golf clubs in his trunk or a camper in his driveway, I
don't hire him."

> LOU HOLTZ, football coach, University of Notre Dame, on his
> criteria for choosing assistant coaches ("Tonight Show," January 7, 1992)

"It is all one to me if a man comes from Sing Sing or Harvard. We hire a man, not his history."

Attributed to HENRY FORD, founder, Ford Motor Co.

HISTORY

"Things are not getting worse; things have always been this bad. Nothing is more consoling than the long perspective of history. It will perk you up no end to go back and read the works of progressives past. You will learn therein that things back then were also terrible, and what's more, they were always getting worse. This is most inspiring."

MOLLY IVINS, columnist,
on the Reagan administration (*Molly Ivins Can't Say That*, p. 84)

"The Industrial Revolution marks the most fundamental transformation of human life in the history of the world recorded in written documents. For a brief period it coincided with the history of a single country, Great Britain. An entire world economy was thus built on, or rather around, Britain, and this country therefore temporarily rose to a position of global influence and power unparalleled by any state of its relative size before or since, and unlikely to be paralleled by any state in the foreseeable future. There was a moment in the world's history when Britain can be described, if we are not too pedantic, as its only workshop, its only massive importer and exporter, its only carrier, its only imperialist. . . . "

E. J. HOBSBAWM, historian (*Industry and Empire*, 1968)

"History, despite its wrenching pain,
Cannot be unlived, but if faced
With courage, need not be lived again."

MAYA ANGELOU, poet (poem read at President Clinton's 1993 inaugural)

"History is, in fact, the fragmentary record of often inexplicable actions of innumerable bewildered human beings, set down and interpreted according to their own limitations by other human beings, equally bewildered."

C. V. WEDGWOOD (quoted in Clifford, *Counsel to the President*, p. 403)

"The past is a foreign country; they do things differently there."

L. P. HARTLEY (*The Go-Between*, 1953, prologue)

"History is more or less bunk. It's tradition. We don't want tradition. We want to live in the present and the only history that is worth a tinker's damn is the history we make today."

HENRY FORD, founder, Ford Motor Co.
(Chicago Tribune, May 25, 1916); often simply cited "History is bunk."

"History is a set of lies agreed upon."

NAPOLEON (Maxims)

"1885—Gus Swift buys cows"
"1984—Beatrice buys Esmark."

DONALD KELLY, former CEO, Esmark, on the important dates
in his former firm's history (Bianco, Rainmaker, p. 242)

"News is the first rough draft of history."

Attributed to BEN BRADLEE, editor, Washington Post

HIT

"When I pass a belt, I can't resist hitting below it."

ROBERT MAXWELL, on his negotiations with unions at the New York Daily
News, which Maxwell was buying (Bower, Maxwell, The Outsider, p. 433)

"A hit record is one thing; a hit career is another."

AL TELLER, general manager, Columbia Records
(Wall Street Journal, May 21, 1985)

"It is not enough to aim; you must hit."

Italian proverb

HOLLYWOOD

"When I remember the desperate, lie-telling, dime-hunting Hollywood I knew only a few years ago, I get a little homesick. It was a more human place than the paradise I dreamed of and found."

MARILYN MONROE, c. 1950s (Corey, Man in Lincoln's Nose, p. 114)

"It's a mining town in lotus land."

F. SCOTT FITZGERALD, writer (The Last Tycoon, 1941)

"If we made cars the way we make movies—not that we do such a good job of making cars in this country—we'd all be pedestrians."

KARL LUEDTKE, screenwriter
(Naked Hollywood, "Funny Money," TV documentary, 1992)

"Here, if you don't want to be a director, it's like a captain who doesn't want to be a major."

JOSH GREENFIELD, novelist and screenwriter
(*New York Times*, April 25, 1982)

"To 'pitch' equals to grovel shamelessly.
To 'network' equals to spread disinformation.
To 'freelance' equals to collect unemployment."

From *The Cynical Screenwriters' Dictionary of Hollywood Lexicon*,
an anonymous fax making the rounds in Hollywood
(*New York Times*, May 31, 1992)

HONESTY

"An honest politician is one who, when he is bought, will stay bought."

SIMON CAMERON, nineteenth-century politician
(Sherrin, *Cutting Edge*, p. 143)

"We are more dishonest about money than our grandfathers were."

C. P. SNOW, novelist (quoted in Moskin, *Morality in America*, p. 239)

"Give me six lines written by an honest man and I will find something in it with which to hang him."

Attributed to Cardinal RICHELIEU

HUMANITY

"It is easier to love humanity as a whole than to love one's neighbor."

ERIC HOFFER, labor leader and commentator
(*New York Times Magazine*, February 15, 1959)

HUMAN NATURE

"The propensity to truck, barter, and exchange . . . is common to all men, and to be found in no other race of animals."

ADAM SMITH, economist (*The Wealth of Nations*, 1776)

"Man is not what he thinks he is, he is what he hides."

Attributed to ANDRÉ MALRAUX, French author

"Nature, Mr. Allnut, is what we were put on this earth to rise above!"

KATHARINE HEPBURN to Humphrey Bogart in *The African Queen*
(screenplay by James Agee)

"Subdue your appetites and you have subdued human nature."
Charles Dickens' MR. SQUEERS (*Nicholas Nickleby*, 1838)

HUMILITY

"Ours was a life of fleeting anonymity. Every morning Johnson
poured spoonfuls of humility through our clenched teeth."
JACK VALENTI, speechwriter for President Lyndon B. Johnson
(quoted in Noonan, *What I Saw at the Revolution*, p. 92)

"I cannot agree with those who rank modesty among the virtues."
Arthur Conan Doyle's SHERLOCK HOLMES to Watson
("The Greek Interpreter, " *The Memoirs of Sherlock Holmes*, 1894)

HURT

"Complaints are only a sign that you've been hurt. Keep the
wounds out of sight." CHARLIE MacARTHUR to fellow screenwriter Ben Hecht
(*Movie Talk*, p. 60)

"I never set out to hurt anybody deliberately unless it was, you
know, important. Like a league game or something."
DICK BUTKUS, Chicago Bears linebacker (*Sports Illustrated*, 1987)

"Do not think yourself hurt and you remain unhurt."
MARCUS AURELIUS (*Meditations*, c. 150)

IDEA

"You look at any giant corporation, and I mean the biggies, and
they all started with a guy with an idea, doing it well."
IRVINE ROBBINS, co-founder, Baskin-Robbins Ice Cream
(Henderson, *Winners*, p. 17)

"It seemed like a good idea at the time."
RICHARD BARTHELMESS, author (*The Last Flight*, 1931)

IDEALISM

"It doesn't matter who gives them as long as you never wear
anything second-rate. Wait for the first-class jewels, Gigi. Hold
on to your ideals."
ISABEL JEANS to Leslie Caron in *Gigi* (screenplay by Alan Jay Lerner)

"Idealism is the noble toga that political gentlemen drape over their will to power."

ALDOUS HUXLEY, writer, recalled on his death
(*New York Herald Tribune*, November 24, 1963)

"I'm an idealist without illusions."

President JOHN F. KENNEDY (Winokur, *True Confessions*, p. 90)

"Ideas are great arrows, but there has to be a bow. And politics is the bow of idealism."

BILL MOYERS, journalist (*Time*, October 29, 1965)

IDEOLOGY

"Nothing political is correct."

Graffiti (quoted in *Esquire*, May 1993)

IMAGINATION

"Microsoft's only factory asset is the human imagination."

FRED MOODY, on Microsoft founder Bill Gates
(*New York Times Magazine*, August 25, 1991)

"Imagination is one of the last remaining legal means you have to gain an unfair advantage over your competition."

PAT FALLON, Fallon McElligott Rice, advertising agency in Minneapolis
(Henderson, *Winners*, p. 113)

"Today's Imagination, a three-layer, elongate (flat) company. I read a book on Disney somewhere where they described his role as that of a bumblebee: floating around pollinating ideas— providing the creative spark, but with no line responsibility as such."

GARY WITHERS, founder, Imagination, an $80-million, 200-employee
company offering "a full range of creative services" to handle projects as
diverse as product launches, architectural designs, issue analysis
(Peters, *Liberation*, p. 165)

IMMIGRANTS

"I have a question about that sign on the Statue of Liberty. Do we have to *specify* the wretched refuse of the earth?"

Jerry Seinfeld, comedian
("The Jerry Seinfeld Show, " NBC-TV, June 17, 1993)

"We are the Romans of the modern world—the great assimilating people."

OLIVER WENDELL HOLMES, physician (*The Autocrat of the Breakfast Table*, 1858)

IMPLEMENTATION

"To reflect is noble, to realize is servile."

> LEONARD DA VINCI, who felt that execution of his many ideas was beneath him (Bramly, *Leonardo: Discovering the Life of Leonardo da Vinci*, 1991)

IMPORTANT

"Some people in this world are important. All the rest wish they were."

> RICHARD FALK, New York publicist, on one of the principles of his career (*New York Times*, November 6, 1991)

"You don't know how important *The Globe* is—you make it possible for me and the Kennedys to be liberal."

> Senator PAUL TSONGAS to Martin Nolan, editor, *Boston Globe* (recalled by Nolan on acquisition of *The Globe* by the *New York Times*, June 13, 1993)

"See, this game's a little bit more important than life. It's not life and death. It's more important than life."

> JOHN McCAY, football coach, University of Southern California, on his team's rivalry with the University of Notre Dame in the 1980s (NBC-TV, "Halftime Report, " November 28, 1992)

"Stew Leonard, Jr., tells a story about his father, whose name adorns a famous Norwalk, Connecticut, food store. Stew Jr., 36, runs the store now, under his father's watchful eye. A couple of years ago, Stew Jr. and his brother, Tom, and some other managers from the store were getting ready to meet with a high-powered, high-priced consultant. Stew Sr. couldn't attend the meeting, so Stew Jr. asked him on the phone if there was anything particularly important he wanted discussed. 'I bought some corn yesterday, ' Stew Sr. replied, 'and had it for dinner last night, and it wasn't really sweet.'

"Stew Jr. gently remonstrated with his father: 'Dad, this isn't that kind of meeting. We're talking about strategy, we're talking about merchandising. Isn't there anything really important that you want me to mention?'"

"'Yeah. The corn isn't really, really sweet.'"

> STEW LEONARD, JR., grocer (*Nation's Business*, June 1991)

"Good and bad is not important in the movie business. All that's important is successful or unsuccessful."

> WILLIAM GOLDMAN, screenwriter (quoted in Brown, *Shoptalk*, p. 65)

INCOME

"Our incomes are like our shoes; if too small, they gall and pinch us; but if too large, they cause us to stumble and to trip."
> CHARLES C. COLTON, English clergyman (*Lacon*, 1820)

"The worker should have enough income to provide for himself and his family sufficient to live a life in keeping with their Christian dignity."
> Pope LEO XIII (encyclical, 1893); cited by Father Conti in his successful argument to the SEC to force Bell Atlantic to put executive compensation to proxy vote (quoted in *Wall Street Journal*, February 13, 1992)

INDEPENDENT

"A damn independent boy; independent as a hog on ice."
> Congressman SAM RAYBURN, on Lyndon B. Johnson (quoted in Steinberg, *Sam Johnson's Boy*, 1968)

"A good independent can run circles around a chain store by offering better service."
> BRIAN BAXTER, operator of independent book store, on financial success (*The Economist*, April 25, 1992)

"Follow the path of the unsafe, independent thinker. Expose your ideas to the danger of controversy. Speak your mind and fear less the label of 'crackpot' than the stigma of conformity."
> THOMAS J. WATSON, founder of IBM (Safire and Safir, *Good Advice*, p. 336)

INERTIA

"It is always wiser, where there is a choice, to trust to inertia. It is the greatest force in the world."
> Rex Stout's NERO WOLFE responding to questions about whether a damaging piece of information should be freely revealed (*Fer-de-lance*, 1934)

INFERIORITY

"During one of my first sessions in the Senate, J. Hamilton Lewis came over and sat down by me. He was from Illinois and was the Whip of the Senate at that time. 'Don't start out with an inferiority complex,' he told me. 'For the first six months you'll wonder how you got here—and after that you'll wonder how the rest of us got here.'"
> Former President HARRY S TRUMAN (quoted in Hyman, *Washington Wind and Wisdom*, p. 77)

INFLATION

"Stop inflation? That crowd? They couldn't stop a sink! They don't care about food prices because they never tasted anything worth eating. You know what Nixon has for lunch? Cottage cheese. On a big day he eats Presbyterian meat loaf on Wonder Bread. What does he care about how much it costs a human being to buy a decent pastrami on rye and a side of chopped liver made with real schmalz?"

Calvin Trillin's character, MAX GOLD
("The Inquiring Demographer, " *The New Yorker*, May 27, 1974)

"Steel prices cause inflation like wet sidewalks cause rain."

ROGER BLOUGH, president, U.S. Steel Corporation (*Forbes*, August 1, 1967)

INFORMATION

"All of economics is information processing. You like green running shoes with air bubbles showing? Fine. I like blue ones, no bubbles. Figuring out who likes what—information!—and serving those specialized needs more quickly than the next person are what 'steer' the firm, innovation, and the overall marketplace."

TOM PETERS, business consultant (*Liberation*, p. 110)

"We are to the information world what transportation was to the industrial world. We are the transportation system of the future."

WILLIAM G. MCGOWAN, founder and CEO, MCI Communications
(Henderson, *Winners*, p. 189)

"In the information society, nobody thinks. We expected to banish paper, but we actually banished thought."

Michael Crichton's mathematician (*Jurassic Park*, p. 72)

"I do not like the words 'You can't.' They are *not* fun."

MICHAEL BENNETT, choreographer and creator of *A Chorus Line*
(*New York Observer*, October 19, 1992)

"I tinker with sensations. A good ride alters the way your body processes information. My job is to turn you on your head. When I see an F-16 climb or dive or roll, I don't just watch, I ask, 'Why can't we do that?' And that's what this new ride does. It flies like a jet plane."

RON TOOMER, president and CEO, Arrow Dynamics, an amusement-ride
manufacturer (*American Way Magazine*, December 1, 1992)

"The very existence of new information channels, operating in real time and across all frontiers, will be a powerful influence for civilized behaviour. If you are arranging a massacre, it will be useless to shoot the cameraman who has so inconveniently appeared on the scene. His pictures will already be safe in the studio five thousand miles away and his final image may hang you."

> ARTHUR C. CLARKE, science fiction writer and first conceiver of the idea of satellite communications (quoted in Shawcross, *Murdoch*, p. 179)

INGENUITY

"Never tell people how to do things. Tell them *what* to do and they will surprise you with their ingenuity."

> General GEORGE S. PATTON (*War As I Knew It*, 1947)

"Anybody who has any doubt about the ingenuity or the resourcefulness of a plumber never got a bill from one."

> GEORGE MEANY, president, AFL (CBS -TV, January 8, 1954)

INHERITANCE

"A lifetime supply of food stamps."

> WARREN BUFFETT, CEO, Berkshire Hathaway, on why he planned to leave his three adult children a very small proportion of his fortune— $5 million each (*Fortune*, 1991)

"Inherited wealth is a big handicap to happiness. It is as certain death to ambition as cocaine is to morality."

> WILLIAM K. VANDERBILT, financier (interview, 1905)

"Some people's money is merited,
And other people's is inherited."

> ODGEN NASH (*The Terrible People*, 1933)

"The very very able, and the very very smooth, inherit the world."

> Attributed to HARVEY SCHEIN, executive vice president, News America Publishing, Inc.

"What do you do with it? You can't give it to the kids—it would ruin their lives."

> STEPHEN JARISLOWSKY, sole owner of an investment management company with assets of $11 billion, referring to his personal fortune of $200 million (speech at the 40th reunion of the Harvard Business School's class of 1949)

"Leisured for life."   HENRY JAMES, father of the writer, on being told the size
of his inheritance from his father, whose fortune was greater
than any other New Yorker except John Jacob Astor's
(Lewis, *The Jameses: A Family Narrative*, 1991)

"The meek shall inherit the earth but not its mineral rights."
JOHN PAUL GETTY, financier (Lenzner, *The Great Getty*, 1985)

INNOVATION

"I'd climb in the car as it went down the assembly line and
introduce myself. Then I'd ask for ideas."
JOHN RISK, Ford manager in charge of developing the Taurus, describing
how he elicited useful suggestions from Ford employees (interview, 1991)

"Discovery consists of seeing what everybody has seen—and
thinking what nobody has thought."
ALBERT SZENT-GYORGYI, biologist (Foster, *Innovation*, p. 82)

"IBM's failure to adapt its business model to new technologies
and markets raises a fundamental question: Can IBM—or any
other computer company—devise a corporate strategy and
design an organization that encourages business model
innovation, especially when such innovations threaten the
people, culture, and business practices that made for the
company's original success?"
MARK STAHLMAN, president of New Media Associates
(a New York City consulting firm) and computer industry
financial analyst (*New York Times*, December 21, 1992)

"It takes five years to develop a new car in this country. Heck, we
won World War II in four years."
H. ROSS PEROT, founder, Electronic Data System (interview, 1970)

"When I was at Oldsmobile, there was something I learned that
I've never forgotten. There was an old guy there who was an
engineer, and he had been at GM a long time, and he gave me
some advice. He told me, whatever you do, don't let GM do it
first."   Peter Estes, president, General Motors (Halberstam, *The Reckoning*, p. 23)

"A wide screen just makes a bad film twice as bad."
Attributed to SAM GOLDWYN, film producer

"The AHA! experience."

MARTIN GARDNER, editor, *Scientific American*,
on brilliant discoveries (Foster, *Innovation*, p. 83)

"I hate it. I just do. *That*, local news, the IRS, and hair dryers are the four worst inventions of this century."

BEANO COOK, football analyst, on artificial turf (quoted in *Sport*, 1985)

"We keep moving forward, opening up new doors, and doing new things, because we're curious and curiosity keeps leading us down new paths."

WALT DISNEY (*The Man Behind the Magic*, p. 154)

"He who will not apply new remedies must expect new evils; for time is the greatest innovator."

FRANCIS BACON, seventeenth-century British essayist
(*Of Innovations*, 1612)

". . . it ought to be remembered that there is nothing more difficult to take in hand, more perilous to conduct, or more uncertain in its success, than to take the lead in the introduction of a new order of things. Because the innovator has for enemies all those who have done well under the old conditions, and lukewarm defenders in those who may do well under the new."

MACHIAVELLI (*The Prince*, 1532)

INSTINCT

"It's a sensual thing. I can feel it in my balls."

Dealer who made $30-40 million finding lost or unrecognized
masterpieces by great painters (Broyard, *Intoxicated by My Illness*, p. 28)

"Johnson's instinct for power is as primordial as a salmon's going upstream to spawn."

THEODORE H. WHITE, on President Lyndon B. Johnson
(*The Making of the President*, 1964)

INSULT

"Open insults openly arrived at."

BERNARD BERENSON, Renaissance art expert,
on modern diplomacy (quoted in McCullough, *Truman*, 1992, p. 954)

"Never insult an alligator until you've crossed the river."

Attributed to CORDELL HULL, diplomat

"He loved to make everybody mad, and used insults the way other people use simple declarative sentences."

JAMES THURBER, cartoonist, on Alexander Woolcott
(*The Years with Ross*, 1957)

INSURANCE

"Look, there's only one reason why anyone goes to Bermuda to start an insurance company—and it isn't the weather."

TONY SCHRADER, deputy commissioner for insurance, State of Iowa
(*Chronicle of Higher Education*, December 14, 1983)

"Americans have an abiding belief in their ability to control reality by purely material means. Hence . . . airline insurance replaces the fear of death with the comforting prospect of cash."

CECIL BEATON, photographer (*All About Money*, p. 181)

"In the insurance business, there is no statute of limitations on stupidity."

WARREN BUFFETT, CEO, Berkshire Hathaway
(annual report, 1991)

INTEGRITY

"They tell a story about a Hollywood agent's young son who asked his father what the word integrity meant. 'Let me give you an example, son. Let's say Kirk Douglas sent me a check for the agency's commission on the new picture we got for him. And let's say a few days later his business manager sends me another check in error for the same commission. Integrity is whether or not I tell my partner.'"

TONY RANDALL and MICHAEL MINDLIN (*Which Reminds Me*, p. 153)

"I ran the wrong kind of business, but I did it with integrity."

SYDNEY BIDDLE BARROWS, Mayflower Madam
("'Mayflower Madam' Tells All, " *Boston Globe*, September 10, 1986)

INTELLIGENCE

"The test of a first-rate intelligence is the ability to hold two opposed ideas in mind at the same time and still retain the ability to function."

F. SCOTT FITZGERALD, writer (*The Crack-Up*, 1936)

"I won't eat anything that has intelligent life, but I'd gladly eat a network executive or a politician."

MARTY FELDMAN, comedian (Calder, Eat These Words, p. 84)

INTERNATIONAL

"Whether we are ready or not, mankind now has a completely integrated international financial and informational marketplace capable of moving money and ideas to any place on this planet in minutes."

WALTER WRISTON, former CEO and chairman, Citicorp
(Risk and Other Four-Letter Words, p. 132)

"Mexico has no tax on capital gains and no tax on dividends. If the U.S. doesn't get serious about capital formation, you may soon see American millionaires swimming across the Rio Grande to the land of plenty."

JAMES M. MYERS, investor (Fortune, November 16, 1992)

"Our sales curve has been a barometer of East-West relations."

JOHN SWANHAUS, president, Pepsico, on the 40-percent drop in sales of
Pepsico's Stolichnaya vodka after the Soviet invasion of Afghanistan
(New York Times, September 6, 1992)

INTUITION

"We have to recognize that intuition is not a flaky concept. Basically, intuition is accumulated knowledge."

ANDRE ALKIEWICZ, founder and managing partner, Perception
International of Ridgefield, Connecticut (Manhattan, Inc., January 1990)

"His nose is pretty good; he can find the truffles."

STEVE TISCH, producer, on Peter Guber, partner, Guber-Peters
Entertainment Company (Premiere, March 1990)

"Only intuition can protect you from the most dangerous individual of all, the articulate incompetent."

ROBERT L. BERNSTEIN, president, Random House, on his experience
interviewing MBA graduates (to author, 1993)

INVENT

"I do not invent anything, even the weather."

BARBARA TUCHMAN, historian
(Phi Beta Kappa address at Radcliffe College, April 1993)

INVESTING

"To turn $100 into $110 is work. To turn $100 million into $110 million is inevitable."

Attributed to EDGAR BRONFMAN, chairman,
Joseph E. Seagram and Co., 1990

"Lethargy bordering on sloth remains the cornerstone of our investment style."

WARREN BUFFETT, CEO, Berkshire Hathaway, on why he hadn't bought or
sold a single share of five of his company's six major holdings recently
(*Newsweek*, May 20, 1991)

"Like the groundhog, we think it's time to be looking for the sun."

DAN W. LUFKIN, on being named general partner
of GLH Partners, L. P., a $556-million investment fund
in which he had been a limited partner
(*Wall Street Journal*, September 13, 1991)

"We have arrived at the age of the militant investor."

SANFORD C. SIGOLOFF, former chairman, Wickes Co.
(*Business Week*, November 1991)

"It's the new way investors are acting. They're not selling; they're screaming and voting."

SARAH TESLIK, executive director, Council of Institutional Investors
(*Wall Street Journal*, April 27, 1992)

"I was the only guy around here who knew a debenture from an equity."

RICHARD E. CHENEY, chairman, Hill and Knowlton, former
director of investor relations for Mobil Oil, on how
well equipped he was for the takeover era
(*New York Times*, October 24, 1989)

INVESTMENT

"Will Rogers once said it is not the original investment in a Congressman that counts; it is the upkeep."

Attributed to President JOHN F. KENNEDY

"In an information-based economy much of what we now consider 'expenditure' or 'social overhead' is actually 'capital investment,' and should—perhaps, must—produce a high return and be self-financing."

PETER DRUCKER, management consultant
(quoted in Wriston, *Risk and Other Four-Letter Words*, p. 128)

"Gentlemen prefer bonds."

ANDREW MELLON, financier (*All About Money*, p. 165)

INVESTMENT BANKING

"Wall Street's old comedy of manners."

FRED JOSEPH, CEO, Drexel Burnham Lambert,
on the politics of underwriting (Bianco, *Rainmaker*, p. 307)

"Investment banking has become to productive enterprise in this country what mud wrestling is to the performing arts."

MARK RUSSELL, PBS-Television comedian

"Male debutantes."

JEFF BECK, investment banker, Donaldson, Lufkin and Jenrette,
on his fellows (Bianco, *Rainmaker*, p. 78)

"Don, you've still got the big hat but all the cattle are gone."

MARTIN SIEGEL, investment banker, Kidder Peabody,
to Donald Kelly, former CEO, Esmark, who still wanted
to do deals after selling his company (Bianco, *Rainmaker*, p. 252)

INVESTMENT STRATEGY

"If the share price of a company with a great product is dropping, go back and look at the product. If it's still good, hold on."

PETER LYNCH, manager, Fidelity Magellan Fund
(*Fortune*, March 11, 1991)

"I learned two things from Peter Lynch. When times get tough, forget everything else and go back to basic company fundamentals. The other idea is to be objective. If you buy a stock at $10, sell it at $15, and it goes to $20, and you know objectively it is still a good buy, you should buy it again."

JEFF VINIK, Fidelity Investments, summarizing advice
from his former boss (*Fortune*, March 9, 1992)

"Never invest your money in anything that eats or needs repairing."

BILLY ROSE, producer (*New York Post*, October 26, 1957)

"We shy away from technology companies. We admit from the start we don't know how to manage technology risk."

GLENN OKUN, pension fund manager, IBM,
on his investment criteria (*Fortune*, March 9, 1992)

"I live by a Warren Buffett maxim: 'Buy stocks like you buy your groceries, not like you buy your perfume.'"

> THOMAS RUSSO, Gardner Investments, Lancaster, Pennsylvania, on his strategy of buying companies with strong, global brand names
> (*Fortune*, March 9, 1992)

"It takes patience, discipline and courage to follow the 'contrarian' route to investment success; to buy when others are despondently selling, to sell when others are avidly buying. However, based on a half century of experience, I can attest to the rewards of the end of the journey."

> JOHN TEMPLETON, CEO and founder, the Templeton Growth Fund
> (quoted in Sharp, *The Lore and Legends of Wall Street*, p. 217)

"If we can assume that it is the habit of the market to overvalue common stocks which have been showing excellent growth or are glamorous for some other reason, it is logical to expect that it will undervalue—relatively at least—companies that are out of favor because of unsatisfactory developments of a temporary nature. This may be set down as a fundamental law of the stock market, and it suggests an investment approach that should prove most conservative and promising."

> BENJAMIN GRAHAM, author of *The Intelligent Investor*
> (quoted in Sharp, *The Lore and Legends of Wall Street*, p. 217)

"To help the homeless after I make my first 100 million."

> JON HSU, entrepreneur and Harvard College junior, who co-founded *Inside Edge*, a magazine "by guys for guys"
> (*New York Times*, May 23, 1993)

JAPAN

"They have the money. Isn't that what we're talking about? It's impossible to have a savings rate of 14 percent in Japan and 3 percent here and for us to be competitive. If those people are going to work the way they do—students in Japan go to school 46 weeks a year, 6 days a week. My grandson is always on holiday."

> LEW WASSERMAN, chairman, MCA, on its acquisition by Matsushita
> (Bruck, "The World of Business, " *The New Yorker*, October 9, 1991)

"We've believed for 50 years that the Japanese are small Americans who wanted to be like us. They are not."

> LESTER THUROW, economist (*Fortune*, July 27, 1992)

"When the phone is out of order,
        and the roof has sprung a leak,
When the money in your paycheck
        barely gets you through the week,
When the baby has the colic,
        and your dog is full of fleas,
Don't complain to Washington—
        just blame the Japanese.

When the crooks are running rampant,
        and the judges are too lax,
When letters from the IRS
        demand some extra tax,
When your son is quitting college,
        and your daughter's getting D's,
Just do what Iacocca does—
        and curse the Japanese.

When your taxes keep on rising,
        while your bank-book starts to shrink,
When pollution clouds your city,
        so the air begins to stink,
When the temperature is falling,
        and your pipes are sure to freeze,
Call upon your Congressman
        to bash the Japanese.

When everyone around you
        is complaining of the news,
And some condemn the Arabs
        while others blast the Jews,
Stiffen up your lip, my son,
        and never bend your knees—
Just be a true American,
        and blame the Japanese."

GEORGE DAWSON, emeritus professor of economics, Empire State College
of the State University of New York (*New York Times*, January 29, 1992)

"If Americans want to worry about something, they ought to
worry about what Japanese companies are investing in Japan."

WILLIAM FRANKLIN, president, Weyerhaeuser Far East, on Japanese
investment in the United States (*Fortune*, February 11, 1991)

"Germany has to pay $150 billion for East Germany and is about to be deluged with Russian immigrants, and everybody knows Japan's problems. You think we have problems? Go live in Frankfurt or Tokyo."

PAUL ERDMAN, former Swiss banker and author of best-selling financial thrillers (*Forbes*, November 23, 1992)

"At least superficially smooth, affable, mild, and formally correct."

EDWIN O. REISCHAUER, on the Japanese businessman (quoted in Bruck, "The World of Business, " *The New Yorker*, October 9, 1991)

"Don't blame the Japanese. We did it to ourselves."

W. EDWARDS DEMING, a consultant on industrial quality who left the unreceptive ears of the United States for Japan where he taught his quality-control principles (*U.S. News and World Report*, April 22, 1991)

"Trade is the goose that laid Japan's golden egg. And Japan just happens to be the bad boy of trade internationally."

CARLA HILLS, United States Trade Representative (interview, 1990)

"Japan is a great nation. It should begin to act like one."

JOHN C. DANFORTH, chairman, U.S. Senate Subcommittee on Trade (speech in Tokyo, January 13, 1986)

"Nobody in the world is as good at making decisions as the Japanese."

PETER DRUCKER, management consultant (interview, 1990)

"Much of Japan's success can be traced to the country's economic disadvantages. Lacking resources, Japanese firms were forced to develop the skills and technologies needed to process its precious resources into higher-value goods."

MICHAEL PORTER, Harvard economist (*The Comparative Advantage of Nations*, 1990)

"The Japanese climb into a uniform at four years old and stay in uniform until they retire."

ROBERT NOYCE, founder and CEO, Intel Corp., and inventor of the integrated circuit (*Esquire*, December 1983)

"This is our revenge for Pearl Harbor."

Hollywood executive on the disastrous performance of Columbia Pictures after its purchase by Sony and MCA's Universal Studio after its purchase by Matushita (*Newsweek*, October 14, 1991)

"The Japanese have a saying: fix the problem, not the blame. In American organizations it's all about *who* fucked up. Whose head will roll. In Japanese organizations it's about *what's* fucked up, and how to fix it. Nobody gets blamed. Their way is better."

Character quoted in MICHAEL CRICHTON (*Rising Sun*, p. 72)

JUSTICE

"The universe is on the side of justice."

MARTIN LUTHER KING, JR., civil rights leader
(Garrow, *Bearing the Cross*, p. 80)

"There's little justice and certainly no mercy in this world."

ELLERY QUEEN (*The Roman Hat Mystery*, 1929)

"If I had to choose between justice and disorder, on the one hand, and injustice and order, on the other, I would always choose the latter."

HENRY KISSINGER, Secretary of State, paraphrasing Goethe
(quoted in Isaacson, *Kissinger: A Biography*, p. 653)

KILL

"If you keep working at it, in the last analysis, you win. We're like old Ho Chi Minh. They've got to kill us one hundred times. All we have to do is kill them once."

FREDERICK C. SMITH, founder, Federal Express, on the Civil Aeronautics
Board's refusal to let Fed Ex fly bigger, more fuel-efficient jets
(Henderson,*Winners*, p. 173)

"What doesn't kill you makes you stronger."

Sign attributed to NIETZSCHE in office of Donny Deutsch, executive vice
president, Deutsch Inc., a New York advertising agency known for its
hard-edged campaigns (*New York Times*, October 14, 1992)

"I don't care if it does kill you."

Sign attributed to DONNY DEUTSCH,
sitting alongside above quote (*New York Times*, October 14, 1992)

"Give me some scratching, diving, hungry ballplayers who come to kill you."

LEO DUROCHER, baseball manager (*Nice Guys Finish Last*, 1975)

KNOWLEDGE

"There's no fool like the guy who gets a hit movie. Whether it's the actor, the director, the marketing head, the chairman of the

company, or the key grip. You start to think you know something.
Well, wait two weeks until your next movie."

NED TANNEN, former president, Universal and Paramount Pictures
("Naked Hollywood: Eighteen Months to Live,"
Channel 13, October 31, 1992)

"The person who knows 'how' will always have a job. The
person who knows 'why' will always be his boss."

DIANE RAVITCH, professor, Columbia University Teachers College
(Time, June 17, 1985)

"Things were run on a need-to-know principle: if you needed to
know, you weren't told."

PETER JAY, former executive, Maxwell Communications, on his former
boss's management practices (Newsweek, January 6, 1992)

"Man, if you gotta ask you'll never know."

Attributed to LOUIS (Satchmo) ARMSTRONG, on being asked what jazz is

"How in the hell would I know why there are Nazis? I don't even
know how this can opener works."

LEO POSTREL to Woody Allen, in Hannah and Her Sisters
(screenplay by Woody Allen)

"Man knows so much and does so little."

R. BUCKMINSTER FULLER, futurist
(quoted in Fadiman, The Little, Brown Book of Anecdotes, 1985)

"Everybody's talking, but nobody knows."

Attributed to SONNY BOY WILLIAMSON, bluesman

"I am rather like a mosquito in a nudist camp; I know what I
ought to do, but I don't know where to begin."

STEPHEN BAYNE, on becoming first executive officer of
the Anglican Communion (Time, January 25, 1960)

"I definitely feel that we cannot do the fantastic things based on
the real unless we first know the real."

WALT DISNEY, directing his artists to study deer and animal life for Bambi
(The Man Behind the Magic, p. 81)

"Noel Coward told me never to work with anybody unless they
knew more than I did. Well, that's great if you can swing it
financially, but in this business, baby, you could starve to death."

ELAINE STRITCH, actress (New York Times, April 11, 1993)

"I read about an Eskimo hunter who asked the local missionary priest, 'If I did not know about God and sin, would I go to hell?' 'No,' said the priest, 'not if you did not know.' 'Then why,' asked the Eskimo earnestly, 'did you tell me?'"

ANNIE DILLARD, writer (*New York Daily News*, December 10, 1992)

LABOR

"We must be part of the general staff at the inception, rather than the ambulance drivers at the bitter end."

LANE KIRKLAND, president, AFL-CIO
(*New York Times*, May 4, 1986)

"American liberals, even American radicals, have more in common with the Reagan Right than with us. All of them, the whole bunch, are middle-class Emersonian individualists. Emerson, Thoreau, all of these guys are scabs. Lane Kirkland is outside the American consensus in a way that even Abbie Hoffman never was."

THOMAS GEOGHEGAN, labor organizer
(Geoghegan, *Which Side Are You On?*, 1991)

"The last thing this industry needs is a shoot-out at the OK Corral."

MICHAEL CONNOR, vice president, Chicago, Central and Pacific Railroad, on the railroad companies' hostile response to a union strike
(*Wall Street Journal*, May 30, 1986)

"The worst crime against working people is a company which fails to operate at a profit."

SAMUEL GOMPERS, president, American Federation of Labor (AFL)

"You can't mine coal with bayonets."

United Mine Workers (UMW) saying
(Geoghegan, *Which Side Are You On?*, p. 19)

LAS VEGAS

"Las Vegas may be a preview of what we are coming to. It's a community in which everyone works very hard to have fun. They are almost grim about it. We make more and more out of having fun."

LESTER A. KIRKENDALL, professor, Oregon State University
(quoted in Moskin, *Morality in America*, p. 55)

LAUGH

"Life holds no more wretched occupation than trying to make the English laugh."

MALCOLM MUGGERIDGE, editor, *Punch* from 1953 to 1957
(*Newsweek*, April 6, 1992)

"Don't laugh, it's paid for."

A Lizzie Label (slogans painted on Model T's in the mid-1920s)
(Patton, *Made in USA*, p. 177)

"If an idea makes me laugh, that's a sure sign it's a good idea. All commercials should be entertaining, no exceptions made. Somebody's made the business too rational, which is wrong. Everybody ought to have fun. If you're not having fun, then you're getting screwed."

LOU CENTLIVRE, executive managing director,
Foote, Cone and Belding (interview, 1985)

THE LAW

"I say that you cannot administer a wicked law impartially. You can only destroy. You can only punish. I warn you that a wicked law, like cholera, destroys everyone it touches—its upholders as well as its defiers."

SPENCER TRACY as defense attorney Henry Drummond in *Inherit the Wind*
(screenplay by Nathan E. Douglas and Harold J. Smith)

"If Moses had gone to Harvard Law School and spent three years working on the Hill, he would have written the Ten Commandments with three exceptions and a saving clause."

CHARLES MORGAN, former head of the ACLU (interview, 1988)

"I don't want to know what the law is, I want to know who the judge is."

ROY COHN, litigator
(quoted by Tom Wolfe in the *New York Times Book Review*, April 3, 1988)

"One hires lawyers as one hires plumbers, because one wants to keep one's hands off the beastly drains."

AMANDA CROSS, pseudonym of Carolyn Heilbrun, mystery writer
(*The Question of Max*, 1976)

"Law is born from despair of human nature."

JOSE ORTEGA Y GASSET, writer (recalled on his death, October 18, 1955)

"At Harvard Law, you learn what the law is; at Yale you learn what it ought to be."
A Yale Law School credo (*Newsweek*, October 26, 1992)

"I use the rules to frustrate the law. But I didn't set up the ground rules."
F. LEE BAILEY, lawyer (Winokur, *True Confessions*, p. 63)

"What looks like a stone wall to a layman is a triumphal arch to a corporation lawyer."
Lawyer of J. P. MORGAN, financier, on the Sherman Antitrust Act of 1890

"I am the law."
FRANK HAGUE, mayor, Jersey City, New Jersey
(*New York Times*, November 11, 1937)

"Out here, due process is a bullet."
JOHN WAYNE explaining the law of the land to David Janssen in
The Green Berets (screenplay by James Lee Barrett)

"It is difficult to improve our material condition by the best laws, but it is easy enough to ruin it by bad laws."
Attributed to President THEODORE ROOSEVELT

"What do I care about the law? Hain't I got the power?"
Attributed to CORNELIUS VANDERBILT, financier
(quoted in Heilbroner, *The Wordly Philosophers*, 1972)

"A multitude of laws in a country is like a great number of physicians, a sign of weakness and malady."
VOLTAIRE
(quoted in Wriston, *Risk and Other Four-Letter Words*, p. 77)

"*Fex urbis, lex orbis.*" ("Dregs of the city, law of the world.")
St. JEROME
(quoted in Sante, *Low Life: Lures and Snares of Old New York*, preface)

"The law, in its majestic equality, forbids the rich as well as the poor to sleep under bridges."
Attributed to ANATOLE FRANCE, author

"Why does a hearse horse snicker
Hauling a lawyer away?"
CARL SANDBURG, poet (*Complete Poems of Carl Sandburg*, p. 189)

"Circumstantial evidence is a very tricky thing. It may seem to point very straight to one thing, but if you shift your own point of

view a little, you may find it pointing in an equally
uncompromising manner to something entirely different."

Arthur Conan Doyle's SHERLOCK HOLMES to Watson
("Bascombe Valley Mystery," *Adventures of Sherlock Holmes*, 1892)

"There's no law against making silk purses."

WILLIAM ARROWSMITH, translator, on being asked if he ever improved the
quality of work he translated (quoted by William Weaver, translator of
Umberto Eco and Italo Calvino, New York City, February 9, 1993)

LAWYERS

"There was a young lawyer who showed up at a revival meeting
and was asked to deliver a prayer. Unprepared, he gave a prayer
straight from his lawyer's heart: 'Stir up much strife amongst thy
people, Lord,' he prayed, 'lest thy servant perish.'"

Senator SAM J. ERVIN, JR. (Behrman, *The Lawyer Joke Book*, p. 119)

"I read recently that they're now using lawyers instead of rats in
scientific experiments. They're doing this for two reasons. One,
the scientists become less attached to the lawyers. And two, there
are some things even rats won't do."

ROBIN WILLIAMS as grown-up Peter Pan, a mergers and acquisition
lawyer, in *Hook* (screenplay by Jim V. Hart and Malia Scotch Marmo)

"Keynes did not like lawyers. He thought the United States 'a
lawyer-ridden land' and believed that 'the Mayflower, when she
sailed from Plymouth, must have been entirely filled with
lawyers.'"

DEAN ACHESON, former U.S. Secretary of State
(*Present at the Creation*, p. 83)

"How many lawyers does it take to screw in a light bulb? How
many can you afford?"

Retold by SID BEHRMAN (Behrman, *The Lawyer Joke Book*, p. 81)

"Behind every sportsman in America stands a lawyer."

JAMES K. COYNE, president, American Tort Reform Association
(Sperber, *College Sports Inc.*, p. 120)

"If your lawyers tell you that you have a very good case, you
should settle immediately."

RICHARD INGRAMS, editor, *Private Eye*, on losing a major libel suit brought
by Robert Maxwell (Bower, *Maxwell, The Outsider*, p. 357)

"There is never a deed so foul that something couldn't be said for the guy; that's why there are lawyers."

MELVIN BELLI, criminal lawyer (*Los Angeles Times*, December 18, 1981)

"The first thing we do, let's kill all the lawyers."

DICK THE BUTCHER (Shakespeare, *Henry VI*, Part II Act 4, Scene 2)

LEADER

"You give a good leader very little and he will succeed; you give a mediocrity a great deal and he will fail."

General GEORGE MARSHALL
(quoted in McCullough, *Truman*, p. 261)

"Strong men can accomplish a lot even with poor organization, but weakness at the top cannot be overcome by the best."

DEAN ACHESON (*Present at the Creation*, p. 47)

"When I die, in the newspapers they'll write that the sons of bitches of this world have lost their leader."

VINCENT GARDENIA's pep talk to his team, The New York Mammoths, in
Bang the Drum Slowly (screenplay by Mark Harris)

"The leader of genius must have the ability to make different opponents appear as if they belonged to one category."

ADOLF HITLER (*Mein Kampf*, 1935)

"Disraeli cynically expressed the dilemma when he said: 'I *must* follow the people. Am I not their leader?' He might have added: 'I *must* lead the people. Am I not their servant?'"

EDWARD L. BERNAYS, publicist (*Propaganda*, 1928)

LEADERSHIP

"Example is leadership."   Attributed to Dr. ALBERT SCHWEITZER, humanitarian

"You can never know the agonies and the lonely moments of leadership."   MARTIN LUTHER KING, JR., to an audience in Chicago as he was leading
the demonstrations in Selma, Alabama (Garrow, *Bearing the Cross*, p. 408)

LEARN

"Learn to obey before you command."

SOLON of Athens (*Fragment*, c. 600 B.C.)

"A tough lesson in life that one has to learn is that not everybody wishes you well."

DAN RATHER, newscaster (Safire and Safir, *Good Advice*, p. 286)

"I learned you have to get a fast start, and you have to have sharp elbows." DONNA E. SHALALA, Secretary of Health and Human Services, on her early days in Washington as Assistant Secretary for Policy at HUD (*New York Times*, December 12, 1992)

"Son, you got to learn to catch those bugs in your mouth."

CASEY STENGEL, baseball manager, to a young pitcher who had balked the winning run home when a bug flew in his eye (*The Gospel According to Casey*, p. 61)

"I have learned that *nothing matters but the final picture*."

DAVID O. SELZNICK, producer (Corey, *The Man in Lincoln's Nose*, p. 140)

"They say princes learn no art truly but the art of horsemanship. The reason is, the brave beast is no flatterer. He will throw a prince as soon as his groom."

BEN JOHNSON, playwright (*Discoveries*, c. 1635)

LEAVE

"Never leave well enough alone."

RAYMOND LOEWY, American industrial designer of the 1930s (*Business Week*, December 3, 1990)

"Joyce was a synthesizer, trying to bring in as much as he could. I am an analyzer, trying to leave out as much as I can."

SAMUEL BECKETT, playwright (quoted in Gussow, "Beckett at 75—An Appraisal," *New York Times*, April 19, 1981)

"Leave them while you're looking good."

ANITA LOOS (*Gentlemen Prefer Blondes*, 1925)

"As a last resort, all any multinational company can do in its relations with a sovereign state is to make an appeal to reason. If that fails, capital, both human and material, will leave for countries where it is more welcome. Since men and money in the long run go where they are wanted and stay where they are well treated, capital can be attracted but not driven."

WALTER WRISTON, former CEO and chairman, Citicorp (*Risk and Other Four-Letter Words*, p. 198)

"The time to leave this place is when all white people begin to look alike."

> PAUL HOFFMAN, *New York Times* correspondent in what was then the Congo (quoted in Halberstam, *The Making of a Quagmire*, 1964)

"And then I was no doubt discharged by baseball in which I had to go back to the minor leagues as a manager, and after being in the minor leagues as a manager, I became a major-league manager in several cities and was discharged, we call it discharged, because there is no question I had to leave."

> CASEY STENGEL, manager, New York Yankees, testifying before the Subcommittee on Antitrust and Monopoly of the Committee of the Judiciary of the United States Senate, 1958 (*The Gospel According to Casey*, p. 157)

LESS

"There is less in this than meets the eye."

> TALLULAH BANKHEAD, actress, on a Maeterlinck play (Woollcott, *Shouts and Murmurs*, 1922)

"Less is a bore."

> ROBERT VENTURI, architect, in reaction to Mies van der Rohe's "Less is more," recalled on the 100th anniversary of Mies's birth (*Time*, March 3, 1986)

LEVERAGE

"It is a mark of this limited financial intelligence that the miracle of leverage is rediscovered approximately every ten years. It is also a measure of the intellectual subtlety of the innovation in these matters that the most celebrated financial discovery in recent times is that high interest rates, if high, even exorbitant, enough, will be sufficient to sell high-risk bonds."

> JOHN KENNETH GALBRAITH, economist, on Ivan Boesky, Michael Milken, and Drexel Burnham in a review of *The Predators' Ball* (*New York Review of Books*, December 24, 1988)

"Lusus cure pecunia mutua sumpta tibi ludendus est." ("The name of the game is leverage.")

> HENRY BEARD (*Latin for More Occasions*, p. 14)

LIBERAL

"A liberal is a man who is willing to spend somebody else's money."

> Senator CARTER GLASS (Associated Press wire, September 24, 1938)

"If God had been a Liberal there wouldn't have been ten commandments. There would have been ten suggestions."
MALCOLM BRADBURY and CHRISTOPHER BIGSBY ("After-Dinner Game,"
Harper's Religious Quotation Companion, p. 94)

LIE

"My point of view is that if somebody asks you a question he shouldn't ask, you have every right to tell him a lie."
ALLAN ("Ace") GREENBERG, managing partner, Bear, Stearns and
Company, on denying that his client, T. Boone Pickens, controlled a
significant amount of Gulf stock, shortly before Pickens took over Gulf
(quoted in Davis, "The Biggest Knockover," *Harper's*, January 1985)

"A lie can travel halfway around the world while the truth is putting on its shoes."
MARK TWAIN (quoted in Burrough,
Vendetta: American Express and the Smearing of Edmond Safra, 1992)

"If there's something in my past that's found
That contradicts the views I propound
Here's what I do: I lie
I simplify, boldly falsify
I look the other fella in the eye
And deny, deny, deny."
PETE SEEGER (*New York Times*, October 13, 1992)

"It's a dirty lie."
JOHN LENNON, responding to the question "Are you a part of social
rebellion against the older generation?"at the Beatles' first press
conference in America in 1963 (Sherrin, *Cutting Edge*, p. 128)

LIFE

"Life is too short to stuff a mushroom."
SHIRLEY CONRAN, business executive and novelist
(Calder, *Eat These Words*, p. 35)

"Listen, you son of a bitch, life isn't all a god-damn football game!
You won't always get the girl! Life is rejection and pain and loss."
FREDERICK EXLEY, writer (*A Fan's Notes*, 1977)

"The geometry of life."
Playwright JOHN GUARE, on the chance encounters and random
coincidences that lead to larger events (quoted in Brown, *Shoptalk*, p. 160)

"Life can only be understood backwards, but it must be lived forwards."

SÖREN KIERKEGAARD, philosopher (*Journals and Papers*, 1843)

"All life is six to five against."

DAMON RUNYON, writer (*Money from Home*, 1935)

LIFESTYLE

"I've been trying for some time now to develop a lifestyle that doesn't require my presence."

GARY TRUDEAU, cartoonist, on avoiding Washington parties
(McLellan, *Ear on Washington*, p. 34)

LISTENING

"What do I see in him? What do I *hear* is more like it. Listen to the name. *Henry Ford.*"

ANNE MCDONNELL, of the "golden clan" of McDonnells, responding
to her sister's question of what she saw in Henry Ford II, whom
she would marry (Collier and Horowitz, *The Fords*, p. 173)

"It's an ear job, not an eye job."

DONALD T. REGAN, on his job as former White House Chief of Staff
(*New York Times*, January 25, 1985)

"If they want to survive, they've got to start listening."

MICHAEL SANGER, chairman, Old Line Plastics, supplier to General
Motors, on GM (*New York Times*, September 23, 1992)

"Who in the hell wants to hear actors talk?"

HARRY WARNER, founder of Warner Bros. Studio
(Cerf and Navasky, *The Experts Speak*, p. 172)

"The government only hears its own voice, knows that it only hears its own voice, yet acts under the illusion that it hears the voice of the people, and demands from the people that they should accepts this illusion too."

KARL MARX, on a censored press; saying hangs
on the office wall of Leslie Fong, editor, *Straits Times*,
Singapore's leading English-language newspaper
(*The Economist*, August 3, 1991)

"Be swift to hear, slow to speak, slow to wrath."

James 1:19

LITIGATION

"I hope that you will not be tempted into litigation. Life is too short for that."

JUNIUS MORGAN's advice to his son, J. P.
(Chernow, *Hourse of Morgan*, 1990)

LIVING

"The cost of living is going up and the chance of living is going down."

Attributed to FLIP WILSON, comedian

"I can't make a living off purists."

KENNETH FELD, president, Ringling Brothers and Barnum and Bailey
Combined Shows Inc., on critics who say he panders to low tastes by
using rock music, skateboarders, and break dancers
(*New York Times*, October 4, 1987)

"I dream for a living."

STEVEN SPIELBERG, producer and director (*Time*, July 15, 1985)

"I would live all my life in nonchalance and insouciance
Were it not for making a living, which is rather a nouciance."

OGDEN NASH, poet (*Hard Lines*, 1931)

"I have always earned my living by the pen and by my tongue."

WINSTON CHURCHILL
(*The Life of the Podium*, p. 192)

"I don't want to be a doctor, and live by men's diseases; nor a minister to live by their sins; nor a lawyer to live by their quarrels. So I don't see there's anything left for me but to be an author."

Attributed to NATHANIEL HAWTHORNE, author

"You must not suppose, because I am a man of letters, that I never tried to earn an honest living."

GEORGE BERNARD SHAW, playwright (*Writers*, p. 34)

"Don't be misled into believing that somehow the world owes you a living. The boy who believes that his parents, or the government, or anyone else owes him a livelihood and that he can collect it without labor will wake up one day and find himself working for another boy who did not have that belief and, therefore, earned the right to have others work for him."

DAVID SARNOFF, founder and CEO, RCA (Safire and Safir, Good Advice, p. 94)

LOANS

"We don't like to make loans. We prefer to make deposits."

EDMOND SAFRA, financier, to Christina Onassis, daughter of the late
billionaire Aristotle Onassis (quoted in Burrough, Vendetta:
American Express and the Smearing of Edmond Safra, 1992)

"Son, never loan money to a church. As soon as you start to close in on them, everybody thinks you're a heel."

GENE LOCKHART in Going My Way
(screenplay by Frank Butler and Frank Cavett)

LOCATION

"Location, location, location."

Long-standing real estate principle

"Geography is irrelevant."

CHRISTOPHER LEINBERGER, real estate consultant,
on the ability of corporations to decentralize, moving different divisions
to widely dispersed areas (Forbes, November 23, 1992)

LONDON

"When it's three o'clock in New York, it's still 1938 in London."

BETTE MIDLER, actress (London Times, October 21, 1978)

"London clubs remain insistent on keeping people out, long after they have stopped wanting to come in."

ANTHONY SAMPSON (The Anatomy of Britain, 1962)

"Certainly London fascinates. One visualizes it as a tract of quivering grey, intelligent without purpose, and excitable without love; as a spirit that has altered before it can be chronicled; as a heart that certainly beats, but with no pulsation of humanity."

ROBERT HUGHES, author
(Culture of Complaint: The Fraying of America, p. 108)

LONG RUN

"Recently I was talking to one of Japan's best foreign-exchange dealers, and I asked him to name the factors he considered in buying and selling. He said, 'Many factors, sometimes very short-term, and some medium, and some long-term.' I became very interested when he said he considered the long term and asked him what he meant by that time frame. He paused a few seconds and replied with genuine seriousness, 'Probably ten minutes.' That is the way the market is moving these days."

> Toyoo Gyothen, former vice-minister, Japanese Ministry of Finance
> (*Changing Fortunes* [with Paul Volcker])

"But this *long run* is a misleading guide to current affairs. *In the long run* we are all dead."

> John Maynard Keynes, economist
> (*Tract on Monetary Reform*, 1923, chapter 3)

LOOKING BACK

"Entrepreneurship was the sacred mushroom of the 1980s. It seemed delusively greater and grander than it was."

> Ted Levitt,
> former editor, *Harvard Business Review* (*Thinking About Management*, 1990)

"It has turned out to be an *annus horribilis*."

> Queen Elizabeth on 1992 (*U.S. News & World Report*, December 7, 1992)

"Huge brains, small necks, weak muscles and fat wallets—these are the dominant characteristics of the '80s, the generation of swine."

> Hunter S. Thompson, gonzo journalist (*Generation of Swine*, 1988)

"Money is the long hair of the '80s."

> Elizabeth Ashley, actress (interview, 1986)

LOOKS

"We suffer for what the gods gave us, and I'm afraid Dorian Gray will pay for his good looks."

> Lowell Gilmore in *The Picture of Dorian Gray*
> (screenplay by Albert Lewin)

"The Lord knew from all eternity I was going to be Pope and you'd think he would have made me more photogenic."

> Pope John XXIII to photographer Yousef Karsh
> (Michaels, *Pope John XXIII*, p. 66)

"You would look a great deal better for your face is so thin."

> 12-year-old Grace Bedell's advice to Abraham Lincoln
> that he grow a beard ("The Furrows of His Face,"
> *U.S. News & World Report*, October 5, 1992)

LOS ANGELES

"It's like paradise. With a lobotomy."

JANE FONDA as a New Yorker in Los Angeles in *California Suite*
(screenplay by Neil Simon)

"A circus without a tent."

CAREY McWILLIAMS (*Southern California Country*, 1946)

"Nineteen suburbs in search of a metropolis."

H. L. MENCKEN (*Americana*, 1925)

"I soon discovered that if you were a writer who couldn't speak English, there was one place in which this was no way a handicap: Los Angeles."

JEREMY IRONS, as a Hungarian-speaking German writer who fled the
Nazis, in *Tales from Hollywood* (screenplay by Christopher Hampton)

"A big hard-boiled city with no more personality than a paper cup."

RAYMOND CHANDLER (*The Little Sister*, 1949, chapter 26)

LOSE

"They've shown me ways to lose I never knew existed."

CASEY STENGEL, baseball manager, on his team, the New York Mets
(*The Gospel According to Casey*, p. 18)

"I'm not going down. I don't go down for nobody."

ROBERT DENIRO, as prizefighter Jake LaMotta, refusing to take a fall in
Raging Bull (screenplay by Martin Scorcese)

"I know why we lost the Civil War. We must have had the same officials."

BUM PHILLIPS, coach, New Orleans Saints, on losing the Senior Bowl
(*Sporting News*, 1983)

"If you're old and you lose, they say you're outmoded. If you're young and you lose, they say you're green. So don't lose."

TERRY BRENNAN, football coach, University of Notre Dame
(*Life*, March 25, 1957)

"While you're trying to save your face, you're losing your ass."

President LYNDON B. JOHNSON
(Geyelin, *Lyndon B. Johnson and the World*, 1966)

"Burke got his ass sent packing home."

> Congressman RONALD COLEMAN, responding to someone noting that
> Edmund Burke said a representative should exercise his own opinion
> (*The Economist*, June 27, 1992)

LOSER

"People don't listen to losers. Now, when I say something, people listen."

> ARTHUR ASHE, tennis champion, after winning the 1968 U.S. Open
> (*New York Times*, February 8, 1993)

"You know what his demise was? He couldn't win on the road."

> MARV LEVY, coach, Buffalo Bills, on Hitler (*Newsday*, January 31, 1993)

"Don't make no waves; don't back no losers."

> A Chicago alderman to political scientist Milton Rakove (interview, 1964)

"Rockne wanted nothing but 'bad losers.' Good losers get into the habit of losing. Rockne wanted boys who would tear their hair out by the handfuls on the rare occasions when Notre Dame lost."

> GEORGE E. ALLEN, writer
> (*Presidents Who Have Known Me*, 1950)

LOSING

"No one knows what to say in the loser's locker room."

> MUHAMMAD ALI, heavyweight champion

"Losing my virginity was a career move."

> MADONNA (Winokur, *True Confessions*, p. 132)

"You gotta lose 'em sometime. When you do, lose 'em right."

> CASEY STENGEL, baseball manager
> (*The Gospel According to Casey*, p. 11)

"You can take your wars and your starvation and your fires and your floods, but there's no heartbreak in life like losing the big game in high school."

> DAN JENKINS (*Semi-Tough*, 1972)

"When you're losing, everyone commences to play stupid."

> CASEY STENGEL, baseball manager
> (*The Gospel According to Casey*, p. 20)

LOSS

"Your loss is our gain."

> T-shirt given as party favor at the Creditors' Ball, held annually since 1986 by bankruptcy lawyer Robert Miller in the Hamptons
> (*New York Times*, August 15, 1991)

"Take care to sell your horse before he dies. The art of life is passing losses on."

> ROBERT FROST, poet ("The Ingenuities of Debt")

"One thing our capitalists are always willing to socialize is a loss."

> KENNETH BURKE, social critic
> (quoted in *Fortune*, September 11, 1989)

LOST

"Nothing is lost save honor."

> JIM FISK, financier, after losing a battle over a railroad to J. P. Morgan
> (quoted in Josephson, *The Robber Barons*, p. 141)

"Next to a battle lost, the greatest misery is a battle won."

> DUKE OF WELLINGTON, victor at the Battle of Waterloo
> (letter, June 19, 1815)

LOYALTY

"You want loyalty, hire a cocker spaniel."

> The head trader of British government bonds at Salomon Brothers' London office rejecting management's appeal to higher principles in urging that he stay rather than leave for more money at another firm
> (quoted in Lewis, *Liar's Poker*, 1989)

"Son, you're on your own."

> MEL BROOKS's *Blazing Saddles*; favorite Wall Street quote for situations in which a once fatherly firm is about to abandon you

"He has every characteristic of a dog except loyalty."

> HENRY FONDA discussing a politician in *The Best Man*
> (screenplay by Gore Vidal)

"Every great man has his disciples and it is usually Judas who writes the biography."

> OSCAR WILDE, writer

"Ministers and merchants love nobody."

> THOMAS JEFFERSON (letter to John Langdon, September 11, 1785)

"I went to work for Mr. Walton in 1972, when he only had 16 tractors on the road. The first month, I went to a drivers' safety meeting, and he always came to those. There were about 15 of us there, and I'll never forget, he said, 'If you'll just stay with me for 20 years, I guarantee you'll have $100,000 in profit sharing.' I thought, 'Big deal. Bob Clark never will see that kind of money in his life.' I was worrying about what I was making right then. Well, last time I checked, I had $707,000 in profit sharing, and I see no reason why it won't go up again. I've bought and sold stock over the years, and used it to build on to my home and buy a whole bunch of things. When folks ask me how I like working for Wal-Mart, I tell them I drove for another big company for 13 years—one they've all heard of—and left with $700. Then I tell them about my profit sharing and ask them, 'How do you think I feel about Wal-Mart?'" BOB CLARK, Wal-Mart truck driver (*Sam Walton*, p. 133)

"There is a great deal of talk about loyalty from the bottom to the top. Loyalty from the top down is even more necessary and much less prevalent." General GEORGE S. PATTON (*War As I Knew It*, 1947)

LUCK

"Luck is a dividend of sweat. The more you sweat, the luckier you get." RAY A. KROC, Chairman, McDonald's
(Love, *McDonald's: Behind the Arches*, 1986)

"At gambling, the deadly sin is to mistake bad play for bad luck." IAN FLEMING (*Casino Royale*, 1953)

"I know what you're thinking: 'Did he fire six shots or only five?' Well, to tell you the truth, in all this excitement I've kinda lost track myself. But being this is a .44 Magnum, the most powerful handgun in the world, and would blow your head clean off, you've got to ask yourself one question—'Do I feel lucky?' Well do ya, punk?" HARRY CALLAHAN in *Dirty Harry*
(screenplay by Harry Julian Fink, R. M. Fink, and Dean Riesner)

"I don't know anything about luck. I've never banked on it, and I'm afraid of people who do. Luck to me is something else: hard work—and realizing what is opportunity and what isn't." LUCILLE BALL, actress (Harris, *The Real Story of Lucille Ball*, 1954)

"The harder you work the luckier you get."

Attributed to GARY PLAYER, golfer

"Luck is the residue of design."

BRANCH RICKEY, baseball owner (Cosell, *Like It Is*, 1974)

"You know what luck is? Luck is believing you're lucky. That's all."

MARLON BRANDO in *A Streetcar Named Desire*
(screenplay by Tennessee Williams)

"Has he luck?"

Napolean's habitual question about his officers
(Taylor, *Politics in Wartime*, 1964)

LUNCH

"Sharing a meal goes back to primitive times, when you'd have the group feeding around the animal they've caught."

FRANK PRICE, former chairman, Columbia Pictures
(*New York Times*, March 8, 1992)

"Making lunch appointments is a lot like dating pretty girls in high school. They say they'll go out with you until a better offer comes along."

MARK HOROWITZ, screenwriter (*New York Times*, March 8, 1992)

MAD

"Coach, I've played with all the great players. And you aren't good enough to get mad."

Pinehurst pro to Notre Dame football coach Lou Holtz, who had just
thrown his golf clubs in anger; told by Holtz on his radio show
(interview, September 1992)

"Only the amateurs stay mad."

SAM DONALDSON, TV reporter
(quoted in Noonan, *What I Saw at the Revolution*, p. 294)

"I used to get mad and blow my top—a Donald-Duck-type thing."

WALT DISNEY (*The Man Behind the Magic*, p. 87)

MAKING IT

"I'm not a little girl from a little town makin' good in a big town. I'm a big girl from a big town makin' good in a little town."

MAE WEST, actress, on moving from Broadway to Hollywood, 1932
(Corey, *Man in Lincoln's Nose*, p. 113)

"It's funny the way most people love the dead. Once you are dead, you are made for life."

JIMI HENDRIX, musician (Rolling Stone, December 2, 1976)

MANAGEMENT

"We hire eagles and teach them to fly in formation."

D. WAYNE CALLOWAY, CEO, PepsiCo (Fortune, January 30, 1989)

"I would be a billionaire if I was looking to be a selfish boss. That's not me."

JOHN GOTTI, Mafia don (New York Times, August 3, 1991)

"It was good for baseball when the most glamorous team, the Yankees, had glamor. To be blunt, Steinbrenner's mismanagement of the Yankees matters much more than the mismanagement of the Braves. The Yankees, the source of so much of baseball's most stirring history—Ruth, Gehrig, DiMaggio, Mantle—are simply irreplaceable as carriers of a tradition that lends derivative glory to teams that compete against them."

GEORGE F. WILL (Newsweek, August 31, 1992)

"For a full week, the boss sells tickets or popcorn, dishes ice cream or hot dogs, loads and unloads rides, parks cars, drives the monorail or the trains, and takes on any of the 100 on-stage jobs that make the entertainment parks come alive."

RED POPE, long-time commentator on Walt Disney Productions,
describing the annual management training ritual
called "cross utilization" (Peters and Waterman,
In Search of Excellence, p. 167)

"We have the poorest productivity growth in any Western industrialized country. And managerial ineptitude has put us into this box. The way to get higher productivity is to train better managers and have fewer of them. Four years ago we had more than 1,200 people at corporate headquarters. We're coming down to 250."

WILLIAM WOODSIDE, chairman, Primerica
(formerly American Can) (interview, 1987)

"I follow the one-ass-to-kick principle."

GEORGE WEISSMAN, chairman, Philip Morris, on his management style—
he makes suggestions to subordinates that turn into orders immediately
if not followed; staff and line functions are separate so that a staff person
can get a line decision overruled only by Weissman
(Forbes, October 10, 1980)

"An army of deer led by a lion is more to be feared than an army of lions led by a deer."

CHABRIAS, Athenian general, 357 B.C.

"You can't 'manage' people. But you can bribe them."

DAVID AYCOCK, former CEO, Nucor Steel,
a highly profitable steel company that gives frequent
productivity bonuses and large amounts of stock to its employees
(*New York Times*, January 14, 1992)

"The world is disgracefully managed, one hardly knows to whom to complain."

Attributed to Mrs. PATRICK CAMPBELL, actress

"A manager is an *assistant* to his men."

THOMAS WATSON, SR., to Thomas Watson, Jr., on the personal relationship
between the worker and the supervisor that, said Watson, Jr.,
became the "IBM equivalent of the social contract"
(Watson and Petre, *Father Son & Co.*, p. 74)

MANAGEMENT, ADVICE

"Hire good people and let 'em do their jobs. Otherwise, why hire 'em?"

BILL VEECK, baseball club owner (*Veeck as in Wreck*, 1962)

"The worst rule of management is 'If it ain't broke, don't fix it.' In today's economy, if it ain't broke, you might as well break it yourself, because it soon will be."

WAYNE CALLOWAY, CEO, PepsiCo (*Fortune*, March 11, 1991)

"You can't direct a Laughton picture. The best you can hope for is to referee."

ALFRED HITCHCOCK, film director (*Movie Talk*, p. 48)

"The environment in many companies is ' Perform or die.' Regressive behavior is rampant."

ALAN E. SCHNUR, consultant (*Fortune*, March 9, 1992)

"The secret of managing is to keep the five guys who hate you away from the guys who are undecided."

CASEY STENGEL, baseball manager (*The Gospel According to Casey*, p. 33)

"The secret in talking to a pitcher in a crucial situation is not so much what you say as how you say it. You want to say something to relax him so that he can be himself and not show pressure. Casey would never say, 'Don't throw a high curve' and put a negative thought in your head. He'd say, 'Oh, Mr. Craig, you know this guy can't hit a low slider. Why don't you throw one and we'll be out of the inning and in the clubhouse.'"

ROGER CRAIG, pitcher, on Casey Stengel
(*The Gospel According to Casey*, p. 32)

"I don't dictate. I sit in my office and watch them start to get frightened when things go badly. When they're frightened enough they ask my help. I give it and they take it."

EARL WEAVER, manager, Baltimore Orioles, responding to Heywood Hale Broun who had asked how an "undersized, undertalented person like himself could dictate to large and talented players"
(*New York Times*, July 7, 1992)

"The general must be first in the toils and fatigue of the army. In the heat of summer he does not spread his parasol nor in the cold of winter don thick clothing. In dangerous places he must dismount and walk. He waits until the army's wells have been dug and only then drinks; until the army's food is cooked before he eats; until the army's fortifications have been completed, to shelter himself."

PING FA (Military Code, fifth century B.C.)

MANAGERS, COMMANDERS, AND CEOs

"A man should have dinner with his friends, and the commanding officer has no friends."

General CURTIS LEMAY,
on his refusal to eat with fellow officers (*Look*, 1965)

"The executive is inevitably a father figure. To be a good father, whether it is to his children or to his associates, requires that he be understanding, that he be considerate, and that he be human enough to be affectionate."

Dr. WILLIAM MENNINGER (quoted in Ogilvy, *Ogilvy on Advertising*, p. 47)

"He was a warrior, and a warrior, he was certain, was not a victim. Never a victim."

WILLIAM KENNEDY (*Ironweed*, 1983)

"There are no easy matters that will come to you as president. If they are easy they will be settled at a lower level."

President DWIGHT D. EISENHOWER to John F. Kennedy
(Winokur, *Friendly Advice*, p. 200)

"No man is fit to command another that cannot command
himself."
                    WILLIAM PENN, founder of Pennsylvania (*No Cross, No Crown*, 1669)

"The graveyards are full of indispensable men."
                    Attributed to CHARLES deGAULLE, French president

"If you can't be captain, don't play."
                    Attributed to JOSEPH P. KENNEDY, financier

"Corporate America operates by the John Wayne school of
management. There are one or two powerful guys at the top who
have the power to bet the company on a new project or a huge
investment, and that requires John Wayne-type pay. The Germans
and Japanese, by contrast, run companies collegially, spreading
the responsibility around among the top managers."
                    ALAN M. JOHNSON, executive-compensation consultant
                    (quoted in Wolff, *Where We Stand,* p. 151)

MANAGERS, MIDDLE

"Most middle managers are really 'human message switchers.'
They gather information, they collate it, collect it, distort it a little
bit, hold on to it a lot—because information is power; and then
they distribute it. All that takes a long time and is very expensive.
It stops the decision-making process cold."
                    WILLIAM G. MCGOWAN, founder and CEO, MCI Communications
                    (quoted in Peters, *Liberation,* p. 306)

MANNERS

"I think it's bad manners in the Southern sense to be sharp and
critical of it. I did cash the check."
                    TOM WOLFE, author, on the filming of his novel,
                    Bonfire of the Vanities (Salamon, *The Devil's Candy,* p. xii)

MARKETS

"We feel the spear of the marketplace in our back."
                    ANTHONY J. F. O'REILLY, CEO, Heinz (*Fortune,* April 9, 1990)

"If the marketplace has gone bonkers, you better have a bonkers
organization. Straitlaced folks are not going to make it in a world
that's not straitlaced."
                    TOM PETERS, business consultant (*Business Week,* August 31, 1992)

"The market is mostly a matter of psychology and emotion, and all that you find in balance sheets is what you read into them; we're all guessers to one extent or another, and when we guess wrong they say we're crooks."

Major L. L. B. Angas (Mayer, *Stealing the Market*, p. 15)

"It's a seller's market. The studios desperately need product, which puts filmmakers in a stronger position than they have ever known. When pictures hit, they hit for higher revenues than ever before. There are many huge hits and many terrible flops, but very few moderately successful pictures."

Sidney Pollack, director (*The Movie Business Book*, 1983)

"If it swells, ride it."

University of Chicago T-shirt

"Marketing is warfare."

Robert L. Dilenschneider, ceo, Hill and Knowlton public relations firm (*Manhattan, Inc.*, July 1990)

"A B picture isn't a big picture that just didn't grow up; it's exactly what it started out to be. It's the $22 suit of the clothing business; it's the hamburger of the butchers' shops; it's a seat in the bleachers—and there's a big market for all of them."

Nick Grinde, director of B films (Corey, *Man in Lincoln's Nose*, p. 150)

"Every morning, to earn my bread,
I go to the market where lies are bought.
Hopefully, I take up my place among the sellers."

Bertolt Brecht, poet

"There ought to be in the world a market for art where the artist would only have to bring his works and take as much money as he needed."

Attributed to Beethoven

"If fools went not to market, bad wares would not be sold."

Spanish proverb

MARKETS, BEAR

"There is nothing in the business situation to warrant the destruction of values that has taken place in the past week, and

my son and I have for some days past been purchasing sound
common stocks."
JOHN D. ROCKEFELLER, SR., October 30, 1929; in response,
said comedian Eddie Cantor, on October 31: "Sure he's buying.
Who else has any money left?" (Sharp, *The Lore and Legends*, p. 209)

"Remember, my son, that any man who is a bear on the future of
this country will go broke."
J. P. MORGAN, financier, quoted by his son
(speech, Chicago, December 11, 1908)

"Never sell the bear's skin until you have killed the bear."
LA FONTAINE (*Fables*, 1668). This saying occurs in many variations and is
thought to be the origin of the term "bear" to designate those who sell
short with the expectation of covering at a lower price

MARX

"M is for Marx
And clashing of classes
And movement of masses
And massing of asses."
CYRIL CONNOLLY, poet (Sherrin, *Cutting Edge*, p. 36)

"Much of the world's work, it has been said, is done by men who
do not feel quite well. Marx is a case in point."
JOHN KENNETH GALBRAITH, economist (*Age of Uncertainty*, 1977)

"All I know is that I am not a Marxist."
KARL MARX, quoted in Friedrich Engels
(letter to Conrad Schmidt, August 3, 1890)

MEASURE

"Every child of the Saxon race is educated to wish to be first. It is
our system; and a man comes to measure his greatness by the
regrets, envies, and hatreds of his competitors."
RALPH WALDO EMERSON, essayist (*Representative Men*, I, 1850)

"Measure not dispatch by the times of sitting, but by the
advancement of the business."
FRANCIS BACON (*Of Dispatch*, 1625)

MEDIA

"I don't care what's written about me as long as it isn't true."
KATHARINE HEPBURN, actress (interview, 1954)

"All the News That's Fit to Print."

New York Times slogan

"All the News That Fits."

Rolling Stone slogan (*Vanity Fair*, June 1992)

"Listen, Mario, media is the plural of mediocre."

JIMMY BRESLIN, columnist, to New York Governor Mario Cuomo
(interview, 1978)

"The Gulf War was quite a victory. Yet who could not be moved
by the sight of that poor demoralized rabble—outwitted,
outflanked and outmaneuvered by the U.S. military. But I think
the press will bounce right back."

JAMES A. BAKER, III, Secretary of State
(speech at the annual Gridiron Club dinner, 1991)

"I feel slimy already."

JOHN SUNUNU, former governor and co-host of CNN's "Crossfire," after a
journalist said, "Welcome to our trade." (*People*, March 6, 1992)

"They've been operating jointly on me for years."

COLEMAN YOUNG, mayor, Detroit, on the joint operating agreement
between the *Detroit Free Press* and the *Detroit News*
(*Newsweek*, October 28, 1991)

"When you're talking to the media, be a well, not a fountain."

MICHAEL DEAVER, former White House Press Secretary
(interview, 1982)

"Mr. Brady, it's the duty of a newspaper to comfort the afflicted
and to flick the comfortable."

GENE KELLY explaining the ethics of
journalism to Frederic March in *Inherit the Wind*
(screenplay by Nathan E. Douglas and Harold Jacob Smith)

"TV news is for people who think they're getting an in-depth
report if the sign on the bank gives both time and temperature."

CHARLES W. BAILEY, Minneapolis newsman
(quoted in *Nieman Reports*, Winter 1990, p. 24)

"I didn't go to any college, but I know what makes a good story
because, before I ever worked on a paper, I sold 'em on a street
corner. You know the first thing I found out? Bad news sells best
because good news is no news."

KIRK DOUGLAS, as a journalist in *The Big Carnival*
(screenplay by Billy Wilder, Lesser Samuels, and Walter Newman)

"One general characteristic of the American press, which seems inexplicable, is the basic antipathy toward business and industry, which I believe exists in our journalism."

CHET HUNTLEY, NBC newscaster
(quoted in Wriston, *Risk and Other Four-Letter Words*, p. 31)

"Reporters are not required to read you your Miranda rights."

CHRISTOPHER MATTHEWS, White House official during the Carter Administration (Winokur, *Friendly Advice*, p. 191)

"I let people tell their own versions of their history. What difference does it make?"

LIZ SMITH, then columnist *New York Daily News* (*Spy*, October 1991)

"Freedom of the press belongs to the man who owns one."

A. J. LIEBLING, writer (*The Press*, 1961)

"This is the West. When the legend becomes a fact, print the legend."

CARLETON YOUNG to fellow newspapermen in *Who Shot Liberty Valance?* (screenplay by James Warner Bellah and Willis Goldbeck)

"Backward ran sentences until reeled the mind."

WOLCOTT GIBBS parodying Henry Luce's *Time* magazine (*The New Yorker*, November 28, 1936); he added: "Where it will all end, knows God!"

"Nothing has really happened until it's been described."

VIRGINIA WOOLF, writer (*Creators*, p. 265)

"That the editorial and news policies of many newspapers are controlled by their business offices no one can deny."

JOHN COWLES, publisher
(*America Now*, edited by Harold Stearns, p. 360)

"Newspapers are unable, seemingly, to discriminate between a bicycle accident and the collapse of civilization."

GEORGE BERNARD SHAW, playwright (*Too True to Be Good*, preface, 1932)

"Has any reader ever found perfect accuracy in the newspaper account of any event of which he himself had inside knowledge?"

E. V. LUCAS, British writer (*Of Accuracy*, 1937)

"No man but a blockhead ever wrote except for money."

SAMUEL JOHNSON, English essayist (Boswell, *Life of Johnson*, 1776)

MEDIOCRITY

"Some men are born mediocre, some men achieve mediocrity, and some men have mediocrity thrust upon them."

JOSEPH HELLER (*Catch-22*, chapter 9, 1961)

"Mediocrity knows nothing higher than itself; but talent instantly recognizes genius."

Arthur Conan Doyle's SHERLOCK HOLMES (*Valley of Fear,* chapter 1, 1915)

MEETINGS

"The success of a meeting often depends on having the right documents—proofs, artwork, schedules, research charts, etc.— present at the start of the meeting. All too often we arrive like plumbers, leaving our tools behind."

DAVID OGILVY, former chairman, Ogilvy and Mather
(The Unpublished David Ogilvy, 1987)

"They should consider giving Oscars for meetings: Best Meeting of the Year, Best Supporting Meeting, Best Meeting Based on Material from Another Meeting."

WILLIAM GOLDMAN, screenwriter (*Adventures in the Screen Trade*, 1983)

MEMO

"When I went to Paramount I found, to my joy, a memo paradise."

DAVID O. SELZNICK, producer (Corey, *Man in Lincoln's Nose*, p. 131)

"A memorandum is written not to inform the reader but to protect the writer."

DEAN ACHESON, former U.S. Secretary of State
(*Wall Street Journal*, October 8, 1977)

MERGERS AND ACQUISITIONS

"It is a simple fact that most acquisitions go awry."

THOMAS J. PETERS and ROBERT H. WATERMAN, JR.
(*In Search of Excellence*, p. 293)

"Peter, you've become a pirate."

VANESSA REDGRAVE, grandmotherly Wendy, to Robin Williams, Peter Pan,
who has grown up to be an investment banker in *Hook*
(screenplay by Jim V. Hart and Malia Scotch Marmo)

"Watching these deals get done is like watching a herd of drunk drivers take to the highway on New Year's Eve. You cannot tell who will hit whom, but you know it is dangerous."

THEODORE J. FORSTMANN, senior partner, Forstmann Little and Co.
(Burrough and Helyar, *Barbarians at the Gate*, p. 241)

"We're not ready for you yet, sonny."

President RICHARD NIXON, confirming the SEC's decision to turn down
Saul Steinberg's proposed acquisition of Chemical Bank, 1969
(Stone, *April Fools*, p. 31)

"The pressures of M & A, like the pressures of gold prospecting, caused normally sociable individuals to threaten to cut each other's balls off."

JOHN ROTHCHILD, writer (*Going for Broke*, p. 69)

"Shearson taking over Lehman is like McDonald's taking over 21."

A Lehman Brothers partner, on the merger
(Burrough and Helyar, *Barbarians at the Gate*, p. 156)

"We really want to have more than our neighbor across the street."

J. IRWIN MILLER, CEO, Cummins Engine
(quoted in Moskin, *Morality in America*, p. 236)

"What are refrigerators but boxes with motors?"

BILLY DURANT of General Motors on buying the Frigidaire Company
in 1918 (Patton, *Made in USA*, p. 242)

"Boys, I'm reminded of the story of the prostitute: I had it, I sold it, and I got it back again."

ARTHUR TEMPLE, former CEO, Texas-based Temple Industries, whose
company had been acquired by Time, Inc., in 1973 and spun off in 1983,
(quoted in Anson, "Greed and Ego in Gotham City,"
Manhattan, Inc., August 1989)

MESS

"Here's another fine mess you've gotten me into."

OLIVER HARDY to Stan Laurel, recurring line in their movies together

"I can tell whether a player is on offense or defense just by looking at his locker. The offensive players keep their lockers clean and orderly, but the lockers of the defensive men are a mess. In fact, the better the defensive player, the bigger the mess."

ARNOLD J. MANDELL, psychiatrist (*Saturday Review*, 1974)

"Stupidity got us into this mess—why can't it get us out?"
Attributed to WILL ROGERS, comedian

MESSAGE

"If you want to send a message, go to Western Union."
SAM GOLDWYN, who disparaged message films
(Marx, Goldwyn, 1976)

"We've fired our receptionist and are passing the savings on to you."
Answering machine messsage for Jeff Slutsky, CEO,
Retail Marketing Institute in Columbus, Ohio
(Henderson,Winners, p. 115)

MIDDLE CLASS

"That which in England we call the Middle Class is in America virtually the nation."
MATTHEW ARNOLD (A Word About America, 1882)

"It is manifest that the best political community is formed by citizens of the middle class."
ARISTOTLE (Politics, book 4)

MIDWEST

"You know, I've never been able to understand why, when there's so much space in the world, people should deliberately choose to live in the Middle West."
CLIFTON WEBB in The Razor's Edge (screenplay by Lamar Trotti)

MILITARY

"The American electronics industry is spoiled by the emphasis on military and space applications. In the U.S. you put your energy into fundamental research to develop technologies that you apply first to military uses. Only later does it makes its way into business and consumer products."
MASARU IBUKA, founder and honorary chairman, Sony,
who invented the pocket-size transistor radio, the VCR,
and the Walkman, on why Japanese companies are
so successful in developing new products from new
technologies even though Americans are thought
to be more creative (Fortune, February 24, 1992)

MILLION DOLLARS

"If someone's dumb enough to offer me a million dollars to make a picture, I am certainly not dumb enough to turn it down."

ELIZABETH TAYLOR, actress (*People*, February 1988)

"One million, two million. . . "

JOHN MADDEN, former Raiders coach, on Lamar Hunt, owner of the Kansas City Chiefs, learning to count (*Sports Illustrated*, 1980)

"Hollywood is one of the few places on earth where a person with absolutely *no* talent can make a million dollars and where a guy who is loaded with talent can starve to death."

DAN DAILE, actor (*People*, February 1988)

"Another day, another million dollars."

RICHARD DONAT, store manager, Marshall Field and Co., Chicago, on the Christmas shopping season (*The Wall Street Journal*, November 29, 1984)

"Millions are to be grabbed out here and your only competition is idiots. Don't let this get around."

HERMAN J. MANKIEWICZ, screenwriter, telegram urging Ben Hecht to come to Hollywood (Corey, *Man in Lincoln's Nose*, p. 113)

MISTAKES

"We tell our young managers: 'Don't be afraid to make a mistake. But make sure you don't make the same mistake twice.'"

AKIO MORITA, CEO, Sony Corporation (Lyons, *The Sony Vision*, p. 101)

"Two, and they are both sitting on the Supreme Court."

President DWIGHT D. EISENHOWER, referring to his appointment of Earl Warren and William Brennan to the Supreme Court, responding to Fred Friendly's question if he had made any mistakes in office (interview, 1959)

"It was a mistake that I bought it. It was an even bigger mistake that I didn't sell it."

CARL C. ICAHN, former CEO, on Trans World Airlines (*New York Times*, January 9, 1993)

"The physician can bury his mistakes, but the architect can only advise his client to plant vines."

FRANK LLOYD WRIGHT (*New York Times Magazine*, October 4, 1953)

"You're gonna make mistakes. You can't worry about them second-guessers."

> CASEY STENGEL, baseball manager, after trying the aging centerfielder Joe
> DiMaggio at first base (*The Gospel According to Casey*, p. 12)

"I am humble enough to recognize that I have made mistakes, but politically astute enough to know that I have forgotten what they are."

> MICHAEL HESELTINE, British politician (*The Economist*, April 11, 1992)

"When I make a mistake, it's a good one."

> President HARRY S TRUMAN (McCullough, *Truman*, p. 467)

"I'll go to my grave with $200 a share on my tombstone."

> RICHARD MUNRO, the former CEO of Time, Inc., who agreed to avoid a
> shareholders' vote and buy Warner for $14 billion, incurring $11 billion
> in debt, rather than accept Marvin Davis's Paramount bid of $200 a share
> (*New York Times*, February 24, 1992)

"Live all you can; it's a mistake not to."

> HENRY JAMES, writer (*The Ambassadors*, 1903)

"The greatest mistake I made was not to die in office."

> DEAN ACHESON, former U.S. Secretary of State, on listening to funeral
> eulogies for his successor John Foster Dulles
> (interview, March 27, 1959)

"You will drop passes. You will make mistakes. But not very many if you want to play for the Green Bay Packers."

> Coach VINCE LOMBARDI (*Football's Greatest Quotes*, p. 138)

"Dontopedology is the science of opening your mouth and putting your foot in it. I've been practicing it for years."

> Prince PHILIP, Duke of Edinburgh (*New York Times*, December 30, 1959)

"No one who accomplished things couιu expect to avoid mistakes. Only those who did nothing made no mistakes."

> President HARRY S TRUMAN (McCullough, *Truman*, p. 516)

"I remember a very good bit of advice Fred used to give me right before we'd do a number: 'Don't be nervous, but don't make any mistakes.'"

> BARRIE CHASE, talking about dancing partner Fred Astaire
> (Safire and Safir, *Good Advice*, p. 223)

"I keep making mistakes, like God."

Attributed to Picasso

MISUNDERSTANDING

"I always enjoy animal acts."

President Calvin Coolidge, on being introduced to Chicago Bears coach
George Halas and star running back Red Grange
(Wall Street Journal, June 20, 1989)

"I think in terms of quarterly profits and annual results and they think in terms of the millennium."

Alfred J. Luciani, former CEO of Foxwoods High Stakes Bingo & Casino,
on his management differences with Connecticut's Mashantucket Pequot
Indians who own the casino (New York Times, October 21, 1992)

MOBILITY

"One of the longest journeys in the world is the journey from Brooklyn to Manhattan."

Norman Podhoretz, political commentator (Making It, p. 3)

"You don't have to be nice to people on the way up if you're not planning to come back down."

Dan G. Stone, vice president of Institutional Equity Sales,
Drexel Burnham (Stone, April Fools, 1991)

MOMENT

"Poets are like baseball pitchers. Both have their moments. The intervals are the tough things."

Robert Frost, poet (The Writer's Quotation Book, p. 37)

"Do not delay; the golden moments fly!"

Henry Wadsworth Longfellow, poet ("The Masque of Pandora," 1875)

MONEY

"Another day, another dollar."

Actor Michael Douglas, shrugging off questions about steamy sex
scenes in Basic Instinct (New York Times, May 9, 1993)

"Early Money Is Like Yeast."

Ellen Malcolm, founder and president, EMILY's List, a major funder of
federal campaigns (EMILY brochure, June 1993)

"Darling, don't regret it. If *you* had made that film it wouldn't
have made any money."

> Director ELAINE MAY telling director (and former partner) Mike Nichols
> not to worry that he had turned down directing *The Exorcist*, one of the
> most profitable films in history (*New York Times*, March 15, 1993)

"Congress received more mail in 1990 on the Arts Endowment,
which cost each citizen 68 cents for everything we did, than on
the savings and loan scandal, which will cost each of us at least
$2,000."

> JOHN FROHNMAYER, former chairman, National Endowment for the Arts
> (*New York Times*, April 18, 1993)

"Money knows no fatherland."

> Ancient saying (quoted in Drucker, *Post-Capitalist Society*, p. 142)

"The show is doing so well, they're shipping the money in by
barge from Boston down the East River."

> MOSS HART on *South Pacific*
> (Keith with Tapert, *Slim: Memories of a Rich and Imperfect Life*, p. 142)

"Money speaks all languages."

> LARRY HAGMAN as J. R. Ewing ("Dallas," 1982)

"Money is like manure. If you spread it around, it does a lot of
good."

> CLINT W. MURCHISON, oil man and financier, quoted by his son
> (*Time*, June 16, 1961)

"I want to do something that will allow me to make money while
I'm sleeping."

> REGINALD LEWIS, CEO, TLC Beatrice International Holdings Inc.,
> as a young corporate lawyer (*Wall Street Journal*, October 15, 1992)

"No one would remember the Good Samaritan if he'd only had
good intentions. He had money as well."

> MARGARET THATCHER, British prime minister, quoting Kenneth Kelton,
> Bishop of Lichfield (Diocesan Synod, March 5, 1983)

"A fool and his money are soon invited everywhere."

> A porcelain plaque at the entry to the Omaha headquarters
> of Berkshire Hathaway

"Money talks and bullshit walks."

> JOHN JACKLEY, aide to Congressman Ronald Coleman
> (Jackley, *Hill Rat*, 1992)

"Money's just a way of keeping score."

> H. L. HUNT, oil man (quoted in *Molly Ivins Can't Say That*, p. 50)

"There's a lot more money to be made in a large-scale software business than in their traditional hardware businesses."

> BILL PADE, consultant, McKinsey and Co., on Matsushita's $7 billion acquisition of MCA/Universal and Sony's $3.4 billion acquisition of Columbia Pictures and its $2 billion acquisition of CBS Records (Peters, *Liberation*, p. 4)

"I don't have to worry about money, thank God. When you don't have it, you have to have it. Only when you get it, you realize you don't need it. But to get the ego experience, you have to go through it."

> RICHARD THALHEIMER, founder and CEO, Sharper Image (interview, 1987)

"If all you want to do is make money by whatever means, let's just open a string of whorehouses across the country."

> ARTHUR TEMPLE, board member, Time, Inc. (quoted in John Gregory Dunne, *New York Review of Books*, April 23, 1992)

"Funny thing about that. I only seem to be able to sing for money."

> BARBRA STREISAND, after singing off-key for Michael and Julia Phillips (*You'll Never Eat Lunch in This Town Again*, p. 92)

"You better give the have-nots some money, or they'll shoot you."

> WARREN BEATTY, actor, summarizing his movie, *Bonnie and Clyde* (*Fortune*, February 24, 1992)

"I have always found it curious that the two things a human being must cope with all his life, his body and his money, are never explained to him at school. Few adults ever know where their liver is until too late, and few ever know where their money is—until the savings and loan system collapses."

> GORE VIDAL, writer (*Screening History*, 1992)

"George Halas throws nickels around like they were manhole covers."

> MIKE DITKA, then a tight end for the Chicago Bears, after negotiating a one-year contract with the Bears' owner (Whittingham, *Bears*, p. 64)

"I had a better year."

> Attributed BABE RUTH in 1930, on reports that he made more than President Herbert Hoover

"The best way to keep money in perspective is to have some."
LOUIS RUKEYSER (Winokur, *Friendly Advice*, p. 167)

"Look, when we sit down to clip a guy we have to remember what's at stake here. There's some hazard. Guys forget that. They get a guy behind in his vig payments, right away they wanna whack him. But what I say is, 'Hey, you're making a living with this guy. He gets you aggravated and right away you wanna use the hammer? How do you get your money *then*?'"
PAUL CASTELLANO, on his dislike for unnecessary violence (O'Brien and Kruns, *Boss of Bosses, the Fall of the Godfather*, August 5, 1991)

"'I hope to risk things all my life.'
'Oh, Margaret, most dangerous.'
'But, after all,' she continued with a smile, 'there's never any great risk as long as you have money.'
'Oh, shame! What a shocking speech!'
'Money pads the edges of things,' said Miss Schlegal. 'God help those who have none.'"
E. M. FORSTER, writer (*Howard's End*, p. 60)

"Runners-up make more money."
RICHARD GELB, chairman, Bristol-Myers, on his strategy of putting "two second-bests together," namely: "We may never be as strong a consumer-goods company as Procter and Gamble or as powerful in ethical drugs as Merck" (*Forbes*, October 13, 1980)

"It's just as easy to be happy with a lot of money as a little."
MARVIN TRAUB, CEO, Bloomingdale's (*7 Days*, October 25, 1989)

"If I weren't earning $3 million a year to dunk a basketball, most people on the street would run in the other direction if they saw me coming."
CHARLES BARKLEY, power forward, Phoenix Suns (*Newsweek*, February 1992)

"The point is to get so much money that money's not the point anymore."
WILLIAM HAMILTON cartoon (*The New Yorker*, December 7, 1992)

"I don't want to make money. I just want to be wonderful."
MARILYN MONROE, actress (*All About Money*, p. 101)

"A nickel ain't worth a dime anymore."
YOGI BERRA, baseball player (Berra, *It Ain't Over*, 1989)

"You can be young without money. But you can't be old without it."
ELIZABETH TAYLOR to husband Paul Newman in *Cat on a Hot Tin Roof*
(screenplay by Richard Brooks and James Poe)

"The bus companies are not prepared to lose money to save segregation."
BAYARD RUSTIN, New York civil rights leader,
to Martin Luther King, JR., correctly predicting that the
Montgomery bus boycott would succeed (Garrow, *Bearing the Cross*, p. 80)

"The only kind of money to have—not quite enough."
Ian Fleming's JAMES BOND (*On Her Majesty's Secret Service*, 1963)

"There's no money in poetry; but then there's no poetry in money."
ROBERT GRAVES, writer (George Plimpton, *The Writer's Chapbook*, 1989)

"Carnegie exemplifies to me a truth about American money men that many earnest people fail to grasp—which is that the chase and the kill are as much fun as the prize, which you then proceed to give away."
ALISTAIR COOKE, journalist, on Andrew Carnegie (*America*, 1973)

"Ah! those artistic pale green rugs issued by the Treasury Department."
S. J. PERELMAN, humorist, on dollar bills

"That's what I like—everything done in contrasting shades of money."
BOB HOPE, on George Sanders's luxury apartment in *That Certain Feeling*
(screenplay by Norman Panama, Melvin Frank, I.A.L. Diamond, and
William Altman)

"When you get a sex story in biblical garb, you can open your own mint."
DARRYL F. ZANUCK, producer (*Movie Talk*, p. 104)

"Money, it turned out, was exactly like sex, you thought of nothing else if you didn't have it and thought of other things if you did."
JAMES BALDWIN, writer
("Black Boy Looks at White Boy," *Esquire*, May 1961)

"Money, what is money? It is only loaned to a man, he comes into the world with nothing and he leaves with nothing."
WILLIAM DURANT, founder, General Motors, who lost his fortune
trying to save GM during the 1920 recession
(quoted in Sharp, *The Lore and Legends of Wall Street*, p. 206)

"Mugger: 'Your money or your life!'
        (pause)
"Mugger: 'Look, Bud, I said your money or your life!'
"Jack Benny: 'I'm thinking it over!'"
JACK BENNY radio skit
(quoted in Sharp, The Lore and Legends of Wall Street, p. 155)

"Big Daddy! Now what makes him so big? His big heart? His big belly? Or his big money?"
PAUL NEWMAN thinking about his father
in Cat on a Hot Tin Roof (screenplay by Richard Brooks and James Poe)

"The arrogance of big money is one of the most unappealing of characteristics, and it goes very deep. To see a grown man groveling in order to keep his job is a horrible sight."
BROOKE ASTOR in Footprints
(quoted in New York Times Magazine, November 17, 1991)

"I asked 10 or 25 people for suggestions . . . finally one lady friend of mine asked me the right question, 'Well, what do you love most?' That's how I started painting money."
ANDY WARHOL, on his enormously successful dollar sign paintings
(The Andy Warhol Diaries, 1989)

"Money doesn't talk anymore; it shrieks."
AILEEN MEHLE (the gossip columnist Suzy)

"We know how to make the tools of abundance but not how to manage abundance so we can share it. What good is productive power if people don't have the money to buy things we know how to make?"
WALTER P. REUTHER, labor union leader
(quoted in Moskin, Morality in America, p. 53)

"You drive for show but putt for money."
BOBBY LOCKE, golfer (recalled on his death, March 9, 1987)

"Always try to rub up against money, for if you rub up against money long enough, some of it may rub off on you."
DAMON RUNYON (Guys and Dolls, 1931)

"Most people don't realize there's just as much money to be made when a society's falling down as when it's rising up."
RHETT BUTLER, Civil War profiteer, to Scarlett O'Hara in
Gone with the Wind (screenplay by Sidney Howard)

"I don't think it's going to ruin any of us to make some money on our work."   LANFORD WILSON, playwright (quoted in Brown, *Shoptalk*, p. 7)

"Her voice is full of money."
F. SCOTT FITZGERALD, writer (*The Great Gatsby*, 1925, chapter 1)

"The trouble, Mr. Goldwyn, is that you are only interested in art—and I am only interested in money."
GEORGE BERNARD SHAW, playwright, refusing Goldwyn's offer of a job
(Johnson, *The Great Goldwyn*, 1937, chapter 3)

"I believe there are two things necessary to salvation. . . . Money and gunpowder."   ROBERT MORLEY to Rex Harrison in *Major Barbara*
(screenplay by George Bernard Shaw)

"Money, which represents the prose of life, and which is hardly spoken of in parlors without an apology, is, in its effects and laws, as beautiful as roses."
RALPH WALDO EMERSON, essayist
(*Nominalist and Realist*, 1844)

"Dangerous human proclivities can be canalised into comparatively harmless channels by the existence of opportunities for money-making and private wealth, which, if they cannot be satisfied in this way, may find their outlet in cruelty, the reckless pursuit of personal power and authority, and other forms of self-aggrandizement. It is better that a man should tyrannize over his bank balance than over his fellow-citizens; and whilst the former is sometimes denounced as being but a means to the latter, sometimes as least it is an alternative."
JOHN MAYNARD KEYNES, economist
(*The General Theory of Employment, Interest, and Money*, 1936, chapter 24)

"I don't like money actually, but it quiets my nerves."
Attributed to JOE LOUIS, prizefighter

"They say money doesn't stink. I sometimes wonder."
RAYMOND CHANDLER (*Farewell, My Lovely*, 1940)

"The money is always there, but the pockets change; it is not in the same pockets after a change; and that is all there is to say about money."
GERTRUDE STEIN, writer
(quoted in Wriston, *Risk and Other Four-Letter Words*, p. 83)

"People look at me and say 'The guy has no regard for money.' That is not true. I have had regard for money. There's some people who worship money as something you've got to have piled up in a big pile somewhere. I've only thought of money in one way—and that is to do something with."

WALT DISNEY (*The Man Behind the Magic*, p. 79)

"A heavy purse makes a light heart."

Irish proverb

"Of course I despise money when I haven't got any. It's the only dignified thing to do."

Agatha Christie's CEDRIC CRACKENTHORPE (*4:50 from Paddington*, 1957)

"You can't blame money for what it does to people. The evil is in the people, and money is the peg they hang it on. They go wild for money when they've lost their other values."

Ross Macdonald's LEW ARCHER
(*The Moving Target*, 1949)

"But there's no doubt that money is to the fore now. It is the romance, the poetry of our age."

WILLIAM DEAN HOWELLS (*The Rise of Silas Lapham*, 1885)

"For that kind of money I would have played the part myself."

ARMAND HAMMER, on learning that Marlon Brando
had been paid a quarter of a million dollars a day
to play an unscrupulous oil millionaire modeled
on Hammer in *The Formula* (Edward Jay Epstein,
New York Times Magazine, November 29, 1981)

"The almighty dollar, that great object of universal devotion through our land."

WASHINGTON IRVING (*Wolfert's Roost*, 1855)

Money makes "foul fair, wrong right, base noble, old young, coward valiant/ [Money is] this yellow slave [that] will knit and break religions, bless the accursed, make the hoar leprosy adored, place thieves and give them title, knee and approbation."

SHAKESPEARE (*Timon of Athens*)

"The populace may hiss me, but when I go home and think of my money, I applaud myself."

HORACE (*Epistles*, c. 29 B.C.)

"Money is mourned with deeper sorrow than friends or kindred."
JUVENAL (Satires)

"I know of nothing more despicable and pathetic than a man who devotes all the hours of the waking day to the making of money for money's sake."
Attributed to JOHN D. ROCKEFELLER, SR., financier

"The love of money is the root of all evil."
I Timothy 6:10

"The most grievous kind of destitution is to want money in the midst of wealth."
SENECA (Epistles, c. 40)

"In 280 B.C., the Epirian king Pyrrhus—he of 'Pyrrhic victory' fame—launched an attack on the Italian mainland, and thousands of Roman soldiers were sent out to meet him. The Romans faced numerous difficulties in this campaign, and at one point they feared they were running short on the funds required to sustain it. A few wise heads among them appealed to their trusty counselor Juno, who issued a brief statement to the effect that those who wage war upon just principles would never lack the necessary cash.

The Romans, who assumed that all their wars were just, were naturally delighted by this piece of advice; so they decided that thenceforth all their money should be coined under Juno's auspices. They established a mint in the Temple of Juno Moneta, after which moneta came to mean 'mint' and eventually 'minted coins.'"
MICHAEL MACRONE
(By Jove! Brush Up Your Mythology, pp. 18–19)

"Bad money drives out good money." [Gresham's Law]
Sir THOMAS GRESHAM (Royal Proclamation of 1560)

MONEY AND POLITICS

"If you're chairman of the Banking Committee, you don't have to speak at all. All you have to do is show up. You can read the phone book, and they'll be happy to pay your honoraria."
Senator WILLIAM PROXMIRE, former chairman of the Banking Committee,
on the drop in his annual lecture fees from $100,000 to under $12,000
when he lost the chairmanship to the Republicans (interview, 1982)

"The truth is that money has replaced brains and hard work as the way for a lobbyist to get something done for his client."

KENNETH SCHLOSSBERG, Washington, D.C., lobbyist (interview, 1986)

MORALITY

"Those individuals who give moral considerations a much greater weight than considerations of expediency represent a comparatively small minority, five percent of the people perhaps. But, in spite of their numerical inferiority, they play a major role in our society because theirs is the voice of the conscience of society."

Dr. LEO SZILARD, atomic scientist
(quoted in Moskin, *Morality in America*, p. 17)

"The Ten Commandments were not a suggestion."

PAT RILEY, coach, New York Knicks, on his upbringing
(*New York*, November 25, 1991)

"If Socrates and Plato had trouble defining what morality was, how can people come along, just like that, and lay down that gambling is immoral?"

MEYER LANSKY, gangster
(Lacey, *Little Man: Meyer Lansky and the Gangster Life*, 1991)

"The ultimate test of a moral society is the kind of world it leaves to its children."

Reverend DIETRICH BONHOEFFER, philosopher
(quoted in The William T. Grant Foundation's annual report, 1991)

"Personal morality has slipped. Too many of us today lack the self-discipline to do our work thoroughly, or to be punctual, or to meet our financial obligations by paying our debts on time."

EDWARD DECOURCY, editor of the weekly *Argus-Champion* of Newport,
New Hampshire (quoted in Moskin, *Morality in America*, pp. 246–47)

"It is not necesary that people be wicked but only that they be spineless."

JAMES BALDWIN, writer (*The Fire Next Time*, 1963)

"It is not impossible that this could be a Golden Age. We have solved our technological and economic problems. We only have moral problems left."

J. IRWIN MILLER, CEO, Cummins Engine, and past president
of the National Council of the Churches of Christ
(quoted in Moskin, *Morality in America*, p. 14)

"The growing forces in this country are the forces of common human decency and not the forces of bigotry and fear and smears." President Lyndon B. Johnson, accepting the Democratic nomination on August 27, 1964 (quoted in Moskin, *Morality in America*, p. 13)

"Because I'm a fine fellow and go to church, everything goes." J. Irwin Miller, CEO, Cummins Engine, and church leader, on what he calls the "split morality" of Americans (quoted in Moskin, *Morality*, p. 176)

"My job is to create an environment that relaxes morality." Robert DiLeonardo, on Atlantic City casinos (*Wall Street Journal*, January 10, 1983)

"Morality comes from self-esteem which comes from making decisions which require risk." Professor Chris Argyris, Yale University (quoted in Moskin, *Morality in America*, p. 137)

"First comes eating, then comes morality." Attributed to Bertolt Brecht, playwright

"We never try to know the reason why. It's not our job to make moral judgments." Boyd Jefferies, founder and CEO, Jefferies Group, on his March 1985 execution of the second largest block trade in history— 6.7 million shares of Unocal stock for T. Boone Picken's raid (Johnston, "The Takeover Wars," *California*, May 1987)

"Mercantile morality is really nothing but a refinement of piratical morality." Nietzsche, philosopher (*Thus Spake Zarathustra*, 1883–1891)

MOTIVATION

"Three people were at work on a construction site. All were doing the same job, but when each was asked what his job was, the answers varied. 'Breaking rocks,' the first replied. 'Earning my living,' said the second. 'Helping to build a cathedral,' said the third." Attributed to Peter Schultz, Porsche CEO

"To beat his father, Keith. And to run the world." Clay Felker, editor, *New York* magazine, on the motives of Rupert Murdoch, who had just acquired *New York* in a bitter battle with the writers and editors (Shawcross, *Murdoch*, p. 141)

"A head coach is guided by this main objective: dig, claw, wheedle, coach that fanatical effort out of the players. You want them to play every Saturday as if they were planting the flag on Iwo Jima."

DARRELL ROYAL, coach, University of Texas
(*Darrell Royal Talks Football*, 1963)

"The motivational moment."

CONAGRA's joking reference to
the heart attack of their CEO, Charles M. Harper, who, on being forced to
eat nutritionally to stay alive, started the successful Healthy Choice
frozen food label (*New York Times*, February 26, 1992)

"I'm not going to claim that we fought the Battle of Wapping because we wanted to bring a silver age to British journalism. When the beaver gnaws down a tree, he isn't thinking of his vital ecological role either. But nevertheless he has one."

RUPERT MURDOCH, chairman, News Corporation,
on his company's confrontation with the press unions
at the Wapping plant (speech, New York City, 1989)

"You can't kiss an oil well."

JOSEPH J. GIOGUARDI, former oilman, on why he invested in a play
(*New York Times*, August 17, 1983)

MOVIES

"Over all, Rambo has probably made as much money as the war cost us, and so the managers of our great nation can point with pride to the books."

GORE VIDAL, writer
(*New York Times Book Review*, August 30, 1992)

"It was an art in which words were subordinate to images, where personality was worn down to the inevitable low gear of collaboration."

F. SCOTT FITZGERALD, writer, on screenwriting
(quoted in the *New York Times*, April 25, 1982)

"I know that Steven really likes his movies. He thinks of himself as the owner of a huge silver mine. So he'll make sequels to *Raiders* and *ET* because the silver is down there and someone has to bring it up."

JOHN MILIUS on Steven Spielberg (*Movie Talk*, p. 190)

"Communal art."

F. SCOTT FITZGERALD, writer, on the movies
(quoted in the *New York Times*, April 25, 1982)

"Distribution is a freemasonry like the kitchens of a restaurant. They have deep, dark secrets. I have never yet been able to discover how much it costs to distribute a film."

ALFRED HITCHCOCK, producer (Corey, *The Man in Lincoln's Nose*, p. 149)

"Directing ain't that tough a gig."

LARRY GORDON, director (*You'll Never Eat Lunch in This Town Again*, p. 189)

"Movies are like wars. The guy who becomes an expert is the guy who doesn't get killed."

ROBERT TOWNE, screenwriter (Brady, *The Craft of the Screenwriter*)

MUSIC

"Rap is the CNN of the streets."   GERALD M. LEVIN, vice chairman, Time Inc.
(*New York Times*, November 29, 1992)

"Probably blue jeans and rock 'n' roll had more effect in undermining the Iron Curtain idea—that you can close off millions of people from the rest of the world—and showed it to be a sham. Forget about it. It won't be the hydrogen bombs or the missiles, it will be something quite simple. . . . [Rock 'n' roll] is probably the best work the English have done since the empire. We took it and ran with it. . . . It was one of the biggest weapons the English had and they didn't know it. Maybe the Berlin Wall would still be up without it. You can't stop music at the border. Music is one of the most powerful and insidious and subtle weapons. It can penetrate areas that no K.G.B. or C.I.A. can possibly get to. It's a beautiful armor-piercing weapon, man."

KEITH RICHARDS, guitarist, Rolling Stones
(quoted in Appleyard, *Vanity Fair*, December 1992, p. 272)

"Most people get into bands for three very simple rock and roll reasons: to get laid, to get fame, and to get rich."

BOB GELDOF (*Melody Maker*, August 27, 1977)

"Don't overly concern yourself with the union pension fund. Musicians mostly die in harness, and for good reason: we're doing something we love (even as we rejoice having escaped the family law office, furniture store, junkyard). Much of the child remains unadulterated in us long after other careerists have journeyed irrevocably into adolescence and beyond. It has to do with our toys—our instruments—that we have been tooting, sucking, breathing into, strumming, plucking, caressing since childhood; they have now been approximately mastered and are used to make both music and a livelihood."

DON ASHER, author ("Never Share the Bill with a Chimp," *Harper's Magazine*, May 1992)

"Music you can see and pictures you can hear."

WALT DISNEY on *Fantasia* (recalled during suit by the Philadelphia Orchestra against the Walt Disney Company, *New York Times*, May 7, 1992)

"Rock journalism is people who can't write interviewing people who can't talk for people who can't read."

FRANK ZAPPA (quoted in Botts, *Loose Talk*, p. 177)

"Extraordinary how potent cheap music is."

NOEL COWARD (*Private Lives*, 1930, act 1)

NAME

"It's sorta like being named Al Capone Jr."

JOHN ROBERTS, marketing manager, Hoechst Celanese, on learning that the company's new, improved microfiber cloth must still be called "polyester" (*Newsweek*, December 7, 1992)

"If my boss calls, be sure to get his name."

WILLIAM S. RUKEYSER, managing editor, *Fortune*, quoting an unnamed ABC executive on the fast changes in management at the network (*Fortune*, April 14, 1986)

"There are teams that are fair-haired and there are teams that aren't. There are teams named Smith and teams named Grabowski. . . . We're a Grabowski."

MIKE DITKA, coach, Chicago Bears (*Bears*, p. 1)

"It's traditional among scientists to name species after a patron as a gesture of thanks. [The *Eruga gutfreundi*] has a revolting life cycle. When it's time to reproduce, she looks for a money spider; she stings and paralyzes the insect, and then lays her egg on its back. The hatched larva feeds off its host's blood for about six months before devouring the money spider."

IAN GAULD, taxonomist, British Museum of Natural History, speaking of the species of female wasp recently discovered in Costa Rica and named after John H. Gutfreund, CEO, Salomon Brothers (interview, 1993)

"I'm starting to like the name 'Euro Jerry.' They said I can't have my name—but they didn't say I couldn't have theirs."

JERRY DELLA FEMINA, former president, Della Femina, McNamee Inc., which had been bought by Euro RSCG (*Wall Street Journal*, August 11, 1992)

NATIONALITY

"If my theory of relativity is proven correct, Germany will claim me as a German and France will declare that I am a citizen of the world. Should my theory prove untrue, France will say that I am a German and Germany will declare that I am a Jew."

ALBERT EINSTEIN, physicist (address at the Sorbonne, Paris, December 1929)

"National borders are no longer defensible against the invasion of knowledge, ideas, or financial data."

WALTER WRISTON, former CEO and chairman, Citicorp (*Risk and Other Four-Letter Words*, p. 133)

"Even underwear has national characteristics."

JOHN BRYAN, CEO, Sara Lee, owner of Hanes, which dominates American women's underwear (*The Economist*, November 14, 1992)

NEGOTIATION

"The Baroness Von Trapp was amusing, eccentric, and, in the end, as eager for a hit as Leland [Hayward] was. I had to admire her negotiating techniques. At their first meeting, Leland offered her 5 percent of the show—not bad considering the composers would be Rodgers and Hammerstein, the book would be by Lindsay and Crouse, and Mary Martin would play the Baroness. 'Well, I'll have to think about it a little bit,' she said. At teatime, she returned with her answer. 'You know, Mr. Hayward, whenever I have a puzzle in my head, or a decision to make, I always pray to the Holy Ghost. And I prayed to the Holy Ghost, and the Holy Ghost says ten percent.'"

SLIM KEITH (*Slim: Memories of a Rich and Imperfect Life*, p. 306)

"What's the beef, boys? So I'm trading. Everybody here is trading. So maybe I trade a little sharper. Does that make me a collaborator?"

WILLIAM HOLDEN facing his bunk-mates in *Stalag 17* (screenplay by Billy Wilder and Edwin Blum)

"Negotiating with one's self seldom produces a barroom brawl."
> WARREN BUFFETT, CEO, Berkshire Hathaway, on executive compensation
> practices (annual report, 1985)

"Don't call it stubborn. Call it conviction."
> WILLIAM PALEY to Adolf Zukor, sticking to what was considered an
> extraordinary price Paley demanded for selling half of CBS to Paramount
> (Smith, *In All His Glory*, p. 84)

"I'm not kind. I'm just tempting you. I never give anything without expecting something in return. Now, I always get paid."
> CLARK GABLE to Vivien Leigh in *Gone with the Wind*
> (screenplay by Sidney Howard)

"If we have done anything wrong, send your man to my man and they can fix it up."
> J. P. MORGAN, financier, to President Theodore Roosevelt
> (quoted in Josephson, *The Robber Barons*, p. 449)

"In a successful negotiation, everybody wins."
> GERARD NIERENBERG, president, Negotiation Institute
> (*Wall Street Journal*, June 24, 1987)

"An appeaser is one who feeds a crocodile, hoping it will eat him last."
> WINSTON CHURCHILL, British prime minister
> (speech, House of Commons, October 2, 1938)

"Any negotiator who seduces himself into believing that his personality leads to automatic breakthroughs will soon find himself in the special purgatory that history reserves for those who measure themselves by acclaim rather than by achievement."
> HENRY KISSINGER (quoted in Isaacson, *Kissinger: A Biography*, p. 511)

"Let me give you some advice. You wanna negotiate for yourself, go ahead and do it. If you negotiate with me, by the time we're finished, I'll own your house."
> MICHAEL MEDAVOY, chairman,
> Tristar Pictures, to fledgling screenwriter Karl Luedtke, who had just
> pitched the story that became *Absence of Malice*—and who had no agent
> ("Naked Hollywood: Funny Money," PBS, October 24, 1992)

"Remember the time Allen Funt put a sign up on a major highway leading into Delaware: DELAWARE CLOSED? You'd see guys drive up in their car and they'd pull over and they'd get out and here's this Funt and they'd go, 'Hey, what's going on in Delaware?'

And he'd say, 'You read the sign.' The guy says, 'Yeah, but I've got a family. When do you think it will be open again?' And so I say to you, legitimacy is very potent."

HERB COHEN, *You Can Negotiate Anything*, 1980
(Tobias, *Getting by on $100,000 a Year*, 1980)

"The 11th Commandment of a motion picture negotiation: Thou shalt not take less than thy last deal."

JOHN GREGORY DUNNE, writer

NEPOTISM

"He has set the son-in-law business back 20 years."

JULIUS EPSTEIN, screenwriter, on an unsuccessful producer married
to one of the Warner Brothers' daughters
(*Hollywood Quotations*, p. 22)

"I have a theory of relatives, too. Don't hire 'em."

JACK WARNER, during a 1930s studio visit by Albert Einstein
(quoted in Farber and Green, *Hollywood Dynasties*, 1984)

NEVER

"Never play by the rules. Never pay in cash. And never tell the truth."

The Three Rules of Wall Street, according to F. Ross Johnson, president
and CEO, RJR Nabisco (Burrough and Helyar, *Barbarians*, 1990)

"Never buy anything by the pound in a dark alley in a damp country."

MEL ZIEGLER, Banana Republic founder, on the pitfalls of learning
a mail-order retail business (*Metropolitan Home*, January 1985)

"After this, never sell what you haven't got, Dannie."

CORNELIUS VANDERBILT to Daniel Drew, nineteenth-century speculator,
who launched a huge unsuccessful bear attack on the Harlem Railroad
(quoted in Sharp, *The Lore and Legends of Wall Street*, p. 99)

"Never celebrate, never rest."

ROBERT MAXWELL, CEO, Maxwell Communications Corp.
(*Wall Street Journal*, September 13, 1991)

Never succumb to the temptation of bitterness."

MARTIN LUTHER KING, JR., civil rights leader (*The Strength to Love*, p. 26)

"Never italicize."

RALPH WALDO EMERSON, essayist (*The Superlative*, 1883)

"Never say anything on the phone that you wouldn't want your mother to hear at your trial."

> SYDNEY BIDDLE BARROWS, Mayflower Madam (quoted in Christy, "'Mayflower Madam' Tells All," *Boston Globe*, September 10, 1986)

"My pappy told me never to bet my bladder against a brewery or get into an argument with people who buy ink by the barrel."

> LANE KIRKLAND, president AFL-CIO (*Fortune*, December 23, 1985)

"Never trust a prosecutor."

> WARREN BEATTY's Bugsy Siegel to Meyer Lansky, on the judicially ordered deportation of Charlie Luciano in *Bugsy* (screenplay by James Toback)

"I'll never write a book as good as *Sometimes a Great Notion* for the same reason that Salazar will never win another marathon."

> KEN KESEY, author, on his inability to repeat his initial brilliant success (*Esquire*, September 1992)

"I never played a note I didn't mean."

> Attributed to STAN GETZ, tenor saxophonist

"Never play cards with a man called Doc. Never eat at a place called Mom's. And never, never, no matter what else you do in your whole life, *never* sleep with a woman whose troubles are worse than your own."

> NELSON ALGREN, who said the advice came a convict (Donahue, *Conversations with Nelson Algren*, 1964)

"Never ask for a job, never refuse one."

> British Navy motto

"Once you sink that first stake, they'll never make you pull it up."

> ROBERT MOSES (Caro, *The Power Broker*, 1974)

"Never hate your enemies. It affects your judgment."

> AL PACINO as Don Corleone (*Godfather III*, screenplay by Mario Puzo and Francis Ford Coppola)

NEW YORK CITY

"Times Square is the Bermuda Triangle of New York City real estate development. More money has disappeared here than any place in the city."

> SEYMOUR DURST, New York City developer, on the city government's plan to renew Times Square (*New York Observer*, March 9, 1992)

"Anything that happens on the planet, short of Somalia, happens in New York. You never have a believability problem in New York. You can say there are pygmy serial killers and they're operating in New York and it would be believable."

> DICK WOLF, producer of the successful television series, *Law and Order*
> (*New York Times*, October 18, 1992)

"Wake up, muscles, we're in New York now."

> CASEY STENGEL, baseball player, on being traded from the Phillies to the
> Giants in 1921 (*The Gospel According to Casey*, p. 4)

"If you live in New York, even if you're Catholic, you're Jewish."

> LENNY BRUCE, comedian (*New York Life*, September 27, 1992)

"I miss everything about New York. The dirt. The crime. The congestion. The crumbling infrastructure. I miss it all."

> JERRY SEINFELD, producer, *Jerry Seinfeld Show*, on living in Los Angeles
> (*People*, May 11, 1992)

"Decent people shouldn't live here."

> JACK NICHOLSON, the villain in *Batman*
> (screenplay by Sam Hamm and Warren S. Kaaren)

"I think the Dutch have been trying to buy Manhattan back piece by piece."

> VINCENT J. EVERTS, chairman, CYCO International, the Atlanta-based
> distribution arm of a Dutch software company, on the Dutch investment
> in the U.S., which stood at $49 billion in 1989
> (*New York Times*, October 24, 1989)

"They getcha, boy. They don't let you escape with minor scratches and bruises. They put scars on you here."

> REGGIE JACKSON, New York Yankees outfielder
> (*New York Times*, July 12, 1992)

"Traffic signals in New York are just rough guidelines."

> DAVID LETTERMAN, TV host (*New York Observer*, September 9, 1991)

"I took one little section of New York and made half a million dollars writing about it."

> DAMON RUNYON, writer (*In Pursuit of Gotham*, p. 163)

"This is a middle-class city. Everybody in this country wants to get ahead, get a piece of the action. That's the fundamental

difference between the Old World and the New World. There's
not the self-improvement ethic in England that there is in this
country. If you drop below that level, you're talking about the
ghettoes." RUPERT MURDOCH, on the inability of the *New York Post* to succeed
with the same tabloid format that had worked for London's
working-class *Sun* (Shawcross, *Murdoch*, p. 201)

NONVIOLENCE

"The lion and the calf shall lie down together but the calf won't
get much sleep." WOODY ALLEN, writer
("The Scrolls," *The New Republic*, August 31, 1974)

"If you will protest courageously, and yet with dignity and
Christian love, when the history books are written in future
generations, the historians will have to pause and say, 'There
lived a great people—a black people—who injected new
meaning and dignity into the veins of civilization.'"
MARTIN LUTHER KING, JR., civil rights leader
(address in Montgomery, Alabama, December 31, 1955)

"I say violence is necessary. It is as American as cherry pie."
H. RAP BROWN, activist (speech in Washington, D.C., July 27, 1967)

NOSTALGIA

"That was a golden age." EARL SINCLAIR, the harassed father
on the NBC comedy, "Dinosaurs," recalling the days when dinosaurs
ate their young (*Greensboro News and Record,* November 7, 1991)

"Nostalgia is a seductive liar." GEORGE BALL (*Newsweek*, March 22, 1971)

"My boy, *these* are the good old days."
JACK L. WARNER, film producer (*Movie Talk*, p. 118)

NUMBER TWO

"As an old center, I know what it's like to be number 2."
GERALD R. FORD, then vice president of the United States and former
Michigan University football center (interview, 1973)

"I never wanted to be vice president of anything."
NELSON ROCKEFELLER (interview with Robert Phelps, *Time*, December 1963)

"After Paul Revere rode through town, everybody said what a great job he did. But no one ever talked about the horse."
GENE UPSHAW, Los Angeles Raiders guard,
on offensive linemen

OBSERVATION

"I'm not smart. I try to observe. Millions saw the apple fall, but Newton was the one who asked why."
BERNARD M. BARUCH, financier (*New York Post*, June 24, 1965)

"You see, but you do not observe."
Arthur Conan Doyle's SHERLOCK HOLMES to Watson
("Scandal in Bohemia," *The Adventures of Sherlock Holmes*, 1892)

OFFENSE

"The offense sells the tickets and the defense wins the games."
LINDSEY NELSON, sportscaster
("NFL Football," CBS-TV, 1982)

OFFER

"My father made him an offer he couldn't refuse."
AL PACINO in *The Godfather*
(screenplay by Mario Puzo and Francis Ford Coppola)

OIL

"Oil is ultimately biodegradable."
Attributed to DON CORNETT, Exxon Corporation Alaskan Coordinator, on
Exxon's 11-million-gallon oil spill in Prince William Sound

"Lord, let there be one more Boom. And don't let us screw it up."
Oilfield prayer, on a sign in a Texas diner
(quoted in *People*, November 10, 1986)

"I don't have a lot of faith in what the oil companies say."
JAY ROCKEFELLER, governor of West Virginia and great-grandson of
John D., founder of Standard Oil (interview, 1990)

"Smell that! That's gasoline you smell in there. You can't buy any perfume in the world that smells as sweet."
WILLIAM K. WHITEFORD, chairman, Gulf Corp. (*Forbes*, May 1, 1964)

"I have some good and bad news for you, Mr. President. First, the bad: the Martians have landed in California."
"That's terrible. What's the good news?"
"They're eating oilmen, peeing oil, and heading East."

> Attributed to JAMES BAKER, Secretary of State

"Rockefeller made his money in oil, which he discovered at the bottom of wells. Oil was crude in those days, but so was Rockefeller. Now both are considered quite refined."

> RICHARD ARMOUR, writer, on John D. Rockefeller
> *(It All Started with Columbus, 1961)*

OLD

"These jokes are old enough to vote."

> ANDREA MARTIN, portraying a beleaguered comedy
> writer in the Broadway show, *My Favorite Year*
> *(New York Times, December 20, 1992)*

"To me, old age is always 15 years older than I am."

> BERNARD M. BARUCH, financier, on his 85th birthday
> (reported in the *New York Times*, June 6, 1984)

OPPORTUNITY

"The American system of ours, call it Americanism, call it Capitalism, call it what you like, gives each and every one of us a great opportunity if we only seize it with both hands and make the most of it."

> AL CAPONE, gangster
> (Cockburn, *In Time of Trouble*, 1956)

"It is a place of warring tribes, which is to say, a place of opportunity for such as we."

> MICHAEL CAINE, on setting out with Sean Connery for
> a remote section of India in *The Man Who Would be King*
> (screenplay by John Huston and Gladys Hill)

"There is no security on this earth, only opportunity."

> General DOUGLAS MACARTHUR
> (quoted in Kehrer, *Doing Business Boldly*, p. 65)

"No great man ever complains of want of opportunity."

> RALPH WALDO EMERSON, essayist (*Journals*, 1909–14)

ORDER

"The policeman isn't there to create disorder; the policeman is there to preserve disorder."
RICHARD J. DALEY, mayor, on his police force
after the Chicago Democratic Convention, 1968
(Rakove, *Don't Make No Waves: Don't Back No Losers*, p. 45)

"The objective is to find the right balance between order and disorder, between rigor mortis and anarchy."
ROY ASH, CEO, AM International

ORGANIZATION

"Organizations exist to enable ordinary people to do extraordinary things."
TED LEVITT, former editor, *Harvard Business Review*
(*Thinking About Management*, 1990)

"This book is about the organization man. . . . I can think of no other way to describe the people I am talking about. They are not the workers, nor are they are white-collar people in the usual, clerk sense of the word. These people only work for the Organization. The ones I am talking about *belong* to it as well."
WILLIAM H. WHYTE (*The Organization Man*, 1956, chapter 1)

ORGANIZATIONAL STRUCTURE

"Many writers on organization have termed the Catholic Church the most venerable large institution in the West, as it has achieved and maintained a position of leadership and power for over a millennium and a half. A key organizational characteristic of the Church is that despite its size it has avoided excessive layering."
ELI GINZBERG and GEORGE VOJTA, social scientists
(*Beyond Human Scale: The Large Corporation at Risk*, 1985)

"Organizations by and large are not capable of more than marginal changes, while the environment is so volatile that marginal changes are frequently insufficient to assure survival."
HERBERT KAUFMAN, political scientist (*Time, Chance, and Organizations*, 1991)

"The worst of all possible worlds is to change structure continually only to find each time upon reorganization that the environment has already shifted to some new configuration that demands yet a different structure."

MICHAEL HANNAN and JOHN FREEMAN (*Organizational Ecology*, 1989)

OTHER SIDE

"Audi partem alterum." ("Hear the other side.")

St. AUGUSTINE

"Fans sometimes don't understand it. The other team gets paid, too."

FRAN TARKENTON, former quarterback, Minnesota Vikings, and broadcaster ("Monday Night Football," ABC-TV, 1981)

"You can't say yes to everything. When you do say yes, say it quickly. But always take a half hour to say no, so you can understand the other fellow's side too."

FRANCIS Cardinal SPELLMAN's advice to his young colleague, Terence (later Cardinal) Cooke (recalled on Cooke's death, October 6, 1983)

OWNERS

"A lot of the more evil problems of pro football might be cured if the owners were forced to cover one kickoff—and to repeat until they made one tackle, however long that took."

BERNIE PARRISH, former defensive back (*They Call It a Game*, 1971)

"The owners have too much of that born-rich money behind them. They're members of the Lucky Sperm Club."

DAN JENKINS (*Life Its Ownself*, 1984)

"Strictly speaking, a man, to be in business, must be at least part owner of the enterprise which he manages and to which he gives his attention, and chiefly dependent for his revenues not upon salary but upon its profits."

ANDREW CARNEGIE, industrialist and philanthropist, arguing that salaried administrators were not businessmen

PAIN

"There has never been a great athlete who died not knowing what pain is."

BILL BRADLEY, basketball player and U.S. Senator (McPhee, *A Sense of Where You Are*, 1965)

"No pain, no gain."

JANE FONDA, actress and founder of Jane Fonda's aerobics studios
(poster in Fonda's Beverly Hills Studio, 1978)

"No pain, no palm; no thorns, no throne; no gall, no glory;
no cross, no crown."

WILLIAM PENN, founder of Pennsylvania
(*No Cross, No Crown*, 1669)

PARKINSON'S LAW

"Parkinson's First Law: Work expands so as to fill the time
available for its completion.
Parkinson's Second Law: Expenditure rises to meet income.
Parkinson's Third Law: Expansion means complexity, and
complexity, decay. Or: the more complex, the sooner dead."

C. NORTHCOTE PARKINSON (*In-Laws and Outlaws*, 1959)

"The ablest men get the prettiest girls."

Parkinson's Seventh Law,
often delivered by Parkinson in speeches to executive audiences

PARKINSON'S LAW, PREDECESSORS & VARIATIONS

"An order that can be misunderstood will be misunderstood."

Attributed to to HELMUT VON MOLTKE, German military thinker

"If it exists it must be possible."

Boulding's Law

"Anything that can go wrong will go wrong."

Murphy's Law

PARTNER

"We have somehow forgotten that partnerships built the West—
as well as the entire country—and have preferred to think that
individuals alone, or in limited and temporary partnerships,
built what we have today. The history of human achievement is
rich with stories of successful partnerships—while the history of
human failure is rife with tales of fruitless competition and
willful antagonisms."

MARGARET E. MAHONEY, president,
The Commonwealth Fund (annual report, 1987)

"Before you run in double harness, look well to the other horse."

OVID (*Remedia Amoris*)

"There is nothing quite so limited as being a limited partner of George Steinbrenner."

> JOHN MCMULLEN, owner, Houston Astros, and former limited partner in the New York Yankees (*Sports Illustrated*, January 4, 1993)

"You can talk about love all you want. To me, you're nothing but a fucking dollar sign."

> DEAN MARTIN to Jerry Lewis, on splitting up (Tosches, *Dino: Living High in the Dirty Business of Dreams*, 1992)

"Mr. Morgan buys his partners; I grow my own."

> ANDREW CARNEGIE, financier (Hendrick, *Life of Andrew Carnegie*, 1932)

PASSION

"Passions are like the trout in a pond; one devours the others until only one fat old trout is left."

> Attributed to OTTO VON BISMARCK, German chancellor

PATRON

"The money that fuels Novelle Society is the same that fuels the creative process. Where would the Renaissance have been without patrons?"

> CAROLYNE ROEHM, fashion designer and wife of Henry Kravis, investment banker, who underwrote opera and ballet performances (Bartlett, *The Money Machine*, p. 232)

"We are a business concern and not patrons of the arts."

> DAVID O. SELZNICK, film producer (Corey, *Man in Lincoln's Nose*, p. 131)

PAY

"First of all I choose the great ones, and if none of those come, I choose the mediocre ones, and if they don't come—I choose the ones that are going to pay the rent."

> MICHAEL CAINE, actor, on choosing movie roles (*Manhattan, Inc.*, p. 26)

"This raise is simple justice, and justice comes before charity."

> POPE JOHN XXIII, giving a 40 percent raise to workers in Vatican City although that meant cutting back on charitable contributions (Michaels, *Pope John XXIII*, p. 60)

"Incentive pay did nothing but build inventory and bad parts."

> WAYNE BOATMAN, production superintendent, Eaton Corp.'s Lincoln, Illinois, factory, on Eaton's abandoned practice of paying incentives based solely on individual output (*Wall Street Journal*, June 5, 1992)

"I'm getting a Harvard education without paying tuition."

> Senator JOHN CHAFEE, on listening to Senator Daniel Moynihan ruminate
> on his days in India (*Wall Street Journal*, March 26, 1993)

"Would we write if we didn't get paid? Probably. But we'd have to do something to get paid. We have to make a living. We have children and ex-wives and bartenders and in some cases dope dealers to support. People say that someone's 'gone Hollywood.' But they never say that someone's 'gone Iowa Writer's Workshop.' But writers also teach to make a living—it's the same thing."

> JOHN GREGORY DUNNE, novelist and screenwriter
> (*New York Times*, April 25, 1982)

"When you're a writer, you have to write these stories, even if you don't get paid."

> HORTON FOOTE, screenwriter (quoted in Brown, *Shoptalk*, p. 183)

"Hollywood is a place where they'll pay you $50,000 for a kiss and 50 cents for your soul."

> MARILYN MONROE, actress (*People*, February 1988)

"It's charity, Ed. You give a blind man a dime you don't expect the Goldberg Variations."

> ELIZABETH McGOVERN explaining to $100-a-week screenwriter Jeremy
> Irons why his employer, Warner Brothers, never reads his scenarios, in
> *Tales from Hollywood* (screenplay by Christopher Hampton)

"For someone to make $250,000 in the business world, he'd have to generate $60 million to $70 million in sales. When coaches say they're worth it, they don't know what's going on out there."

> BOB MARCUM, former athletic director, University of South Carolina
> (*USA Today*, September 24, 1986)

"Writers don't make a bad wage for a half day's work."

> PETER FLEISCHMANN, publisher of *The New Yorker*
> (quoted in *The Last Days*, p. 106)

"He that cannot pay, let him pray."

> THOMAS FULLER, English cleric (*Gnomologia*, 1732)

PEACE

"In Italy, for 30 years under the Borgias, they had warfare, terror, murder and bloodshed, but they produced Michelangelo,

Leonardo da Vinci, and the Renaissance. In Switzerland, they had brotherly love, 500 years of democracy and peace—and what did they produce? The cuckoo clock."   ORSON WELLES to Joseph Cotton
in *The Third Man* (screenplay by Graham Greene)

"Whenever peace—conceived as the avoidance of war—has been the primary objective of a power or a group of powers, the international system has been at the mercy of the most ruthless member."   HENRY KISSINGER, diplomat (Isaacson, *Kissinger: A Biography*, p. 39)

"If you want to make peace, you don't talk to your friends. You talk to your enemies."
MOSHE DAYAN, Israeli general (Safire and Safir, *Good Advice*, p. 82)

PERQUISITES

"The Indefensible."
Corporate jet named by Warren Buffett, CEO, Berkshire Hathaway, known for decrying corporate perks and who says: "Occasionally a man must rise above principles" (Berkshire Hathaway annual report, 1991)

"It's a little different from the road tour. You don't get to travel around. But you get to put all your toys on the counter in your dressing room and you don't have to move them."
TAYLOR JOHN, 9-year-old lead of *Les Miserables*, which opened on Broadway after 15 months on the road (*Greensboro News & Record*, November 17, 1991)

"When I paint my office, it will be because everybody knows the place is doing well. But before I get mine, I will see that everybody gets theirs."   Attributed to EDWARD J. MULVEY, turnaround expert
and head of Spectrum Communications and Electronics Corp.

"You need an automobile to reach his desk."
SAM GOLDWYN, film producer, on Louis B. Mayer (Marx, *Goldwyn*, 1976)

PERSISTENCE

"If at first you don't succeed, try again. Then quit. There's no use being a damn fool about it."   W. C. FIELDS, actor (*Movie Talk*, p. 111)

"Nothing in the world can take the place of persistence. Talent will not; nothing is more common than unsuccessful men with talent. Genius will not; unrewarded genius is almost a proverb. Education will not; the world is full of educated derelicts. Persistence and determination alone are omnipotent."

RAY A. KROC, Chairman, McDonald's (Boas and Chain, *Big Mac*, pp. 7–8)

"Persistence is to power what carbon is to steel. If a rat gnaws long enough at a dike, it could sink an entire nation."

HERB COHEN, author of *You Can Negotiate Anything* (Tobias, *Getting by on $100,000 a Year*, p. 150)

PHILANTHROPY

"The man who dies rich, dies disgraced."   ANDREW CARNEGIE, financier
("The Gospel of Wealth," *North American Review*, June 1889)

"The good Lord gave me my money, and how could I withhold it from the University of Chicago?"   JOHN D. ROCKEFELLER, SR.,
financier, to first graduating class (Flynn, *God's Gold*, 1932)

"The dead carry with them to the grave in their clutched hands only that which they have given away."

DEWITT WALLACE, publisher, *The Reader's Digest*, recalled on his death
(*Time*, April 13, 1981)

"The best philanthropy is a search for cause, an attempt to cure evils at their source."

JOHN D. ROCKEFELLER, SR., financier (Flynn, *God's Gold*, 1932)

PHILOSOPHY

"I adopted a philosophy I've never wavered from: Yesterday is a cancelled check; today is cash on the line; tomorrow is a promissory note."

HANK STRAM, Kansas City Chiefs coach (*Football's Greatest Quotes*, p. 180)

"Our philosophy is live, live, and *more* live."

REESE SCHONFELD, first president, Cable News Network
(Peters, *Liberation*, p. 30)

PLAGIARISM

"If you're going to plagiarize, go *way* back."

Senator BARRY GOLDWATER to Senator Joseph Biden
(Winokur, *Friendly Advice*, p. 194)

"If you look at any of the Japanese successes, with the possible exception of the tape recorder, you see that they're copies of American ideas."

ROBERT NOYCE, founder and CEO, Intel Corporation, and inventor of the integrated circuit, denying that Japanese would outstrip the U.S. in developing new technology
(*Esquire*, December 1983, p. 374)

"God gave you eyes, plagiarize."

Advice from a Salomon Brothers investment banker to trainee Michael Lewis (*Liar's Poker*, p. 186)

"Of course not. Not when I look up and down Park Avenue and see all those dreadful knock-offs of the Seagram Building and Lever House. But I couldn't have stopped it. No one could, because businessmen found out that that kind of building was cheaper to build."

PHILIP JOHNSON, architect, on being asked if he would still promote modernism if he had it to do over
(*Esquire*, December 1983, p. 281)

PLANNING

"No amount of planning will ever replace dumb luck."

Anonymous

"Ready. Fire. Aim."

Executive at Cadbury's
(quoted in Peters and Waterman, *In Search of Excellence*, p. 119)

"Even New Jersey doesn't want to be New Jersey anymore."

ROBERT YARO, executive director, Regional Plan Association, on New Jersey's eagerness to plan its development
(Hiss, *The Experience of Place*, p. 207)

"Make no little plans; they have no magic to stir men's blood. . . . Make big plans, aim high in hope and work."

Attributed to DANIEL H. BURNHAM, planner

POLITICAL ECONOMY

"Cecily, you will read your political economy in my absence. The chapter on the fall of the rupee you may omit. It is somewhat too sensational. Even these metallic problems have their melodramatic side."

OSCAR WILDE, playwright
(*The Importance of Being Earnest*, 1895)

"John Stuart Mill,
        By a mighty effort of will,
Overcame his natural bonhomie,
        And wrote Principles of Political Economy."

E. C. BENTLEY, writer (*Biography for Beginners*, 1905)

POLITICS

"In Hollywood they would call me a 'product extension.' They call my gubernatorial campaign 'Brown, Sequel III.'"

KATHLEEN BROWN, Treasurer, State of California, on her gubernatorial campaign (speech in New York City, June 22, 1993)

"There's nothing in the middle of the road but yellow stripes and dead armadillos."

JIM HIGHTOWER, radio commentator and former Texas Agriculture Commissioner (*New York Times*, January 17, 1993)

"Being in politics is like being a football coach. You have to be smart enough to understand the game and dumb enough to think it's important."

Senator EUGENE MCCARTHY, then a presidential candidate (interview, 1968)

"There should be a limit on politicians' terms. Let them make the laws for a couple of terms and them let them go home to live under those laws."

R. DAVID THOMAS, founder, senior chairman, Wendy's International (*New York Times*, November 5, 1991)

"The networks are not some chicken-coop manufacturing lobby whose calls nobody returns."

RALPH NADER, on the proposal of NBC president Robert C. Wright that company employees support a political action committee (quoted in Diamond, *New York*, January 19, 1987)

"All politics is local."

THOMAS (Tip) O'NEILL, former Speaker, U.S. House of Representatives (*New York Review of Books*, March 13, 1989)

"That our political system is failing to solve the bedrock problems we face is beyond dispute. One reason is that our public discourse has become the verbal equivalent of mud wrestling."

BILL MOYERS (*New York Times*, Op-Ed, March 22, 1992)

"Everything was a machine, too. The mill was a machine. The Union was a machine. Even the Catholic Church was a machine, with a cardinal, named Cody, who was straight out of *The Untouchables*."
THOMAS GEOGHEGAN, labor lawyer, on Chicago politics
(*Which Side Are You On?*, p. 65)

"God is a Republican and Santa Claus is a Democrat."
P. J. O'ROURKE, writer (*Parliament of Whores*, 1991)

"Ideology is the curse of public affairs because it converts politics into a branch of theology and sacrifices human beings on the altar of dogma."
ARTHUR M. SCHLESINGER, JR.
(*The Cycles of American History*, 1986, p. 65)

"A crucial feature of the political apparatus in America is that greater differences are harbored within each major party than the differences existing between them."
TOM HAYDEN, political activist (*Port Huron Statement*, 1962)

"Politics is the art of the possible, the science of the relative."
Prince OTTO VON BISMARCK, September 29, 1851
(quoted in Isaacson, *Kissinger: A Biography*, p. 109)

"Politics is just like show business."
President RONALD REAGAN
(quoted in Shawcross, *Murdoch*, p. 222)

"You campaign in poetry. You govern in prose."
MARIO CUOMO, governor of New York
(*New Republic*, April 8, 1985)

"In politics nothing is contemptible."
BENJAMIN DISRAELI, British prime minister
(*Vivian Grey*, 1926)

"Man is a political animal."
ARISTOTLE (*Politics, 1*)

POLITICS—CORPORATE

"Don't fuck with me, boys. This ain't my first time at the rodeo."
FAYE DUNNAWAY as Joan Crawford, widow of the former chairman
of Pepsi-Cola, warning the board not to try pushing her out
after the death of her husband, in *Mommie Dearest* (screenplay by
Frank Yablans, Frank Perry, Tracy Hotchner, and Robert Getchell)

POLLUTION

"New Yorkers don't trust any air they can't see."

JOHN LINDSAY, mayor, New York City (interview, 1971)

POOR

"It's hard being black. You ever been black? I was black once—
when I was poor."   LARRY HOLMES, boxer (quoted in Oates, *On Boxing*, 1987)

"A poor man shames us all."

Gabra (Kenya) saying

"I owe much. I have nothing. I give the rest to the poor!"

Attributed to RABELAIS

"Leo, he who hesitates is poor."

ZERO MOSTEL to Gene Wilder in *The Producers*
(screenplay by Mel Brooks)

"Anyone who has ever struggled with poverty knows how
extremely expensive it is to be poor."

JAMES BALDWIN (*Nobody Knows My Name*, 1961)

POVERTY

"Poverty is a great enemy of human happiness; it certainly
destroys liberty and it makes some virtues impracticable, and
others extremely difficult."   SAMUEL JOHNSON, writer (*The Idler*, 1758)

"The getting and borrowing and spending binge didn't make it
into Hunter's Point or East Oakland. The gangs did,
redistributing the income of the poor—most of whom, as
Republicans and many Democrats fail to note, work for a bad
living. Instead of leveraged buyouts, the gangs have other
weapons and organize different raids. Instead of arbitrage, Uzis.
Instead of bond houses, crack houses. The construction folks put
up their steel frames downtown, where their efforts were
subsidized by federal law and tax abatements, not on the little
streets where those Other People, the ones the rest of us would
like to wash our hands of, live and die."

TODD GITLIN ("Uncivil Society," *Image*, April 19, 1992)

"If a free society cannot help the many who are poor, it cannot save the few who are rich."

President JOHN F. KENNEDY (inaugural address, January 20, 1961)

"A man who sees another man on the street corner with only a stump for an arm will be so shocked the first time he'll give him sixpence. But the second time it'll only be a threepenny bit. And if he sees him a third time he will cold-bloodedly have him handed over to the police."   BERTOLT BRECHT *(The Threepenny Opera, 1928)*

"America is an enormous frosted cupcake in the middle of millions of starving people."

GLORIA STEINEM, editor, *Ms.* magazine (interview, 1959)

"A starved body has a skinny soul."

MARLON BRANDO in *Viva Zapata* (screenplay by John Steinbeck)

"Hunger has no conscience."

SYDNEY CHAPLIN in *Limelight* (screenplay by Charles Chaplin)

"We must show them they can get the wrinkles out of their empty bellies without putting their souls in chains."

WALTER P. REUTHER, labor union leader, on the world's poor
(quoted in Moskin, *Morality in America*, p. 89)

"A poor man has no honor."

SAMUEL JOHNSON, writer (Boswell, *Life of Johnson*, 1777)

"A call girl is just a girl who hates poverty more than she hates sin."

SYDNEY BIDDLE BARROWS, Mayflower Madam
(*New York Live*, October 6, 1991)

"Beggars mounted run their horse to death."

SHAKESPEARE (III *Henry VI*, I iv.)

"From the wild Irish slums of the 19th century to the riot-torn sections of Los Angeles, there is one unmistakable lesson in American history: A community that allows a large number of young men to grow up in broken families, dominated by women, never acquiring any set of rational expectations about the future—that community asks for, and gets, chaos."

DANIEL PATRICK MOYNIHAN, political scientist (*America*, 1965)

"I see one-third of a nation ill-housed, ill-clad, ill-nourished."
FRANKLIN D. ROOSEVELT (second inaugural address, January 20, 1937)

"Poverty is the openmouthed relentless hell which yawns
beneath civilized society."
HENRY GEORGE (*Progress and Poverty*, 1879)

"For the poor always ye have with you."
John 12:8

"Habemus publice egestatem, privatim opulentiam."
("We have public poverty and private opulence.")
Sallust (*Catiline* 1ii:22)

"I'm one of the undeserving poor, that's what I am. Now think
what that means to a man. It means he's up against middle-class
morality all the time. If there's anything going and I puts in for a
bit of it, it's always the same story: you're undeserving so you
can't have it. But my needs is as great as the most deserving
widow's that ever got money out of six different charities in one
week for the death of the same husband. I don't need less than a
deserving man. I need more. I don't eat less hearty than he does,
and I drink—oh, a lot more."
WILFRED LAWSON expanding on the curse
of poverty in *Pygmalion* (screenplay by George Bernard Shaw)

"Poverty is the parent of revolution and crime."
ARISTOTLE (*Politics, book 2*)

POWER

"In Birmingham we knew in the beginning that Negroes did not
have enough votes to move the political power structure, but we
knew that Negroes had enough money, enough buying power to
make the difference between profit and loss in almost any
business. So we decided to center it on the economic power
structure."
MARTIN LUTHER KING, JR., civil rights leader
(Garrow, *Bearing the Cross*, p. 227)

"Power is based upon perception—if you think you've got it then
you've got it. If you think you don't have it, even if you've got it,
then you don't have it."
HERB COHEN, author of *You Can Negotiate Anything*
(quoted in Tobias, *Getting by on $100,000 a Year*, p. 145)

"Power is fun."
　　　　　Donna E. Shalala, Chancellor, University of Wisconsin
　　　　　(*New York Times*, December 12, 1992)

"Power? I'm about to meet real power."
　　　　　Edward Bennett Williams, Washington lawyer, responding on his
　　　　　deathbed to a comment about all the power and influence
　　　　　he had in Washington (*Newsweek*, July 20, 1992)

"I spent my youth and early manhood worrying about corporate power. Now I worry about corporate incompetence."
　　　　　John Kenneth Galbraith, economist (*Fortune*, May 18, 1992)

"Power wins football games."
　　　　　Bill Parcells, coach, New York Giants, a constantly repeated refrain
　　　　　after winning his second Super Bowl (interview, 1991)

"The modern corporation depends for its effectiveness . . . on the quality of its internal organization, which is to say the extent and depth of the submission of its employees. . . . High salaries are collected for such submission, but it would be wrong to suggest that these are the decisive factor. Belief in the purposes of the corporation—conditioned power—is almost certainly more important."
　　　　　John Kenneth Galbraith, economist (*The Anatomy of Power*, 1985)

"Power is the ultimate aphrodisiac."
　　　　　Henry Kissinger, diplomat (*New York Times*, January 19, 1971)

"Rank is a great beautifier."
　　　　　Edward George Earle, Lord Bulwer-Lytton, English poet
　　　　　(*The Lady of Lyons*, 1838)

"Power wipes out sex. A woman who does acquire power stops arousing the same level of concern about whether or not she will be wanted as a leader."
　　　　　Rosabeth Moss Kanter, professor,
　　　　　Harvard Business School (*Men and Women of the Corporation*, 1977)

"The people can never understand why the President does not use his supposedly great power to make 'em behave. Well, all the President is, is a glorified public relations man who spends his time flattering, kissing and kicking people to get them to do what they are supposed to do anyway."
　　　　　President Harry S Truman (letter to his sister, November 1947)

"When you've got them by the balls, their hearts and minds will follow."

Sign in the den of CHARLES W. COLSON, adviser to
President Richard Nixon

"In this administration, I'm the majority."

FIORELLO H. LAGUARDIA, mayor, New York City
(quoted in *New York Times*, December 29, 1991)

"Sometimes, to those around him, he seemed so idealistic as to be innocent. He never talked about power and he did not seem to covet it. Yet the truth was quite different. He loved power and he sought it intensely, and he could be a ferocious infighter where the question of power was concerned. . . . Part of his strength appeared to be his capacity to seem indifferent, to seem almost naive about questions of power."

DAVID HALBERSTAM, on Robert McNamara
(*The Best and the Brightest*, p. 216)

"He's got them by their limos."

Expression used about Harold Geneen's control
over his top executives at ITT

"The *weak* are the second sex."   ELIZABETH JANEWAY (*Atlantic Monthly*, 1973)

"There are some physical signs that hint at power—a certain immobility, steady eyes, quiet hands, broad fingers, above all a solid presence which suggests that one belongs where one is, even if it's somebody else's office or bed."

MICHAEL KORDA, editor (*Power! How to Get It! How to Use It!*, 1975)

"Power in the system was concentrated at the top. Only top managers, the gospel went, had enough information to make decisions. And that information was expressed in the common language of finance. The system disenfranchised those who were so important in the early stages of American manufacturing, the foremen and plant managers. Instead of being creators and innovators, as in an earlier era, now they depended on meeting production quotas. They lost any stake in stopping the line and fixing problems as they occurred; they lost any stake in innovation or change."

ROBERT MCNAMARA (Shapley, *Promise and Power: The Life and Times of
Robert McNamara*, p. 67)

"Johnson's instinct for power is as primordial as a salmon's going upstream to spawn."
THEODORE H. WHITE on Lyndon B. Johnson
(*The Making of the President—1964*)

"Those who have economic power have civil power also."
GEORGE W. RUSSELL (A.E.), Irish writer, on the general strike of 1913

"The world is given to those whom the world can trust."
WALTER BAGEHOT, English economist and editor

"Power is gradually stealing away from the many to the few, because the few are more vigilant and consistent."
SAMUEL JOHNSON (*Address to Electors of Great Britain*, 1774)

"There was a rankling indignity, that to me had become almost an obsession, in seeing the power of the written word subordinated to another power, a more glittering, grosser power."
F. SCOTT FITZGERALD, writer, on his hunch that "the talkies would make even the best-selling novelist as archaic as silent pictures" (quoted in *New York Times*, April 25, 1982)

"Power is best used quietly, without attracting attention."
Attributed to MALCOLM X

"Power is not sufficient evidence of truth." SAMUEL JOHNSON (*Works*, 1776)

"Power gradually extirpates from the mind every humane and gentle virtue." EDMUND BURKE, British statesman (*A Vindication of Natural Society*, 1756)

POWER CORRUPTS

"Power tends to corrupt, and absolute power corrupts absolutely." Lord ACTON (letter to Bishop Mandell Creighton, April 5, 1887)

"Power corrupts, but the lack of power corrupts absolutely."
ADLAI STEVENSON, statesman (quoted in Bower, *Maxwell*, p. 123)

"Power corrupts, but absolute power is a blast."
Capitol Hill aphorism (*The Economist*, June 27, 1992)

"Power corrupts. You use it, abuse it, then lose it."
Attributed to Henry Kaiser, industrialist

"All weakness tends to corrupt, and impotence corrupts absolutely."
EDWARD Z. FREIDENBERG (*Coming of Age in America*, 1965)

"Powerlessness corrupts. Absolute powerlessness corrupts absolutely."
ROSABETH MOSS KANTER, professor, Harvard Business School
(Peters, *Thriving on Chaos*, p. 286)

PRAISE

"From praise springs virtue."
Inscription on Venetian goblet, c. 1500,
at J. Paul Getty Museum, Santa Monica, California

"You done splendid."
CASEY STENGEL, baseball manager (*The Gospel According to Casey*, p. 9)

PREDATORS

"*The Predators' Ball*" The name given to the annual meeting of Drexel Burnham
Lambert investors and the title of a book on the firm's demise

"In this business it's dog eat dog, and nobody's going to eat me."
Attributed to SAM GOLDWYN, film producer

"Millions of years ago, dinosaurs fed on the leaves of those trees.
The dinosaurs were vegetarians. That's why they became extinct.
They were just too gentle for their size. And then the carnivorous
creatures—the ones that eat flesh—the killers—inherited the
earth. But, then, they always do, don't they?"
KATHARINE HEPBURN in *Suddenly Last Summer*
(screenplay by Gore Vidal and Tennessee Williams)

"If you live among wolves, you have to act like a wolf."
Attributed to NIKITA KHRUSHCHEV, Soviet leader

"Man, biologically considered . . . is the most formidable of all the
beasts of prey, and, indeed, the only one that preys systematically
on its own species."
WILLIAM JAMES, psychologist (*The Principles of Psychology*, 1890)

PREDICTIONS (ON TARGET)

"Anyone who sticks around that fellow will get rich."
ALBERT LASKER, advertising man, on André Meyer
(Reich, *Financier: André Meyer*, p. 81)

"I'm bound to be rich! *Bound to be rich!*"
JOHN D. ROCKEFELLER, SR.,
financier (quoted in Josephson, *The Robber Barons*, 1934)

"I cannot imagine any scenario other than the total collapse of society in which the sales of microcomputer application software will not grow by a factor of 10 in the next five years."
JOHN WALKER, CEO, Autodesk, Inc., 1982; Autodesk's sales increased
nearly ten times to $9.8 million in fiscal 1992
(*Wall Street Journal*, May 28, 1992)

"I believe the new trends include the requirement on the part of the customer that the vehicle will work."
Sir GRAHAM DAY, chairman, Rover Group, the British car maker, on what
car buyers will look for in the 1990s (*Fortune*, January 1, 1990)

"We need a bigger boat."
ROY SCHEIDER, on first spotting
the shark in *Jaws* (screenplay by Peter Benchley)

"You have a better chance of being a brain surgeon than you do an NBA player."
BOB MINNICKS, an NCAA director of enforcement, speaking to high
school athletes at a Nike training camp: only 1 percent of high school
athletes play in the pros; only 2.7 percent play in college, including all
divisions (Moyers, "Sports in America," Public Broadcast System, 1992)

"Ninety-nine percent of the people in those cars are not transporting anything in bulk. If the communications were rich enough, most of them could do their jobs at home."
ROBERT NOYCE, founder and CEO, Intel Corporation, and inventor of the
integrated circuit, looking out his office window in 1976
(quoted by Tom Wolfe, *Esquire*, December 1983, p. 374)

"By the year 2000 there will be no developed country where traditional workers making and moving goods account for more than one sixth or one eighth of the work force."
PETER F. DRUCKER, writer (*Post-Capitalist Society*, p. 5)

"That thing is going to make a hatful of money."
Banker, after sitting silently through Walt Disney's storytelling of Snow
White, for which there was not yet a lot or even script
(*The Prince of the Magic Kingdom*, p. 26)

"The stockholders will always pick up the bills."
BEN STEIN, financial writer, predicting that investment bankers would
retire rich no matter what their wrongdoings
(*New York Observer*, October 14, 1991)

"Young man, there is America—which at this day serves for little more than to amuse you with stories of savage men and uncouth manners; yet shall, before you taste of death, show itself equal to the whole of that commerce which now attracts the envy of the world."   EDMUND BURKE, British statesman *(Speech on Conciliation with America.*
The Thirteen Resolutions, 1775)

"Now we've got all the pieces in place, we're going to grow *au naturel.*"   J. PETER GRACE, CEO, W. R. Grace, on his company's entry into
natural resources *(Forbes,* September 13, 1980)

PREDICTIONS (UNFORTUNATE)

"If you are a patient with heart disease, and you have neither love nor money, your prognosis is worse."
Dr. REDFORD B. WILLIAMS, professor of medicine, Duke University,
summarizing a study showing that people with few social or economic
resources have triple the heart disease death rate of those with money
and friends *(Greensboro News & Record,* November 17, 1991)

"Smoother, rounder, yet bolder."
ROBERTO C. GOIZUETA, CEO, Coca-Cola, describing the new taste that was
to replace the 99-year-old secret formula *(People,* May 13, 1985)

"Can't act. Slightly bald. Can dance a little."
Anonymous summation of Fred Astaire's first screen test
(quoted in Thomas, *Astaire,* 1985, chapter 3)

"There are conditions in America which necessitate the use of such instruments more than here. Here, we have a superabundance of messengers. The absence of servants has compelled Americans to adopt communications systems."   Sir WILLIAM PREECE, chief engineer
of the British Post Office, testifying in 1879 in the House of Commons
that the telephone had little future in Britain

"No Civil War picture ever made a nickel."
Attributed to IRVING THALBERG, MGM producer,
in turning down *Gone with the Wind*

"Cavalry will never be scrapped to make room for the tanks; in the course of time cavalry may be reduced as the supply of horses in this country diminishes. This depends greatly on the life of fox-hunting."   Unsigned contribution
(Journal of the Royal United Services Institution, 1921)

"No legs, no jokes, no chance!"
> Attributed to MIKE TODD, producer, walking out of a 1943 New Haven
> tryout performance of *Away We Go*, shortly to be retitled *Oklahoma*

"I think there is a world market for about five computers."
> THOMAS J. WATSON, chairman of IBM (Peters, *Thriving on Chaos*, p. 199)

"Can't make a double-play, can't throw, can't hit left-handed and can't run."
> PETE ROSE'S scouting report by the Cincinatti Reds
> (quoted in Will, *New York Review of Books*, June 1991)

"When I got to Hollywood, I was discouraged with animation. I figured I had gotten into it too late. I was through with the cartoon business."
> WALT DISNEY (*The Man Behind the Magic*, p. 42)

"There is no reason for any individual to have a computer in their home."
> KEN OLSEN, president of Digital Equipment
> (Peters, *Thriving on Chaos*, p. 199)

"You will be bankrupt."
> ALEXANDER KORDA to John Huston and Sam Spiegel,
> on declining to participate in *The African Queen*
> (quoted in Dunne, *Crooning*, p. 194)

"I believe it is peace for our time."
> British Prime Minister NEVILLE CHAMBERLAIN
> (speech, September 30, 1937)

PREDICTIONS (NO COMMENT)

"The digital intersection of print and video is where this company is headed. It's just so clear."
> GERALD M. LEVIN, vice chairman, Time, Inc.
> (Clurman, *To the End of Time*, p. 10)

"We are leaving the period of money fever that was the Eighties and entering a period of moral fever."
> TOM WOLFE, writer (interview, 1990)

"Like a lot of males, I'll be taking the drug."
> Dr. P. ROY VAGELOS, CEO, Merck and Company, on the long-awaited
> prostate drug, Proscar (*New York Times*, February 16, 1992)

"I've got one word for you—plastics."
> WALTER BROOKE predicting the path to success to Dustin Hoffman in
> *The Graduate* (screenplay by Calder Willingham and Buck Henry)

"The nineties will be a decade in a hurry, a nanosecond culture. There'll be only two kinds of managers: the quick and the dead."
DAVID VICE, vice-chairman, Northern Telecom (Peters, *Liberation*, p. 59)

"Mayor David N. Dinkins: 'See that man over there digging the ditch. I remember you dated him once. If you had married him, you would be the wife of a ditch digger.'
"Mrs. Dinkins: 'No, if I had married him, he would be the mayor of New York City.'"
DAVID N. DINKINS, mayor, New York City (speech, November 12, 1992)

"As we look at the status of nuclear energy development, we see something solid. We find that quietly, without fanfare, the thing we have been waiting for has happened: the age of nuclear power has begun."
GLENN SEABORG, chairman, Atomic Energy Commission
(interview, September 1964)

"Well, I just gave the South to the Republicans for the next 40 years."
Attributed to President LYNDON B. JOHNSON, on signing the Civil Rights
Act of 1964 (quoted in *Commonweal*, December 4, 1992)

"We will bury you."
NIKITA KHRUSHCHEV, Soviet leader (November 18, 1956)

"Then the first thing that happens is I see you, and I thought this is going to be one terrific day so you better live it up, boy, 'cause tomorrow you'll be nothing."
JAMES DEAN to Natalie Wood
in *Rebel Without a Cause* (screenplay by Nicholas Ray)

"Economists are always half right in their predictions, but they don't know which half it will be."
Anonymous

"What all the wise men promised has not happened, and what all the damned fools predicted has come to pass."
Lord MELBORNE, quoted by John W. Gardner, founder, Common Cause
(mimeo speech, February 6, 1977)

PREPARE

"We can't always cross a bridge until we come to it; but I always like to lay down a pontoon ahead of time."
BERNARD M. BARUCH, financier
(quoted in Adams, *The Home Book of Humorous Quotations*, p. 55)

"Be prepared."

Boy Scout motto

PRICE

"If your price isn't right, you can't sell it regardless of fit, quality, or style."

BUD KONHEIM, president, Nicole Miller, an upscale clothing manufacturer, on the increasing bargain hunting among buyers (*Fortune*, March 11, 1991)

"What is a cynic? A man who knows the price of everything and the value of nothing."

OSCAR WILDE, playwright (*Lady Windermere's Fan*, 1892)

"People of the same trade seldom meet together, even for merriment and diversion, but the conversation ends in a conspiracy against the public, or in some contrivance to raise prices."

ADAM SMITH (*The Wealth of Nations*, 1776)

PRINCIPLES

"It's a matter of having principles. It's easy to have principles when you're rich. The important thing is to have principles when you're poor."

ROY A. KROC, Chairman, McDonald's (Love, *McDonald's: Behind the Arches*, 1986)

"No sanctuary."

ROBERT W. GALVIN, CEO, Motorola, on his attitude toward Japanese competitors (*Fortune*, March 11, 1991)

PRIVACY

"I am angry that I was put in the position of having to lie if I wanted to protect my privacy. I didn't commit any crime. I'm not running for public office. I should be able to reserve the right to keep things like that private. After all, the doctor-patient and lawyer-client relationships are private. Just as I'm sure everyone in this room has some personal matter he or she would like to keep private, so did we. There was certainly no compelling medical or physical necessity to go public with my medical condition."

ARTHUR ASHE, tennis champion, on the reporting of his having the fatal disease AIDS (*New York Times*, February 8, 1993)

PROBLEM

"Just because there's a problem doesn't mean there has to be a solution."
ROBERT L. BERNSTEIN, president, Random House (to author, 1993)

"No sooner is one problem solved than another surfaces—never is there just one cockroach in the kitchen."
WARREN BUFFETT, CEO, Berkshire Hathaway (annual report, 1989)

"Problems are only opportunities in work clothes."
HENRY J. KAISER, CEO, Kaiser Steel (recalled on his death, August 24, 1967)

"I find that the three major administrative problems on a campus are sex for the students, athletics for the alumni, and parking for the faculty."
CLARK KERR, president of the University of California
(*Time*, November 17, 1958)

"I'm either part of your problem or part of your solution."
RUBERT MURDOCH, chairman, News Corporation,
to Ian Chapman, deputy chairman, Collins Publishers,
pointing out that he owned 31 percent of the company's stock
and that opponent Robert Maxwell had increased his share to 9 percent
(Shawcross, *Murdoch*, p. 289)

"The problem with having a sense of humor is often that people you use it on aren't in a very good mood."
LOU HOLTZ, football coach, the University of Notre Dame
(*Sports Illustrated*, December 9, 1985)

"No problem is too big to run away from."
Charles M. Schulz's CHARLIE BROWN
(quoted by Ries and Trout, *Positioning: The Battle for Your Mind*, 1981)

PRODUCT

"I'm only a product like a cake of soap. To be sold as well as possible."
CHARLES BRONSON, actor (*Movie Talk*, p. 95)

"One good product or service can support you in style for the rest of your life."
E. JOSEPH COSSMAN, author of *How I Made $1,000,000 in Mail Order*
(Henderson, *Winners*, p. 6)

PRODUCTIVITY

"If all we're looking at is productivity increases by downsizing, it's 'game over' for America."
STEPHEN S. ROACH, senior economist, Morgan Stanley and Co.
(Business Week, "Reinventing America," 1992, p. 22)

"At Ford plants, you see everyone walking somewhere with a purpose—doing something. At a GM plant, guys are just sitting on a bench watching the press line run, waiting for something to break."
JOHN McELROY, editor-in-chief, Automotive Industries magazine, on the
higher productivity of Ford, which takes one-third fewer man-hours to
build cars than GM (Wall Street Journal, December 15, 1992)

"Man is the only creature that consumes without producing. He does not give milk, he does not lay eggs, he is too weak to pull the plow. . . . Yet he is the lord of all the animals."
GEORGE ORWELL (Animal Farm, 1945)

"Poets aren't very useful.
Because they aren't consumeful or very produceful."
OGDEN NASH, poet (The Writer's Quotation Book, p. 57)

PROFIT

"Nobody ever got poor taking a profit."
ANDRÉ MEYER, investment banker, who sometimes sold
businesses that went on to reap even bigger returns
(Reich, Financier: André Meyer, p. 119)

"If we can't make 40 percent profit pretax, we might as well be plumbers."
HARTMUT ESSLINGER, industrial designer and CEO, frogdesign
(Business Week, December 3, 1990)

"I can see in principle no grounds for that low estimation of the creation of wealth which prevails in many Christian circles and which regards nursing as inherently more vocational than oil drilling."
Rev. ANTHONY DYSON, Canon of Windsor, England
(National Catholic Reporter, October 4, 1991)

"The bottom line is in heaven."
EDWIN H. LAND, CEO, Polaroid (shareholders annual meeting, 1977)

"It is no sin to make a profit."

Dean, Harvard School of Business, cited approvingly by Robert
McNamara when he was a student there (Shapley, *McNamara*, p. 20)

"Profits are the lifeblood of the economic system, the magic elixir
upon which progress and all good things depend ultimately. But
one man's lifeblood is another man's cancer." PAUL A. SAMUELSON,
professor of economics, Harvard University (*Time*, August 16, 1976)

"Watch the costs and the profits will take care of themselves."

ANDREW CARNEGIE, financier
(quoted in *Wall Street Journal*, Centennial Edition, 1989)

"It is a socialist idea that making profits is a vice. I consider the
real vice is making losses." WINSTON CHURCHILL, British prime minister
(quoted in *National Catholic Reporter*, October 1991)

"No man profits but by the loss of others."

MONTAIGNE, French philosopher (*Essays*, 1580)

"What is a man profited if he shall gain the whole world and lose
his soul?" *Matthew* 16:26

"Unearned increment."

JOHN STUART MILL, economist (*Dissertations and Discussions*, 1859)

PROPERTY

"Buy the acre, sell the lot." JOHN JACOB ASTOR, fur and real estate magnate
(Rachlis and Marqusee, *The Land Lords*, p. 3)

"Those who hold and those who are without property have ever
formed distinct interests in society. Those who are creditors, and
those who are debtors, fall under a like discrimination. A landed
interest, a manufacturing interest, a mercantile interest, a moneyed
interest, with many lesser interests, grow up of necessity in
civilized nations, and divided them into different classes, actuated
by different sentiments and views."

JAMES MADISON (*The Federalist*, no. 10, 1787)

"Property is desirable, is a positive good in the world."

ABRAHAM LINCOLN (message to Congress, 1861)

"In America, the most democratic of nations, those complaints against property in general, which are so frequent in Europe, are never heard, because in America there are no paupers. As everyone has property of his own to defend, everyone recognizes the principles upon which he holds it."
ALEXIS DE TOCQUEVILLE, French comentator (*Democracy in America,* 1835–1840)

"The great and chief end of men . . . putting themselves under government, is the preservation of their property."
JOHN LOCKE (*Two Treatises on Government,* 1690)

"Doesn't thou 'ear my 'erse's legs, as they canters away?
Proputty, proputty, proputty—that's what I 'ears 'em say."
ALFRED TENNYSON (*Northern Farmer,* 1869)

"Property is theft."
PROUDHON (*Principle of Right,* 1840)

"Invest in land because they've stopped making it."
MARK TWAIN

"If I had it to do over, I'd buy every square foot on the island of Manhattan."
JOHN JACOB ASTOR, financier (on his deathbed, 1848)

PROTEST

"The whole purpose is to arouse a sense of concern within what I call the people of good will so that they will rise up and bring an end to the reign of terror."
MARTIN LUTHER KING, JR., civil rights leader, on his strategy after the Selma, Alabama, murders that shocked the nation in 1965 (Garrow, *Bearing the Cross,* p. 418)

"Don't waste any time mourning, organize."
JOE HILL, labor organizer (letter written to William D. Haywood, November 18, 1915, the day before Hill was executed)

"A riot is at bottom the language of the unheard."
MARTIN LUTHER KING, JR., civil rights leader (*Where Do We Go from Here?,* 1967, chapter 4)

"When genitals are outlawed, only outlaws will have genitals."
Placard carried at 1988 protest of congressional attacks on freedom of expression in the arts (*The Guardian,* September 1989)

"If you don't like the president, it costs you 90 bucks to fly to Washington to picket. If you don't like the governor, it costs you 60 bucks to fly to Albany to picket. If you don't like me, 90 cents."
EDWARD I. KOCH, mayor, New York City
(New York Times, February 28, 1985)

PROTOCOL

"I don't understand the protocol about how such major corporate events are conducted. I can imagine like a Bulgarian wedding—you don't ever see the bride beforehand."
JASON McMANUS, editor-in-chief, Time, Inc.
(Clurman, To the End of Time, p. 11)

PUBLIC

"There's no reason for the public to hear of us. We're not selling anything to the public."
STEPHEN DAVISON BECHTEL, JR., chairman, Bechtel Group, a private
construction company, refusing to talk to a reporter
(McCartney, Friends in High Places, 1988)

"The public be damned."
WILLIAM H. VANDERBILT, president, New York Central Railroad, replying
to a reporter who asked if he was working for the public or his
stockholders (quoted by Stone, Fifty Years a Journalist)

"Consider the public. . . . Never fear it nor despise it. Coax it, charm it, interest it, stimulate it, shock it now and then if you must, make it laugh, make it cry, but above all . . . never, never, never bore the living hell out of it."
NOEL COWARD, advice
to fellow playwrights (recalled on his death, March 26, 1973)

PUBLIC INTEREST

"The notion that a business is clothed with a public interest and has been devoted to the public use is little more than a fiction intended to beautify what is disagreeable to the sufferers."
Justice OLIVER WENDELL HOLMES, JR. (Tyson v. Banton, 1927)

"The public interest is not defined as what is interesting to the public."
KEN MORGAN, chief, British Press Complaints Commission, on why
publication of nude photos of Prince Andrew could not be justified on
public interest grounds (Newsweek, July 29, 1991)

"For years I thought what was good for our country was good for General Motors, and vice versa. The difference did not exist. Our company is too big. It goes with the welfare of the country. Our contribution to the nation is quite considerable."

CHARLES E. WILSON, CEO, General Motors, testimony to the Senate Armed Services Committee on his nomination as Secretary of Defense, January 15, 1952 (quoted in *New York Times,* February 24, 1953)

"The President of the United States is paid to look after the national interest. I am paid to look after the interests of the miners."

JOHN L. LEWIS, president, United Mine Workers of America, and, subsequently, head of the newly formed Congress of Industrial Organizations, refusing President Roosevelt's appeal to put mineworkers back to work after calling a strike against the wage freeze imposed in 1943 during World War II (quoted by Drucker, *Post-Capitalist Society,* p. 98)

PUBLIC RELATIONS

"PR cannot overcome things that shouldn't have been done."

HAROLD BURSON, CEO, Burson-Marsteller public relations (*USA Today,* June 7, 1993)

"I want to be a public relations man, not a pimp."

JACK LEMMON in *Days of Wine and Roses* (screenplay by J. P. Miller)

PUNISH

"The people threw me out. Now the people must be punished."

EDWARD I. KOCH, former mayor, New York City, to a passerby who had shouted to him that he should return to office to save the city (*Wall Street Journal,* March 4, 1992)

"I don't think we ought to execute them right now. Give them another two or three weeks and see if they improve."

MACK BROWN, football coach, Tulane University, on being asked about his team's execution (*Sporting News,* 1986)

"If a contractor builds a house for a man and does not build it strong enough, and the house which he builds collapses and causes the death of the house owner, then the contractor shall be put to death. If it causes the death of the son of the owner, then the son of the contractor shall be put to death."

Code of Hammurabi (c. 1750 B.C.)

"Why is it that scarcely any are executed but the poor?"

THOMAS PAINE *(The Rights of Man,* 1791*)*

PURE

"I am as pure as the driven slush."

TALLULAH BANKHEAD, actress
(quoted in Zolotow, *Saturday Evening Post,* April 12, 1927)

"I was Snow White, but I drifted."

MAE WEST, actress (quoted by Warren Buffett, CEO, Berkshire Hathaway,
discussing his errors in annual report, 1989)

QUALIFICATIONS

"A successful museum director has to be a Ph.D. in art history,
with a great eye; a smuggler; a ward-heeling politician, and an
expert at avoidance of knowledge."

THOMAS HOVING, former director,
Metropolitan Museum of Art *(W,* April 27, 1992)

"No man should be allowed to be President who does not
understand hogs, or has not been around a manure pile."

HARRY S TRUMAN, as quoted by Rep. Paul Findley
(Hyman, *Washington Wind and Wisdom,* p. 109)

QUALITY

"You can't have quality with mass production. You don't want it
because it lasts too long. So you substitute styling, which is a
commercial swindle intended to produce artificial obsolescence.
Mass production couldn't sell its goods next year unless it made
what it sold this year look unfashionable a year from now. . . . We
make the finest packages in the world, Mr. Marlowe. The stuff
inside is mostly junk."

RAYMOND CHANDLER *(The Long Goodbye,* 1953)

"People always apologize for new carpets. But that's absurd.
They should only apologize for bad ones."

GEORGE JEVREMOVIC, president, Philadelphia's Woven Legends, which
directs Turkish and Yugoslav weavers in reproducing classic
nineteenth-century patterns *(Metropolitan Home,* April 1991)

"Griping, groping, grasping, and growing."

A General Motors manager describing the four stages of an employee
Quality Circle (quoted in Augustine, *Augustine's Laws,* p. 84)

"Quality is a common standard; it makes sense to everybody, everywhere. It can bind and build a core of corporate values worldwide."

> Francis Lorentz, chairman, Groupe Bull
> (*Harvard Magazine*, March–April 1991)

QUALITY, CONSUMER SATISFACTION

"Treat each patient as you would a member of your own family."

> Motto of Humana, a health care company

"The United States has been terrible as it applies to customer service. When the history of American business is written, I think that's going to be the most incredible part of the historian's view of what we did during the sixties and seventies. Somehow, management let employees believe the customers weren't important."

> Frederick C. Smith, founder of Federal Express
> (Peters, *Thriving on Chaos*, p. 89)

". . . now all you have to do is hold the chicken, bring me the toast, give me a check for the chicken-salad sandwich—and you haven't broken any rules."

> Jack Nicholson, trying to get a side order of toast from
> an obnoxious waitress in *Five Easy Pieces*
> (screenplay by Adrien Joyce)

QUALITY, SLOGANS AND SAYINGS

"Absolutely, Positively, Overnight"

> Federal Express

"Old Lonely"

> Maytag washer

"No Problem at Nordstrom"

> Nordstrom

"The thinking man's barbell."

> Arthur Jones, inventor of Nautilus exercise equipment

"In God we trust; everything else we check."

> Airline Pilot's Union

"Tell them quick and tell them often."

> William Wrigley, Jr., founder of the chewing gum company,
> on his namesake gum

"Quality, service, cleanliness, and value."

McDonald's

"Do you want it fast or good?"

Hollywood filmmaker query

"Doing common things uncommonly well."

HENRY J. HEINZ, founder, H.J. Heinz & Co.

"No foal, no fee."

Saying in the horse business

QUESTION

"Am I not a man and a brother?"

Kneeling slave in chains pictured on
Wedgwood medallion created for the London Society for the Abolition of
Slavery in 1787 (recalled in letter to the *New York Times*, March 22, 1992)

"Who do you have to sleep with to get *off* this picture?"

OLIVE DEERING, actress, after working on Cecil B. DeMille's *Ten
Commandments* on location in Mojave desert for endless weeks
(Randall and Mindlin, *Which Reminds Me*, p. 146)

"I'm the chairman! If I can't make things happen, how can
anybody else?"

NAJEEB HALABY, chairman, Pan Am, on making changes
at the declining airlines (*Conde Nast Traveler*, July 1991, p. 24)

"That's a good question. Let me try to evade you."

PAUL TSONGAS, presidential contender (*Newsweek*, July 20, 1992)

"Are we going to be a services power? The double-cheeseburger-
hold-the-mayo kings of the whole world?"

LEE IACOCCA
(speech to Japan Society of New York, quoted in *Fortune*, July 7, 1986)

"What was that leopard doing at that altitude?"

MAUREEN DOWD, reporter, *New York Times*, applying the Hemingway
question to Vice President Dan Quayle
(speech, New York City, February 10, 1993)

"Does this boat go to Europe, France?"

MARILYN MONROE in *Gentlemen Prefer Blonds*
(screenplay by Charles Lederer)

"Mice? Who wants mice?"

A representative of Universal Pictures rejecting Walt Disney's request
that his studio finance Mickey Mouse (*The Man Behind the Magic*, p. 54)

QUOTING

"I'm happy. Let's end this right now. I don't care about the championship. Forget the MVP. I got all-quotable."

> CHARLES BARKLEY, power forward, Phoenix Suns,
> on learning during the NBA playoffs that a
> nationwide panel of writers and broadcasters had named him
> to the NBA All-Interview team for the fourth straight season
> (*New York Newsday*, June 16, 1993)

"You know a good quote when you see it."

> JUSTIN KAPLAN, editor, *Bartlett's Familiar Quotations*, 16th ed.
> (*Wall Street Journal*, November 12, 1992)

"Quoting, like smoking, is a dirty habit to which I am devoted."

> Amanda Cross's Professor KATE FANSLER
> (*Mystery Lovers Book of Quotations*, p. 419)

RACE

"No Viet Cong ever called me 'Nigger.'"

> MUHAMMAD ALI, boxer (quoted in Mailer, *The Fight*, 1975)

"Our nation is moving toward two societies, one black, one white, separate and unequal."

> National Advisory Commission on Civil Disorders, 1968

"To be a Negro in this country and to be relatively conscious is to be in a rage almost all the time."

> JAMES BALDWIN, writer (*Time*, August 20, 1965)

"If ever America undergoes great revolutions, they will be brought about by the presence of the black race on the soil of the United States; that is to say, they will owe their origin, not to the equality but to the inequality of condition."

> ALEXIS DE TOCQUEVILLE (*Democracy in America*, 1840)

RADICAL

"If you have a radical idea . . . for God's sake don't be radical in how you carry it out. . . . Become a right-wing conservative in carrying out a left-wing idea."

> JOHN PRESPER ECKERT, computer pioneer ("Revenge Theory,"
> *Harvard Magazine*, March–April 1991)

"Religion often gets credit for curing radicals when old age is the real medicine."

AUSTIN O'MALLEY (*Keystones of Thought*)

READ

"He tries to read Plato's *Republic* every year."

MARILYN QUAYLE, on the reading habits of her husband, Vice President Dan Quayle (*Wall Street Journal*, January 20, 1993)

"Because when I grow up I'm going to be a millionaire and hire someone to read for me."

Sir JAMES GOLDSMITH, financier, as a child on why he would not learn to read (*The Economist*, November 16, 1991)

"They get those weak eyes from reading, you know—those long tiny little columns in the *Wall Street Journal*."

MARILYN MONROE, explaining to Tony Curtis her attraction to businessmen in *Some Like It Hot* (screenplay by Billy Wilder and I. A. L. Diamond)

REAL ESTATE

"What developers do, fundamentally, is run the numbers. And the most impressive number they run is the one in which they manage to divide extremely large dollar figures by 43,560, which is the number of square feet in an acre. By so doing they can and do reduce much of human experience—quite accurately, as it turns out—to the Deal."

JOEL GARREAU, writer (*Edge City*, 1991)

"Everything that is wrong with U.S. housing—high prices, slow production, labor troubles, archaic building codes—can be licked by size."

WILLIAM LEVITT, founder, Levitt & Sons building company, 1937 (Rachlis and Marqusee, *The Land Lords*, p. 231)

"[When] everyone else is getting out, that's usually the time to get in."

CARL C. ICAHN, on buying American Property Investors for $44 million cash at the Integrated Resources bankruptcy auction (*Manhattan, Inc.*, November 1990)

"Were I to characterize the United States, it would be by the appellation of the land of speculations."

WILLIAM PRIEST, an Englishman who toured the country in 1796 (Rachlis and Marqusee, *The Land Lords*, p. 32)

"It's a nice building. You get a better class of cockroaches."
JAMES EARL JONES to Diahann Carroll in *Claudine*
(screenplay by Tina Pine and Lester Pine)

"The best investment on earth is earth."
LOUIS J. GLICKMAN, investment banker (*New York Post*, October 3, 1957)

REALITY

"Reality has come to seem more and more like what we are
shown by cameras."
SUSAN SONTAG, author (*New York Review of Books*, April 18, 1974)

"It is an immutable law in business that words are words,
explanations are explanations, promises are promises—but only
performance is reality."
HAROLD GENEEN, chairman, ITT (*Managing*, 1984)

"Euphoria has a nasty habit of stumbling on reality."
ADAM OSBORNE, founder, Osborne Computer, which started in 1981, did
$93 million in business its first fiscal year, and declared bankruptcy in
1983 (Henderson,*Winners*, p. 166)

RECOVERY

"The economy has a case of Lyme disease brought on in large part
by over-indebtedness. It isn't necessarily fatal, but it is debilitating.
So we're in a 'recover,' but it's not a recovery like recoveries used to
be. It's not at all red-blooded and lusty. It's in fact quite meek and
mild.'
JAMES GRANT, editor,
Grant's Interest Rate Observer, a newsletter (*M*, July 1992)

"Suffering isn't ennobling, recovery is."
CHRISTIAN N. BARNARD, surgeon,
who did the first heart transplant (*New York Times*, April 28, 1985)

REFORM

"We must reform in order to preserve."
EDMUND BURKE, British statesman
(quoted in Blackwell, *Political Thought*, p. 52)

REGRETS

"I don't talk in regrets, it's so boring. Yesterday is so gone."
ELAINE STRITCH, actress (*New York Times*, April 11, 1993)

REJECTION

"NBC's ratings were so low that there were days when, after calling New York for the overnights at 7:00 A.M. California time, I would almost be too depressed to go to work. I had a real connection to those shows, and so I took their failure personally. It's bad enough to be rejected by your friends, your wife, or your family; I felt like I was being rejected by an entire nation."

BRANDON TARTIKOFF, head of programming, NBC-TV
(*The Last Great Ride*, p. 45)

REMEMBER

"Remember, the rooster only crows; it is the hen that delivers the egg."

Texas saying

"Just remember. They're the guys you went to high school with."

R. W. APPLE, Washington bureau chief, *New York Times*, to Maureen
Dowd, reporter, on not being intimidated by President Clinton's White
House staff (quoted in a speech, New York City, February 10, 1993)

"Just remember, beautiful, everything gets old if you do it often enough."

ELLEN BURSTYN to daughter Cybil Shepherd in *The Last Picture Show*
(screenplay by Peter Bogdanovich and Larry McMurtry)

REPUTATION

"Where do I go to get my reputation back?"

Former Secretary of Labor RAY DONOVAN, on being acquitted of
corruption charges (Noonan, *What I Saw at the Revolution*, p. 119)

"Don't be too sure I'm as crooked as I'm supposed to be. That kind of reputation might be good business—bringing in high-priced jobs and making it easier to deal with the enemy."

Dashiell Hammett's SAM SPADE (*The Maltese Falcon*, 1930)

"My father said: 'You must never try to make all the money that's in a deal. Let the other fellow make some money too, because if you have a reputation for always making all the money there is in a deal, you won't make many deals.'"

J. PAUL GETTY, financier (*Getty on Getty*, p. 28)

REQUEST

"I don't know what I'd do without your help, but let me try."
Lou Godstein, social director at Grossinger's, the Catskills resort
(Frommer and Frommer, *It Happened in the Catskills*, 1991)

RESPONSES

"So what?"   MADONNA, performer, on being told of the discovery of pornographic
pictures she posed for as a young woman in New York
(Noonan, *What I Saw at the Revolution*, p. 119)

"I am told that I'm the first commissioner ever to use the word

tsoris."   FAY VINCENT, baseball commissioner, on being asked "Do you feel lately
like you're in a bunker?" (*Newsweek*, July 20, 1992)

"I have to. Otherwise I get all the tax cases."
Justice DAVID SOUTER, on why he sings along with Chief Justice
Rehnquist at Rehnquist's annual Christmas party
(*Wall Street Journal*, February 2, 1993)

"Minsky's burlesque is. Would you invest in a swamp? You
wouldn't. What if I called it Florida?"
ELLIOTT GOULD in *The Night They Raided Minsky's*, responding to comment
that burlesque is not a good investment (screenplay by Arnold Shulman,
Sidney Michaels, and Norman Lear)

"Nah, man, journalism—it was easier."
JOE NAMATH, Jets quarterback, when asked if he had majored in basket
weaving at the University of Alabama (interview, 1970)

"Is it really? Do you worry in a painting about the size of a

canvas?"   Film producer SAM SPIEGEL, on being told that his new film, *Betrayal*,
was small (*New York Review of Books*, March 17, 1988)

"There are no security checks for taste."
KATHARINE GRAHAM, publisher, the *Washington Post*, to Henry Kissinger,
who had angrily asked whether he was supposed to run security
checks on everyone he dated, after the *Post* reported
he had dated two young female strippers
(Isaacson, *Kissinger*, p. 583)

"So was Chanel."   HALSTON to those who said he was only a hatmaker
(*Simply Halston*, p. 97)

"And where does she find them?"

> DOROTHY PARKER, writer, on being told that Clare Boothe Luce was
> always kind to her inferiors (quoted in Drennan, ed., *Wit's End*)

"It's not 1–800–Jonathan."

> JONATHAN TISCH, CEO, Loews Hotels,
> on being asked if he invites all patrons to
> call him personally to make reservations
> (*Fortune*, March 11, 1991)

"Like what?"

> BARRY DILLER, CEO, Fox Television, responding to the comment of Rubert
> Murdoch, chairman, News Corporation and owner of Fox, that "we all
> share certain values" (Shawcross, *Murdoch*, p. 310)

"Impossible. Democracy is a dangerous trade."

> GILBERT CHESTERTON, on Woodrow Wilson's
> efforts to make the world safe for democracy
> (quoted in Wriston, *Risk and Other Four-Letter Words*, p. 231)

"Just a little bit more."

> JOHN D. ROCKEFELLER, SR., financier, on being asked how much money is
> enough (quoted in Sharp, *The Lore and Legends of Wall Street*, p. 233)

"Well, here you are, alone with the President of the United States,
the leader of the free world, and you ask a chickenshit question
like that."

> President LYNDON B. JOHNSON to Charles Mohr, White House
> corespondent for the *New York Times*, who had asked him about a report
> that he had raised his staff's salaries after winning the 1964 election
> (*Esquire*, December 1983, p. 151)

"Because it was the wrong thing to do, kid."

> JOHN HUSTON, director, on being asked why
> he became partners with producer Sam Spiegel
> (quoted in Viertel, *Dangerous Friends: At Large
> with Huston and Hemingway in the Fifties*, p. 25)

"I invented the idea, so I guess I can call it anything I like."

> HENRY LUCE, founder of Time, Inc., answering
> a reporter's question on how he could call
> the highly opinionated *Time* magazine a newsmagazine
> (quoted by William F. Buckley, Jr., *Esquire*, December 1963, p. 257)

"Although your Ford was badly damaged, we have managed to
repair it."

> Alleged reply to a man who had sent a box full of tin cans
> to the Ford plant (Patton, *Made in USA*, p. 177)

RESTRUCTURING

"The housewife, not the soldier, is the key to perestroika."

DWAYNE ANDREAS, chairman, Archer Daniels Midland Company, on
selling soy meal, cooking oils, etc. to Russia

"It's like the coming of civilization."

A Muscovite, on the Soviet Union's first McDonald's

"I Want My Wall Back."

T-shirt in West Berlin

RETAIL

"No sale is really complete until the product is worn out, and the
customer is satisfied."

LEON LEONWOOD BEAN, founder, L. L. Bean, Inc. (*Fortune*, April 5, 1993)

"The store is my theater and my show, and I am the producer and
director." GERALDINE STUTZ, manager, Henri Bendel (*Fortune*, August 25, 1980)

"Retailing is theater."

IRWIN GREENBERG, president, Hess Department Stores
(Henderson, *Winners*, p. 112)

"The store forces people to cleanse their mind and allows them to
do the major damage to their credit cards that we appreciate so
much." TOMMY PERSE, co-owner, Maxfield boutique, Los Angeles, on the
effectiveness of minimalist decor (*Newsweek*, November 10, 1986)

"Retail is very Darwinian. The bookseller species is continuing to
evolve and change, and this is the next step toward bigger,
stronger, faster." LEONARD RIGGIO, CEO, Barnes and Noble, Inc., the country's
second-largest bookseller, which has some 900 stores
(*New York Times*, November 8, 1992)

RETIREMENT

"Part of it is the loss of heroic stature. These are people who were
never just one of the guys."

JEFFREY SONNENFELD, diretor, Center for Leadership and Career Studies,
Emory University, on the depression experienced by many CEOs on
retirement (*New York Times*, April 25, 1993)

"Yup, they threw me out intact, furniture and all."

> WALTER WRISTON, former CEO, Citibank, on his retirement office that is
> down a few floors but otherwise identical to his former office
> (*New York Times*, April 25, 1993)

"You're nothing if you don't have a studio. Now I'm just another millionaire, and there are a lot of them around."

> JACK L. WARNER, after retiring, 1960s (Corey, *Man in Lincoln's Nose*, p. 137)

"The real difficulty with retirement is that you never know when you're finished."

> GENE KLEIN, former San Diego Chargers owner
> (*First Down and a Billion*, 1987)

"They have gone from being everything to nothing—from doer to viewer."

> Dr. WILLIAM P. MURPHY, JR., former chairman, Cordis Corporation, a
> $200-million medical technology company he founded in a garage
> (Henderson, *Winners*, p. 214)

"When Evita Peron was in Barcelona and complained that she had been called 'puta' (prostitute) as she drove through the streets, an old general apologized, saying, 'Why, I've been retired for 12 years and they still call me General.'"

> ADLAI STEVENSON, politician (Sherrin, *Cutting Edge*, p. 146)

"Ninety-five percent of me is very sad. But my knees—the other five percent—are very, very happy."

> DAN DIERDORF, Phoenix Cardinals offensive lineman, on his retirement
> (*Sporting News*, 1983)

"Statutory senility."

> WALTER WRISTON, former CEO, Citibank, on mandatory retirement ages
> (*New York Times*, April 25, 1993)

"We cease from exploration
And the end of all our exploring
Will be to arrive where we started
And know the place for the first time."

> T. S. ELIOT, as quoted by Robert McNamara, Secretary of Defense, when
> he left the Pentagon (Shapley, *McNamara*, p. 558)

"They look upon retirement as something between euthanasia and castration."

> LEON A. DANCO, president, Center for Family Business,
> on company founders (*New York Times*, June 11, 1986)

"John K. probably won't stop working for Winnebago until six weeks after he dies."

> KENNETH J. VAUGHAN, former director, Winnebago Industries Inc., on the company's founder, John K. Hanson (*New York Times*, May 18, 1986)

"Now your limo is yellow and your driver speaks Swahili."

> Friend to Walter Wriston, former CEO, Citibank, on his retirement (*New York Times*, April 25, 1993)

"I call it On Golden Parachute."

> DONALD KELLY, retired CEO, Esmark, on his castle (quoted in Bianco, *Rainmaker*, p. 242)

"From the revolution? From my ideas? No. For me, power is like a form of slavery. I feel like a slave. It's my profession."

> FIDEL CASTRO, Cuba's dictator, on whether, at age 65, he would retire (*Wall Street Journal*, October 10, 1991)

REVENGE

"I do unto others what they do unto me, only worse."

> Attributed to JIMMY HOFFA, president, Teamsters Union

"I don't hold no grudges more'n five years."

> William Kennedy's FRANCIS PHELAN (*Ironweed*, 1983)

"Nothing dates like hate."

> CYRIL CONNOLLY, critic

"An expression of revenge to a company that killed its founder."

> HARTMUT ESSLINGER, industrial designer and CEO, frogdesign, on the black cube of a computer he designed for NeXT, whose founder, Steve Jobs, had been driven from Apple (*Business Week*, December 3, 1990)

"Revenge is a dish that people of taste prefer cold."

> Italian proverb quoted in *Kind Hearts and Coronets* (screenplay by Robert Hamer and John Dighton)

"Revenge is profitable, gratitude is expensive."

> EDWARD GIBBON (*The Decline and Fall of the Roman Empire* II, 1776-88)

RICH

"I've been rich and I've been poor; but believe me, rich is better."

> Attributed to both SOPHIE TUCKER and TEXAS GUINAN

"To be seriously rich means that one no longer counts money."
PAUL GETTY, financier (*Esquire*, November 1991)

"I am not rich. I am a poor man with money, which is not the same thing."
GABRIEL GARCIA MARQUEZ (Winokur, *True Confessions*, p. 254)

THE RICH

"Rich families shed, in each generation, their most passionate and outspoken members. In the shedding the family loses the possibility of renewal, of change. Safety is gained, but a safety that is rigid and judgmental."
SALLIE BINGHAM, estranged heiress to the Louisville *Courier-Journal* newspaper fortune (*Passion and Prejudice: A Family Memoir*, 1989)

"Propagandists, from Shakespeare to Jacqueline Susann, have been telling the unrich that money doesn't buy happiness. The unrich, not being immune to spasms of common sense, sometimes wonder about this."
ANTHONY HADEN-GUEST, British journalist (interview, 1978)

"The tragedy of the Labour Party is not that their aims aren't sincere, it's just that they have this absurd obsession that high earners are rich."
ANDREW LLOYD WEBBER, musical theater producer (*The Economist*, April 11, 1992)

"One has to be as rich as you, Gaston, to be bored at Monte Carlo."
HERMIONE GINGOLD rebuking Louis Jourdan in *Gigi* (screenplay by Alan Jay Lerner)

"Rich people always wash their sins out with art. To snuggle up to Rembrandt is to become as good as Rembrandt."
THOMAS HOVING, former director, Metropolitan Museum of Art (*W*, April, 27, 1992)

"Let me tell you about the very rich. They are different from you and me."
F. SCOTT FITZGERALD (*All Sad Young Men*, 1926); Ernest Hemingway responded: "Yes, they have more money" (*Esquire*, August 1936)

"Solvency is entirely a matter of temperament and not of income."
LOGAN PEARSALL SMITH (*Afterthoughts*, 1931)

"We were not as rich as the Rockefellers or Mellons, but we were rich enough to know how rich they were."
Louis Auchincloss's narrator (*The Book Class*, 1984)

"I have a lot of compassion for the people that need it, but I have very little compassion for the windfalls for the well-off. Do you have to bribe the rich to help the poor? If everyone receives, who pays? That's the political basis of this free lunch: they bribe all of us and we pass the bill on to our kids."
PETER G. PETERSON, chairman, Blackstone Group (Hillary Mills, "Pete and Joan," *Vanity Fair*, August 1993)

"It is easier for a camel to go through the eye of a needle, than for a rich man to enter into the kingdom of heaven."
Mark 10:25

"For any city, however small, is in fact divided into two, one the city of the poor, the other of the rich; these are at war with one another."
PLATO (*The Republic* IV)

"By and large, the rich have the temperaments of lizards."
LEWIS LAPHAM, editor (*Money and Class in America*, 1988)

"One half the world knows not how the other half lives."
GEORGE HERBERT (*Jacula Prudentum*, 1651)

"Abundance and scarcity are never far apart; the rich and the poor frequent the same house."
Somali saying

"The rich have many consolations."
PLATO (*The Republic* I)

"The ways to enrich are many, and most of them foul."
FRANCIS BACON (*Of Riches*, 1625)

RIGHT

"I never called one wrong."
BILL KLEM, umpire (Harwell, *Ernie Harwell's Diamond Gems*, 1991)

"How could this happen? I was so careful. I picked the wrong play, the wrong director, the wrong cast—where did I go *right*?"
ZERO MOSTEL to accountant Gene Wilder in *The Producers* (original screenplay by Mel Brooks)

"A businessman has only to be right 51 percent of the time."
                    LEON SHIMKIN, former CEO, Simon and Schuster (to author)

"Let us have faith that right makes might, and in that faith let us
to the end dare to do our duty as we understand it."
                                            President ABRAHAM LINCOLN
                        (address, Cooper Union Institute, February 27, 1860)

"A hitter's perfection consists of failing only 60 percent of the
time."
                    TED WILLIAMS, baseball player (quoted by George F. Will,
                              New York Times Book Review, April 7, 1991, p. 23)

RISK

"All of life is the management of risk, not its elimination."
                    WALTER WRISTON, former CEO and chairman, Citicorp
                              (*Risk and Other Four-Letter Words*, p. 101)

"If you can make one heap of all your winnings
And risk it on one turn of pitch-and-toss
And lose, and start again at your beginnings
And never breathe a word about your loss"
                                                        KIPLING ("If")

"We won't grow unless we take risks. Any successful company is
riddled with failures."
                    JAMES E. BURKE, chairman, Johnson and Johnson (interview, 1976)

"Anyone who says they never had a chance never took a chance."
                    TED BALESTRERI, co-founder, The Sardine Factory in Monterey, California,
                              quoting his father (American Express ad)

"No-risk managements run both no-win and no-fun businesses."
                    ALLEHN H. NEUHARTH, CEO, Gannett Company
                              (quoted in Kehrer, *Doing Business Boldly*, p. 65)

"Always do what you are afraid to do."   RALPH WALDO EMERSON, essayist
                    (quoted in Wriston, *Risk and Other Four-Letter Words*, p. 221)

"If you're not a risk-taker, you should get the hell out of
business."
                    STEVEN J. ROSS, CEO, Time Warner Inc., the world's largest media and
                              entertainment company (*New York Times*, December 21, 1992)

"Historically, risk takers are people who shatter the illusion of knowledge. They are willing to try something that everyone thinks is outrageous or stupid."

> DANIEL BOORSTIN, former Librarian of Congress
> (quoted in Kehrer, *Doing Business Boldly*, p. 15)

"If no one ever took risks, Michelangelo would have painted the Sistine floor."

> NEIL SIMON, playwright

"You can't run a business without taking risks."

> MILLARD DREXLER, president, The Gap (*Fortune*, February 12, 1990)

"Sometimes it's risky not to take a risk—if you walk backward you never stub your toe."

> HARVEY MACKAY, author
> (quoted in *Home Office Computing* magazine, May 1993, p. 43)

"Every good thing in the world stands on the razor-edge of danger."

> THORNTON WILDER
> (quoted in Wriston, *Risk and Other Four-Letter Words*, p. vii)

ROB

"Officials are the only guys who can rob you and then get a police escort out of the stadium."

> ROB BOLTON, defensive back, Cleveland Browns (*Sports Illustrated*, 1978)

"Mendoza: 'I am a brigand: I live by robbing the rich.'
   Tanner: 'I am a gentleman: I live by robbing the poor.'"

> GEORGE BERNARD SHAW, playwright (*Man and Superman*, act 3)

RUIN

"Italians come to ruin most generally in three ways—women, gambling, and farming. My family chose the slowest one."

> Pope JOHN XXIII (Michaels, *Pope John XXIII*, p. 7)

"Gentlemen: You have undertaken to cheat me. I will not sue you, for the law takes too long. I will ruin you."

> CORNELIUS VANDERBILT (letter to associates who had
> schemed to ruin a Vanderbilt transit company
> and establish one of their own, 1854) (quoted in
> Sharp, *The Lore and Legends of Wall Street*, p. 111)

RULES

"In my lifetime I have seen many runners fail to touch second as they trotted around the bases after clouting the ball out of the park. When the opposing team raised the point, I always said, 'To me he touched second.' And to me he did, the second he hit the ball out of the park."

BILL KLEM, umpire (Harwell, Ernie Harwell's Diamond Gems, 1991)

"They want to play baseball in America, but they want seven strikes, no umpire and a right to cancel the game."

RICHARD BREEDEN, chief, Securities and Exchange Commission,
on German companies that want to list shares on
American exchanges without disclosing financial condition
(The Economist, March 27, 1993)

"In order to survive, Strike went by three unbreakable rules. One: Trust no one. Two: Don't get greedy. Three: Never do product."

Richard Price's Strike, a cocaine dealer and hero (Clockers, 1992)

"He must be 'emotionally stable,' of good appearance, and pass an intelligence test. For his first few weeks he is tutored in driving, delivering, and courtesy. He mustn't 'scuffle or engage in loud talk,' or 'whistle or yell at people on the street,' or splash pedestrians with mud, or walk or drive on people's lawns or gardens, or complain if he's asked to lay a rug or carry a parcel to some remote room. If he breaks a rule, he's fined."

The New Yorker summary of rules for United Parcel Service deliverymen
as developed by founder James E. Casey (Fortune, March 11, 1991)

"Rule number something or other—never tell anybody anything unless you're going to get something better in return."

Sara Paretsky's V. I. WARSHAWSKI (Deadlock, 1984)

"The rule is, jam tomorrow and jam yesterday—but never jam today."

LEWIS CARROLL, author (Alice's Adventures in Wonderland, ch. 5, 1865)

SALARY

"Salary is no object; I want only enough to keep body and soul apart."

DOROTHY PARKER, writer, responding to a job offer
(quoted in Gaines, Wit's End, 1977)

"It is difficult to get a man to understand something when his salary depends upon his not understanding it."
Upton Sinclair, novelist (*Toastmaster*, p. 4910)

SALES TECHNIQUES

"I was so proud that I wore an eight at Halston. But I think it was a twelve marked eight."   Eleanor Lambert, publicist on Halston's technique
of mislabeling the sizes on his dresses (*Simply Halston*, p. 114)

"Basically, it's the same exact talent. Sales is sales."   Bruce Perlowin,
former marijuana smuggler, on his work for the ecologically sound
Rainforest Products Co. (*Newsweek*, February 1992)

"Push once a minute until clerk appears."
Sign placed by Leon Leonwood Bean, founder, L. L. Bean, Inc., outside
his 24-hour retail store to accommodate outdoorsmen driving through
Maine in the middle of the night (*Fortune*, April 5, 1993)

SALESPEOPLE

"Ever since Moses came down from the mountain with the tablets, the world has been moved by salesmen. I'm a salesman."
David Mahoney, chairman, Norton Simon, Inc. (interview, 1988)

"A salesman is got to dream, boy. It comes with the territory."
Arthur Miller's Willy Loman (*Death of a Salesman*, 1949)

"Legend tells of the traveler who went into a country store and found the shelves lined with bags of salt. 'You must sell a lot of salt,' said the traveler. 'Nah,' said the storekeeper. 'I can't sell no salt at all. But the feller who sells me salt—boy, can *he* sell salt.'"
Martin Mayer (*The Bankers*, 1974)

"Life is very long and full of salesmanship, Miss Clara. You might buy something yet."   Paul Newman to Joanne Woodward in
The Long Hot Summer (screenplay by Irving Ravetch and Harriet Frank, Jr.)

SATIRE

"Satire picks a one-sided fight, and the more its intended target reacts, the more the practitioner gains the advantage."
Garry Trudeau, cartoonist (*Wall Street Journal*, January 20, 1993)

SCARED

"All that hair, all those teeth—you gotta run scared."

> Governor WILLIAM WELD of Massachusetts, on rumor that Representative
> Joe Kennedy would run against him in 1994 (*Newsweek*, February 15, 1993)

SCIENCE

"There is no area of the world that should not be investigated by
scientists. There will always remain some questions that have not
yet been answered. In general, these are the questions that have
not yet been posed."

> LINUS PAULING, physicist
> (quoted in Moskin, *Morality in America*, pp. 70–71)

"A scientist has to be neutral in his search for the truth, but he
cannot be neutral as to the use of that truth when found. If you
know more than other people, you have more responsibility,
rather than less."

> C. P. SNOW, scientist and author
> (quoted in Moskin, *Morality in America*, p. 61)

"We have made of the world a neighborhood through our scientific
genius, and now through our moral commitment we must make of
it a brotherhood. We've got to learn to live together as brothers or
we'll perish together as fools."

> MARTIN LUTHER KING, JR., civil rights leader
> (quoted in Moskin, *Morality in America*, p. 71)

SELF-MADE

"A self-made man is one who believes in luck and sends his sons
to Oxford."

> CHRISTINA STEAD, author

"A self-made man may prefer a self-made name."

> LEARNED HAND on Samuel Goldwyn's having changed his name from
> Samuel Goldfish (quoted in Crowther, *The Lion's Share*, 1957, chapter 7)

SELL

"Threshold resistance."

> A. ALFRED TAUBMAN, chairman, Sotheby's Holdings, Inc., and former
> shopping mall magnate, who coined the term when he decided stores in
> malls should have no doors, just wide openings that would induce
> customers to wander in; he successfully applied the same principal to the
> upper-echelon auction house (*7 Days*, October 25, 1989)

"If you can't smell it, you can't sell it."

> ESTEE LAUDER, founder of cosmetics firm (interview, 1976)

"Shoulda brought pants to sell. Pants don't wear worth a hoot in the diggin's."

> Advice given to Levi Strauss, on arriving in San Francisco from Bavaria in 1853; he had brought canvas to make tents and wagon covers for prospectors—instead he made the canvas into pants
> (Patton, *Made in USA*, p. 297)

"You sell a screenplay like you sell a car. If someone drives it off a cliff, that's it."

> RITA MAE BROWN, writer (*Newsweek*, August 19, 1986)

"Life is pain. Anyone who tells you different is trying to sell you something."

> *The Princess Bride* (screenplay by William Goldman)

"We're trying for the Queen. She sells."

> GEORGE HARRISON, answering: "Do you have a leading lady for your film?" (the Beatles' first press conference in America in 1963)

"Give the lady what she wants."

> Attributed to MARSHALL FIELD, department store founder

"Selling art has a lot in common with selling root beer."

> A. ALFRED TAUBMAN, chairman, Sotheby's Holdings, Inc.
> (*7 Days*, October 25, 1989)

"Anyone who doesn't know what it means to have painful feet doesn't know what selling is."

> Attributed to ALFRED "Freddy" HEINEKEN, chairman, Heineken Breweries, on his youthful days peddling his father's beer bar to bar in Times Square

"Beat your gong and sell your candies."

> Chinese proverb

SEX

"People assume you slept your way to the top. Frankly, I couldn't sleep my way to the middle."

> JONI EVANS, president, trade division, Simon and Schuster
> (*New York Times*, July 23, 1986)

"Money is the best sex."

> STEVE RUBELL, owner, Studio 54 (*Simply Halston*, p. 202)

"I never quite understood it—this sex symbol. I always thought symbols were something you clashed together."

MARILYN MONROE, actress (*Life*, August 3, 1962)

"That was the most fun I've had without laughing."

WOODY ALLEN to Diane Keaton in *Annie Hall*
(screenplay by Woody Allen and Marshall Brickman)

"I hope we're going to have some gratuitous sex and violence."

ALGERNON (the inventor) welcoming
back James Bond (Sean Connery) while deploring
how dull things have gotten in *Never Say Never*
(screenplay by Lorenzo Semple, Jr.)

"Sex and money: the forked root of evil."

Ross Macdonald's LEW ARCHER (*The Drowning Pool*, 1950)

SHORT TERM

"In the White House the short run is the only run there is."

PEGGY NOONAN, speechwriter (*What I Saw at the Revolution*, p. 205)

"If you don't win the first year, if you don't win the short term, you're dead."

DAVID W. JOHNSON, CEO, Campbell Soup
(*Fortune*, December 14, 1992)

"The short-term problems are economic—royalties, unions, irresponsible management. The long-term problems are artistic, and they started 40 years ago with the advent of television and the upgrading of films."

EMANUEL AZENBERG, Broadway producer
(quoted in Freedman, "The Last of the Red-Hot Producers,"
New York Times, June 2, 1985)

"I hate to say it, because this is my country, but I see America as an obvious short. As I got closer to home, I was overwhelmed by the impression that the United States is strangling itself while the rest of the world is loosening the ropes. Free markets are spreading almost everywhere, but we're still adding needless regulations that are destroying our competitiveness."

JIM ROGERS, former Wall Street investor,
after travelling through much of the world on a motorcycle
(*Fortune*, February 24, 1992)

SIZE

"The key to the future is the midsize company—big enough to spend on technology, small enough to change."

> Tom Peters, business consultant (*Manhattan, Inc.*, January 1990)

"Hey, size works against excellence."

> Bill Gates, chairman and founder, Microsoft
> (quoted in Peters, *Liberation*, p. 554)

"I've never seen a job being done by a 500-person engineering team that couldn't be done better by 50 people."

> C. Gordon Bell, computer pioneer
> (quoted in Peters, *Liberation*, p. 572)

SKIING

"I wasn't born to ski. I was born to work. But then I got laid off."

> Warren Miller, CEO, Warren Miller Productions,
> which produces videos on skiing (*Skiing*, January 1992)

"One board, one body."

> Nicholas Hartmann, former skier, on the appeals of snowboarding
> (to author)

"In the last decade, Jake Burton has done for snowboards what Henry Ford did for automobiles: He has mass produced them until today that $10 piece of plywood that was called a Snurfer has evolved into a $562 snowboard."

> Warren Miller, CEO, Warren Miller Productions (*Skiing*, January 1992)

SLOGANS

"If you're slow, you're dead."

> George Stalk, Jr., vice president, Boston Consulting Group
> ("Reinventing America," *Business Week*, 1992, p. 65)

"THINK!"

> Thomas Watson, Sr., chairman of IBM, sign executives were expected
> to keep on their desks (The entire slogan: "THINK! ... Think about
> Appearance, Associations, Actions, Ambition, Accomplishment.")

"Or Thwim!"

> Corporate graffiti scrawled below Think! sign
> in IBM's Armonk headquarters

"Your veritas sux if it ain't got that lux."

> A Yale drum at the Harvard–Yale game playing off Harvard's *Veritas*
> (Truth) motto against Yale's *Lux et Veritas* (Light and Truth)
> (*Game Day U.S.A: NCAA College Football,* p. 30)

"KISS—Keep it simple, stupid."

> Motto at Lockheed's Skunkworks advanced development facility

"Better than sex, less filling than beer."

> Underline for *Inside Edge,* a magazine "by guys for guys"
> (*New York Times,* May 23, 1993)

"Eat What You Kill."

> Policy at Baker & McKenzie, a 1640-member lawyer firm; most of the
> money earned stays where the actual work is done and gets divided
> among local partners (*New York Times,* March 14, 1993)

"The maxim of the British people is: Business as usual."

> WINSTON CHURCHILL (speech at the Guildhall, November 9, 1914)

"*L'amour sans stress.*" ("Love without stress.")

> Slogan on condom vending machine at Richard Branson's Paris
> Megastore (*New York Times,* February 28, 1993)

"People dream they can fly
Birds dream they can skate."

> Rollerblade slogan

SMALL

"It turned out that the first big lesson we learned was that there
was much, much more business out there in small-town America
than anybody, including me, had ever dreamed of."

> SAM WALTON, founder and CEO, Wal-Mart stores (*Sam Walton,* p. 50)

"Small is beautiful. A study of economics as if people mattered."

> E. F. SCHUMACHER, economist (*Small Is Beautiful,* 1973)

SMILE

"People at McDonald's smile a lot. Russian workers don't. That's
how we differ from the West."

> VLADIMIR SOLOVIEV, general manager, Meteor Personnel, which places
> workers in multinational firms in Moscow
> (*Wall Street Journal,* June 9, 1992)

"Don't open a shop unless you know how to smile."   Jewish proverb

"If you want to call me that, smile."

> Gary Cooper to Walter Huston in *The Virginian*
> (screenplay by Howard Estabrook)

SOCIAL LIFE

"My definition of a perfect date is one in which, when I look back on my golden memories, I can honestly say, 'No weapons were fired, no lawsuits were filed, and everyone had pretty good hygiene.' And you wonder why I don't go out more?"

> MERRILL MARKOE, head writer on David Letterman's "Late Night" show
> ("What the Dogs Have Taught Me," *People*, July 6, 1992)

"She had limited social experience and apparently unlimited social anxiety."

> JOAN DIDION, writer, on Nancy Reagan (*Women's Wear Daily*, April 1992)

"The best parties are given by people who can't afford them."

> Attributed to ELSA MAXWELL, legendary hostess

SOCIETY

"Are we still a society, even if we are no longer an economy?"

> ROBERT REICH, Secretary of Labor (*Wall Street Journal*, October 28, 1992)

"A 'good' family, it seems, is one that used to be better."

> CLEVELAND AMORY (*Who Killed Society?*, 1960)

"She's taken her good family name and put it on the asses of America!"   GILDA RADNER, comedian, on Gloria Vanderbilt's line of designer jeans

> ("Saturday Night Live," NBC-TV, May 31, 1980)

"Write about society as news and treat it as sociology."

> CLIFTON DANIEL, managing editor, the *New York Times*,
> to fledgling women's page reporter Charlotte Curtis
> (Robertson, *The Girls in the Balcony*, p. 116)

SOFT

"'Soft' now dominates. 'Hard' has been eclipsed."

> TOM PETERS, business consultant (*Liberation*, p. 383)

SORRY

"I felt sorry. I don't know why I felt sorry. John Wayne never felt sorry."

U.S. soldier who had knifed to death a Viet Cong soldier
(quoted in Lifton, *Home from the War*, 1974)

"The football field is no place to say 'I'm sorry.'"

MIKE DAVIS, Los Angeles Raiders safety (*San Francisco Chronicle*, 1981)

"What did you get? You got no apology from me, which you didn't accept."

GEORGE BURNS, noting that Walter Matthau rejected an apology that
wasn't offered in *The Sunshine Boys* (screenplay by Neil Simon)

SPEECH

"The hatred of minorities does not have its source in arson attacks, but in discriminatory remarks to which no resistance is offered."

RITA SÜSSMUTH, president of the German Bundestag, speaking at a
memorial service at the former Dachau concentration camp
(*The Week in Germany*, June 11, 1993)

"Sometimes I get a little hard-of-speaking."

CASEY STENGEL, baseball manager
(*The Gospel According to Casey*, p. 26)

"The best audience is intelligent, well-educated, and a little drunk."

ALBEN W. BARKLEY, former U.S. vice president
(recalled on his death, March 30, 1956)

"Somewhere out in this audience may even be someone who will one day follow in my footsteps, and preside over the White House as the President's spouse. I wish him well."

BARBARA BUSH, spouse
(commencement speech, Wellesley College, June 1, 1990)

"A speech is like an airplane engine. It may sound like hell but you've got to go on."

WILLIAM THOMAS PIPER, president, Piper Aircraft Corporation
(*Time*, January 13, 1961)

"Spartans, stoics, heroes, saints and gods use a short and positive speech."

RALPH WALDO EMERSON, essayist (lecture in Boston, December 18, 1864)

"Speechwriters have a unique distinction in Washington—none of us has ever been indicted."

JACK VALENTI, speechwriter for President Lyndon B. Johnson
(quoted in Noonan, *What I Saw at the Revolution*, p. 91)

SPECIALIST

"I never had much use for specialists. Specialists are inclined to argue why you can't do something, while our emphasis has always been to make something out of nothing."

MASARU IBUKA, founder and honorary chairman, Sony, on why he did not
recruit the top engineering students in each discipline
(*Fortune*, February 24, 1992)

SPECULATE

"To specilate [*sic*] in Wall Street when you are no longer an insider, is like buying cows by candlelight."

DANIEL DREW, nineteenth-century speculator and mentor to Jay Gould
and Jim Fisk (quoted in Sharp, *The Lore and Legends of Wall Street*, p. 89)

"Why does a dog chase his thousandth rabbit? All life is a speculation. The spirit of speculation is born with men."

JAMES R. KEENE, nineteenth-century speculator
(quoted in Sharp, *The Lore and Legends of Wall Street*, p. 135)

STANDARDS

"I like elements which are hybrid rather than 'pure,' compromising rather than 'clean,' distorted rather than 'straightforward.'"

ROBERT VENTURI, Philadelphia architect
(*Complexity and Contradiction in Architecture*, 1966)

"No wire hangers."

JOAN CRAWFORD in *Mommie Dearest*
(screenplay by Frank Yabians, Frank Perry, and Tracy Hotchner)

"Use your best judgment at all times."

Nordstrom's one-sentence policy manual

"A Coke is a Coke, and no amount of money can get you a better Coke than the one the bum on the corner is drinking. All the Cokes are the same, and all the Cokes are good. Liz Taylor knows it, the President knows it, the bum knows it, and you know it."

ANDY WARHOL, artist (Patton, *Made in USA*, p. 23)

"Set exorbitant standards, and give your people hell when they don't live up to them. There is nothing so demoralizing as a boss who tolerates second-rate work."

DAVID OGILVY, former chairman, Ogilvy and Mather
(*The Unpublished David Ogilvy*, 1987)

"When I came here, I heard all the reasons why Notre Dame couldn't win again: no redshirting, tough schedule, tough academics, no special courses for athletes, no athlete dorms. Well, you can't say high standards don't produce *winners*."

LOU HOLTZ, football coach, University of Notre Dame, on winning the
national championship (interview, 1989)

"Produce or get out."

EWING KAUFMANN's maxim for salesmen at Marion Laboratories

"I remember once asking Alfred North Whitehead, who was one of my teachers, how he marked. I said, 'You've given me a B, and I know I don't know anything.' 'Oh, Philip,' he said, 'I always give an A to those who are acceptable and a B to those who are no good.'"

PHILIP JOHNSON, architect, on his dashed ambitions to study philosophy
at Harvard (quoted by Tom Buckley, *Esquire*, December 1983, p. 275)

"I shall stop flying first class when they invent something better."

ROBERT STRAUSS, chairman, Democratic Party (interview, 1979)

STAR

"The great thing about rock and roll is that someone like me can be a star."

ELTON JOHN, on his transformation from a plump piano player
to one of the world's most successful rock stars
(*New York Times*, April 1992)

"Stars don't audition."

TERESA WRIGHT, actress (to author, 1988)

"They gave me star treatment when I was making a lot of money. But I was just as good when I was poor."

BOB MARLEY, band leader (Winokur, *True Confessions*, p. 43)

"You make a star, you make a monster."

SAM SPIEGEL, after casting the unknown Peter O'Toole as Lawrence of
Arabia (Corey, *Man in Lincoln's Nose*, p. 103)

"My father always said, if you want to be a star, don't be
versatile."

JASON ROBARDS, actor (*New York Daily News*, May 16, 1993)

STATISTICS

"I could prove God statistically."

Attributed to GEORGE GALLUP, pollster

"Statistics are like alienists—they will testify for either side."

FIORELLO LA GUARDIA, mayor, New York City

"Beauty is the first test: there is no permanent place in the world
for ugly mathematics."

GODFREY HAROLD HARDY (*A Mathematician's Apology*, 1940, p. 25)

STATUS

"I'm in the 'B' group. But I plan on using the entire alphabet."

ED WYNN, responding to his teenaged son's question on which parties
he's invited to (Wynn, *Beverly Hills*, p. 100)

"At dinner parties I sit below the salt now. There are a lot of
interesting people there."

DONALD T. REGAN, former White House Chief of Staff and former CEO of
Merrill Lynch (*New York Times*, January 25, 1985)

STOCK MARKET

"Something is wrong with our economy when the stock market is
long on hamburgers and short on steel."

Texas Senator LLOYD BENTSEN, warning in 1974 that glamour stocks like
McDonald's were overvalued in relation to traditional companies
(Boas and Chain, *Big Mac*, p. 71)

STRATEGY

"All warfare is based on deception. Hence, when able to attack
we must seem unable; when using our forces, we must seem
inactive; when we are near, we must make the enemy believe that
we are away; when far away, we must make him believe we are
near. Hold out baits to entice the enemy. Feign disorder, and
crush him."

SUN TZU, Chinese army commander and military thinker
(*The Art of War*, 490 B.C.)

"A Coke should always be within arm's reach of desire."

> ROBERT WOODRUFF, former CEO, Coca-Cola; this tenet led to the disastrous
> plan to introduce office syrup machines "BreakMates"
> (*Wall Street Journal*, June 14, 1993)

"The flavors are all out there, in the collective unconscious, floating about 18 miles above the atmosphere. Our job is to just beam them down."

> PETER LIND, Primal Ice Cream Therapist
> (executive in charge of flavors), Ben & Jerry's Homemade, Inc.
> (*New York Times*, March 21, 1993)

"Strategies are okayed in boardrooms that even a child would say are bound to fail. The problem is, there is never a child in the boardroom."

> VICTOR PALMIERI, business takeover financier
> (*Fortune*, February 24, 1992)

"One day [FBI chief J. Edgar] Hoover received [a memo] whose margins were too small. In big red letters he scrawled an angry warning across the top: 'Watch the borders!' The next morning his frightened assistants transferred 200 FBI agents to Canada and Mexico."

> WAYNE CALLOWAY, CEO, PepsiCo, arguing that managers should
> be given a lot of flexibility; Hoover, says Calloway,
> insisted on signing off on every decision
> (*Fortune*, March 11, 1991)

"You see, I said 'fuck' to ruin his audio. Then when I started scratching my ass I was ruining his video. He ain't gonna ask me a question like that again."

> CASEY STENGEL, baseball manager, after a reporter asked him
> if the Yankees had choked in the 1957 World Series
> (*The Gospel According to Casey*, p. 11)

"If you make your quarters, you'll make your year."

> HAROLD GENEEN, chairman, ITT (*Managing*, 1984)

"The best armor is to keep out of range."

> ITALIAN PROVERB

"We're going to sober them up with Pepsi and bring their vodka over here and get the Americans drunk."

> DONALD M. KENDALL, Pepsico chairman, on Pepsico's 1971 contract with
> the Soviet Union to accept payment in Stolichnaya
> (*U.S. News and World Report*)

STRESS

"Some senior managers are the toxic carriers of stress."

ROBERT L. SWAIN, chairman of an outplacement firm
(*Fortune*, February 29, 1988)

"All the staff infighting and squabbling was causing the President many sleepless afternoons."

PATRICK BUCHANAN, on the Reagan administration
(C-Span, October 19, 1991)

"It's ulcers and eventually it's hemorrhoids. I don't want that. I don't want to sit on a donut."

MEL BROOKS, on why he turned down the top job at Twentieth Century
Fox Studios ("Naked Hollywood: Eighteen Months to Live,"
Channel 13, October 31, 1992)

"I'm not the type to get ulcers. I give them."

EDWARD I. KOCH, mayor, New York City
(*New York Times*, January 20, 1984)

"To be under pressure is inescapable. Pressure takes place through all the world: war, siege, and the worries of state. We all know men who grumble under these pressures, and complain. They are cowards. They lack splendor. But there is another sort of man who is under the same pressure, but does not complain. For it is the friction which polishes him. It is pressure which refines and makes him noble."

St. AUGUSTINE (quoted in Ogilvy, *Ogilvy on Advertising*, p. 51)

STUPID

"Stupid is forever."

JOEL SMILOW, CEO, Playtex, cited by *Fortune* magazine in 1964 as one of the
country's toughest bosses (*Wall Street Journal*, December 21, 1991)

"Egotism is the anesthetic that dulls the pain of stupidity."

FRANK LEAHY, University of Notre Dame football coach
(*Look*, January 10, 1955)

"You've heard of people living in a fool's paradise? Well, Leonora has a duplex there."

Playwright GEORGE S. KAUFMAN, on Leonora Corbett who called a terrible
performance she had just given "fantastic" (Sherrin, *Cutting Edge*, p. 105)

"I'm a dope, not a crook. Since I never had a check returned for insufficient funds, I never knew there was a problem."

> Representative SUSAN MOLINARI, Republican of New York, on her overdrawn checking account at the House Bank (*New York Times*, March 14, 1992)

"Thank God people are so stupid."

> EDMOND SAFRA, president, Republic Bank, on the phenomenal success of his bank's offering free color televisions to people who made long-term, low-interest $10,000 deposits (Burrough, *Vendetta*, 50)

"Just remember one thing: there are no dumb Asians."

> ROBERT TRUMBULL, *New York Times* correspondent, to David Halberstam (*The Making of a Quagmire*, 1964)

STYLE

"You must know how to say 'Fuck you' with style."

> DONALD ENGEL, investment banker, Drexel Burnham, on his attitude with clients (Bianco, *Rainmaker*, p. 364)

"I live like a monk, almost. A monk with red lips, short dresses and big hair."

> TINA TURNER, singer (*Newsweek*, December 7, 1992)

"I find extravagance esthetically repulsive. I find the New England Puritan tradition more attractive. And more profitable. It is a matter of posture, manners, style and *habit*."

> DAVID OGILVY, former chairman, Ogilvy and Mather (*The Unpublished David Ogilvy*, 1987)

SUCCESS

"You have to be obsessed with an idea to succeed. It must drive you, instead of your driving it. Any crisis is just for a moment, otherwise you are trapped and won't find the door."

> CHRISTINE VALMY, president, Christine Valmy, Inc., a cosmetics firm (*New York Daily News Magazine*, September 13, 1987)

"A string of successes can kill you if they make you think, 'Hey, I'm smart; I can't make any mistakes.'"

> HARVEY MACKAY (*Swim with the Sharks Without Being Eaten Alive*, 1988)

"Anyone can be pope; the proof of this is that I have become one."

> Pope JOHN XXIII (Fesquet, *Wit and Wisdom of Good Pope John*, p. 112)

"Our success has been chiefly due to luck, I told him. 'No,' he replied, 'to audacity,' and I believe he was right."

General GEORGE S. PATTON, JR., note of a conversation with
General Henri Honore Giraud, March 30, 1945
(Farago, *The Last Days of Patton*, p. 13)

"Success in almost any field depends more on energy and drive than it does on intelligence. This explains why we have so many stupid leaders."

SLOAN WILSON (*The Man in the Gray Flannel Suit*, 1955)

"The penalty of success is to be bored by the people who used to snub you."

Lady NANCY ASTOR (recalled on her death, May 2, 1964)

"Only cream and SOB's rise to the top."

AL NEUHARTH, former chairman, Gannett Company
(*Confessions of an S.O.B.*, 1989)

"To succeed it is necessary to accept the world as it is and rise above it."

MICHAEL KORDA, editor and writer (*Success!*, 1977)

"What we've had to do is succeed in a lot of different businesses. When we first came here to Washington, we were in the raising-venture-capital business. We succeeded in that business. Then we went into the next one, which was lobbying the government to get permission to go into business. We succeeded in that business. Then we raised a lot of money and went into the long-distance telephone business, which I thought we'd be in forever. It turned out we were only in that business for two years, because AT&T thought we should be in another business. So we went into the business of battling in the courts for the absolute right to provide the services we wanted to provide—while surviving in the interim. We succeeded in that business, and went into the one we're in today."

WILLIAM G. McGOWAN, founder and CEO, MCI Communications
(Henderson, *Winners*, p. 188)

"Always remember this. If you have a success, you have it for the wrong reasons. If you become popular it is always because of the worst aspects of your work. They always praise you for the worst aspects. It never fails."

ERNEST HEMINGWAY, writer
(quoted in Callaghan, *That Summer in Paris*, 1973)

"The price of freedom is financial success."
> ALBERTO VITALE, CEO, Random House, Inc., on the independent divisions
> called imprints (Peter, *Liberation*, p. 263)

"Success has ruined many a man."
> BENJAMIN FRANKLIN *(Poor Richard's Almanack*, 1733)

"You can strike your way down, but you have to work your way up."
> British Prime Minister MARGARET THATCHER (Public Broadcast System, 1989)

"When you begin thinking you really are number one, that's when you begin to go nowhere."
> STEVIE WONDER, singer

"Success took me to her bosom like a maternal boa constrictor."
> NOEL COWARD, on having three hit plays running at the same time in
> London (recalled on his death, March 26, 1973)

"Success is a poison that should only be taken late in life and then only in small doses."
> Attributed to ANTHONY TROLLOPE, author

"Fifty percent of an architect's success lies in the ability to go out and get the job."
> Attributed to DANIEL BURNHAM, designer of the first Chicago Master Plan

"Whether you believe you can do a thing or not, you're right."
> Attributed to HENRY FORD

"The exclusive worship of the bitch goddess Success is our national disease."
> WILLIAM JAMES, psychologist (in a letter to H. G. Wells, September 11, 1906)

"Success is counted sweetest
By those who ne'er succeed."
> EMILY DICKINSON, poet *(Poems*, 1890)

SUCCESS, SECRETS OF

"An absolute ungovernable curiosity."
> LARRY KING, talk show host (interview, 1991)

"I leave out the parts that people skip."
> ELMORE LEONARD, on the popularity of his novels
> (Zinsser, *A Family of Readers*, 1986)

"Success comes from good judgment. Good judgment comes from experience. Experience comes from bad judgment."
ARTHUR JONES, founder, Nautilus Sports/Medical Industries
(Henderson, *Winners*, p. 8)

"I suppose it's because I was born with two crystal balls."
ALFRED HITCHCOCK, film director, on why he seemed
so able to cast unknown actresses who became stars
(*Movie Talk*, p. 57)

"The key to success for Sony, and to everything in business, science, and technology for that matter, is never to follow the others."
MASARU IBUKA, founder and honorary chairman, Sony
(*Fortune*, February 24, 1992)

"The main thing is to remix."
TINA BROWN, after being named top editor
at *The New Yorker* (*New York Times*, August 30, 1992)

"After 150 years, we've finally learned how to run a railroad."
JOHN W. SNOW, CEO of CSX, on why the company's third-quarter earnings
rose 19 percent on flat revenues (*Fortune*, December 14, 1992)

"One of the paradoxes of an increasingly specialized, bureaucratized society is that the qualities rewarded in the rise to eminence are less and less the qualities required once eminence is reached."
HENRY KISSINGER, diplomat (*The Necessity for Choice*, 1960)

"Physicist Isador Isaac Rabi, who won a Nobel prize for inventing a technique that permitted scientists to probe the structure of atoms and molecules in the 1930s, attributed his success to the way his mother used to greet him when he came home from school each day. 'Did you ask any good questions today, Isaac?' she would say."
RICHARD SAUL WURMAN (quoted in Peters, *Liberation*, p. 610)

"I had many years that I was not so successful as a ballplayer as it is a game of skill."
CASEY STENGEL, baseball manager
(*The Gospel According to Casey*, p. 157)

"We had so much success for so long, it got embedded in our DNA code."
ROSS COOLEY, head of North American operations
for Compaq Computer (*Fortune*, December 14, 1992)

"I don't dawdle. I'm a surgeon. I make an incision, do what needs to be done and sew up the wound. There is a beginning, a middle, and an end."

RICHARD SELZER, M.D., on writing (*New York Times*, October 28, 1979)

"It can be set down in four words: the best of everything. The best hay, oats, and water."

JAMES ("Sunny Jim") FITZSIMMONS,
on training winning horses (*Life*, June 18, 1963)

SUCCESSFUL STYLES

"A second-class mind but a first-class temperament."

Justice OLIVER WENDALL HOLMES, JR., on Franklin Delano Roosevelt
(*Journals*, March 8, 1933)

"There are only two ways of getting on in the world: by one's own industry, or by the weaknesses of others."

LA BRUYERE, French moralist (*Les Caracteres*, 1688)

"Such was her nature—to float, when it was calm, in a sea of indecision, and, when the wind rose, to tack hectically from side to side."

LYTTON STRACHEY, on Elizabeth I (*Elizabeth and Essex*, 1918)

"Have more than thou showest,
Speak less than thou knowest,
Lend less than thou owest,
Ride more than thou goest,
Learn more than thou trowest,
Set less than thou throwest;
Leave thy drink and thy whore,
And keep in-a-door,
And thou shalt have more
than two tens to a score."

SHAKESPEARE (*King Lear* I, iv, 132)

"Success or failure lies in conforming to the times."

MACHIAVELLI (*Discourse on Livy*, 1518)

SUCCESSION

"The strongest."

ALEXANDER THE GREAT's last words on being asked to name
a successor (quoted in *New York Times Review of Books*, March 18, 1982)

"Very large companies have become islands of entrenchment in the midst of an otherwise extremely promising situation. They pick their own successors. Boards of directors are like the House of Lords." ROBERT A. G. MONKS, arguing that big companies are throttling the American economy (*Esquire*, May 1992)

"You must remember the old saying: *Morto un Papa se ne fa un altro!* (When a Pope dies they make another)" POPE JOHN XXIII, comforting colleagues on his deathbed (Michaels, *Pope John XXIII*, p. 10)

"When you strike at a king, you must kill him." Attributed to essayist RALPH WALDO EMERSON by Justice Oliver Wendell Holmes, Jr. (Lerner, *The Mind and Faith of Justice Holmes*, 1943)

"Ford is dead! Long live Ford!" A voice in the crowd at the funeral of Henry Ford, founder, Ford Motor Corp., who was succeeded by his son, Henry Ford II (Collier and Horowitz, *The Fords*, p. 227)

"I'm the chief executive and I intend to remain here as long as God will permit me." ARMAND HAMMER, chairman, Occidental Petroleum, refusing on his 82nd birthday to announce a successor

"Where there's death there's hope." THEODORE J. LOWI, John L. Senior professor of political science, Cornell University (to author, 1972)

"The Greens eat their children." MICHAEL VESPER, party manager of Germany's Green Party, on its inability to institutionalize itself (*Newsweek*, November 2, 1992)

"To an entrepreneur the business is his baby. Picking a successor is like letting your baby girl go off in the arms of a gorilla." Dr. LEON A. DANCO, founder, Center for Family Business in Cleveland, Ohio (Henderson,*Winners*, p. 212)

SUCKER

"Never give a sucker an even break." W. C. FIELDS, in *Poppy* (screenplay by Dorothy Donnelly)

"Barnum was right." A Lizzie Label (slogans painted on Model T's in the mid-1920s) (Patton, *Made in USA*, p. 177)

"Once a chump, always a chump."
Dashiell Hammett's SAM SPADE (The Maltese Falcon, 1930)

SUFFERING

"I didn't know you could get heartburn from corn flakes."
GEORGE AMES, partner, Lazard Fréres, on senior partner André Meyer's
very early morning breakfasts (Reich, Financier: André Meyer, p. 185)

SUPPORT

"I have been supportive of my wife since the beginning of time, and she has been supportive of me. It's not a sacrifice; it's a family."
MARTIN D. GINSBURG, lawyer, on his relationship with Ruth Bader
Ginsburg, Supreme Court nominee (New York Times, June 16, 1993)

SURVIVAL

"These are nutty times. Nutty organizations, nutty people, capable of dealing with the fast, fleeting, fickle, are a requisite for survival."
TOM PETERS, management consultant (Liberation, 1992)

"It's ridiculous to call this an industry—it's not. This is rat eat rat, dog eat dog. I'll kill 'em, and I'm going to kill 'em before they kill me. You're talking about the American way of survival of the fittest."
RAY A. KROC, chairman, McDonald's (Boas and Chain, Big Mac, p. 1)

"[Executive turbulence] scares the hell out of people. With this fear comes safety behavior, survival behavior. People start pulling back to protect themselves instead of thinking about the business."
RICHARD GOULD, organizational psychologist

"Pro football is like nuclear warfare. There are no winners, only survivors."
FRANK GIFFORD, New York Giants halfback (Sports Illustrated, July 4, 1960)

"Never take top billing. You'll last longer that way."
Attributed to BING CROSBY, singer

"The growth of a large business is merely a survival of the fittest."
JOHN D. ROCKEFELLER, SR., financier
(quoted in Ghent, Our Benevolent Feudalism, 1902)

SWEAT

"Sweat is the cologne of accomplishment."
HEYWOOD HALE BROUN, writer (CBS-TV, July 21, 1973)

"The more you sweat in peace, the less you bleed in war."
Admiral HYMAN RICKOVER (recalled on his death, July 8, 1986)

"Champions don't sweat."
JOE McCARTHY, manager, New York Yankees
(quoted by Heywood Hale Broun in *New York Times*, July 14, 1991)

TAKEOVERS

"Let's make this goddamn deal happen. . . .Time Inc. is gone.
Long live Time Warner."
J. RICHARD MUNRO, chairman, Time, Inc.
(Clurman, *To the End of Time*, p. 10)

"It takes geniuses to build businesses and idiots to run them."
JOSEPH BROOKS, CEO, Ann Taylor, on why he left Lord and Taylor to mount
a leveraged buyout of the women's wear chain (interview, 1991)

"We were charging through the rice paddies, not stopping for
anything and taking no prisoners."
HENRY KRAVIS, general partner, Kohlberg, Kravis Roberts and Co.,
on his strategy in the RJR Nabsico takeover
(Burrough and Helyar, *Barbarians at the Gate*, 1990)

"So, naturalists observe, a flea
    Hath smaller fleas that on him prey;
And these have smaller still to bite 'em
    And so proceed *ad infinitum*."
JONATHAN SWIFT, satirist (*On Poetry: A Rhapsody*, 1733)

"Today money is the only thing that matters. Management is
protected by its golden parachutes, the stockholders will tender
their shares to Ho Chi Minh if the price is right and a lot of the
P.R. function centers on the price tag, not the quality of the offer."
RICHARD E. CHENEY, chairman, Hill and Knowlton
(*New York Times*, October 24, 1989)

"A lot of dogs chase Cadillacs, but few dogs drive Cadillacs."
DONALD KELLY, former CEO, Esmark, on the large number of self-
proclaimed takeover experts on Wall Street (Bianco, *Rainmaker*, p. 353)

"Are these guys really Robin Hood and his Merry Men as they claim, or Genghis Khan and the Mongol hordes?"

> ROBERT MILLER, chairman, Chrysler Financial Corp., on corporate raiders
> (*U.S. News and World Report*, January 26, 1987)

"How can I get angry with him? If a man pulls a rabbit out of his hat, he's entitled to do with it what he will. Make stew or skin it or turn it into another felt hat. That's the ball game."

> DONALD FORST, editor, Boston *Herald-American*, on Rubert Murdoch
> (Shawcross, *Murdoch*, p. 203)

"I'm sick of people calling me a corporate gunslinger."

> T. BOONE PICKENS, CEO, Mesa Limited Partnership
> (Public Broadcast System, 1986)

"All the planes, the penthouses, Premier, the country clubs, the Atlanta headquarters, had to be napalmed."

> J. TOMILSON HILL III, merger chief, Shearson Lehman Hutton,
> on the cost-cutting that would have to be done
> at RJR Nabisco (Burrough and Helyar,
> *Barbarians at the Gate*, 1990)

"'I weep for you,' the Walrus said:
        'I deeply sympathize,'
With sobs and tears he sorted out
        Those of the largest size . . . "

> LEWIS CARROLL, writer (*The Walrus and the Carpenter*, 1865);
> a popular Wall Street jingle during the 1980s
> (*New York Daily News*, August 23, 1992)

TALENT

"There is no substitute for talent. Industry and all the virtues are of no avail."

> ALDOUS HUXLEY (*Point Counter Point*, 1928, chapter 13)

"Trying to sneak a fastball past Hank Aaron is like trying to sneak the sunrise past a rooster."

> CURT SIMMONS, pitcher, Philadelphia Phillies
> (*New York Times*, February 24, 1991)

"You can take an ol' mule and run him and feed him and train him and get him in the best shape of his life, but you ain't going to win the Kentucky Derby!"

> PEPPER MARTIN (quoted in Heywood Hale Broun,
> *Tumultuous Merriment*, 1979)

"The main thing to do is relax and let your talent do the work."
CHARLES BARKLEY, power forward, Phoenix Suns
("NBA Stories," NBC-TV, June 11, 1993)

"You think creative talent can be bought as a commodity. You see guys like Eisner as a little crazy or a little off the wall. But every great studio in this business has been run by crazies. What do you think Walt Disney was? The guy was off the god-dammed wall. His brother Roy kept him in check. This is a creative institution. What's been wrong with this institution over the past 20 years is that it hasn't been run by the crazies. It needs to be run by crazies again. Clean out your image of crazies. We're talking about creative crazies. That's what we ought to have. We can always buy MBA talent."
STAN GOLD, urging the Disney board
to hire Michael Eisner as CEO (*The Prince of the Magic Kingdom*, p. 131)

TALK

". . . talk should precede, not follow, the issuance of orders."
Secretary of State DEAN ACHESON (*Present at the Creation*, p. 456)

"[Johnny] Sain don't say much, but that don't matter much, because when you're out there on the mound, you got nobody to talk to."
CASEY STENGEL, baseball manager, on pitching
(*The Gospel According to Casey*, p. 62)

"There was a time in this business when they had the eyes of the whole world. But that wasn't enough for them. Oh, no! They had to have the ears of the world too. So they opened their big mouths, and out came talk! Talk! Talk! . . . "
GLORIA SWANSON IN *Sunset Boulevard*
(screenplay by Charles Brackett and Billy Wilder)

"They say you can't understand me 'cause I talk Stengelese but what about him. He talks beautiful but when he's done you can't understand him either."
CASEY STENGEL, baseball manager, on Branch Rickey, Dodgers president
(*The Gospel According to Casey*, p. 21)

"He could talk the balls off a brass monkey."
ROBERT F. KENNEDY, on Larry O'Brien, the political operative sent by the
Kennedys to handle politicians (Lemann, *The Promised Land*, p. 113)

"He has a stained-glass voice."
Anonymous on Senator Everett Dirksen of Illinois

TAXATION

"As a U.S. Senator, I probably know more about the inner workings of the KGB than I do about the IRS."
Senator DAVID PRYOR, chairman, Senate Finance Subcommittee on
Oversight of the IRS (Silverman, Battling the IRS, 1992)

"The federal government of the United States of America takes away between a fifth and a quarter of all our money every year. That is eight times the Islamic zakat, the almsgiving required of believers by the Koran; it is double the tithe of the medieval church and twice the royal tribute that the prophet Samuel warned the Israelites against when they wanted him to anoint a ruler."
P. J. O'ROURKE (Parliament of Whores, p. 3)

"I come to Washington to get screwed. I'm a taxpayer, aren't I?"
ROBERT MITCHUM, actor (McLellan, Ear on Washington, p. 47)

"Rich people don't pay taxes—the little people do that."
LEONA HELMSLEY, hotelier, to an employee (The Economist, April 25, 1992)

"It's so simple. Step one: you find the worst play in the world, a surefire flop. Step two: I raise a million bucks. There are a lot of little old ladies in the world. Step three: you go back to work on the books, only list the backers one for the government and one for us. You can do it, Bloom. You're a wizard. Step four: we open on Broadway, and, before you can say step five, we close on Broadway. Step six: we take our million bucks, and we fly to Rio de Janeiro."
ZERO MOSTEL scheming to make a huge profit on a failed play
with Gene Wilder in The Producers
(screenplay by Mel Brooks)

"Thinking is the one thing no one has ever been able to tax."
CHARLES F. KETTERING, American industrialist
(recalled on his death, November 25, 1958)

"A government which robs Peter to pay Paul can always depend on the support of Paul."
GEORGE BERNARD SHAW, playwright
(Everybody's Political What's What?, 1944, chapter 30)

"I'm proud to be paying taxes to the United States. The only
thing is—I could be just as proud for half the money."
Attributed to ARTHUR GODFREY, television host

"Taxes are what we pay for civilized society."
Justice OLIVER WENDELL HOLMES, JR.
(*Companaia de Tabacos v. Collector*, 1904)

"The art of taxation consists in so plucking the goose as to obtain
the largest amount of feathers with the least possible amount of
hissing."   Attributed to J. B. COLBERT, Louis XIV's controller and finance minister

"The current tax code is a daily mugging."   President RONALD REAGAN
(Labor Day address, Independence, Missouri, October 2, 1985)

"What reason is there that he which laboreth much, and, sparing
the fruits of his labor, consumeth little, should be more charged
than he that, living idly, getteth little and spendeth all he gets,
seeing the one hath no more protection from the commmonwealth
than the other?"   THOMAS HOBBES (*Leviathan* II, 1651)

"The power to tax involves the power to destroy."
Chief Justice JOHN MARSHALL (*McCulloch v. Maryland*, 1819)

TAXATION, DEDUCTIONS

"I don't think meals have any business being deductible. I'm for
separation of calories and corporations."
RALPH NADER, consumer activist (*Wall Street Journal*, July 15, 1985)

TECHNOLOGY

"Almost unknowingly, by 1914, armies had come to depend on
weaponry—artillery, rifles, and machine guns—rather than upon
the soldiers themselves. . . .The generals never came to terms with
this power. Time and time again they threw their men forward,
confident that this time a little more preparation, a few more
men, and an extra dash of sheer courage would suffice to break
the enemy's will to resist. They never realized that they were not
fighting his 'will,' but his machine guns."
JOHN ELLIS, historian (*The Social History of the Machine Gun*, 1975)

"The higher the technology, the higher the freedom. Technology enforces certain solutions: satellite dishes, computers, videos, international telephone lines force pluralism and freedom onto a society."
LECH WALESA, leader of Poland's Solidarity (interview, 1989)

"If we hadn't put a man on the moon, there wouldn't be a Silicon Valley today."
JOHN SCULLEY, CEO, Apple Computer
(*U.S. News and World Report*, November 16, 1992)

"We are prone, especially in this fast-moving country, to what I call the displacive fallacy—to believe that every new technology displaces the old technology; that television will replace radio, that electronic news will displace print journalism, that the automobile will displace the human foot, and that television will displace the book. But each of these new technologies has simply given a new role to the earlier technologies. The development of technology is not displacive—it is cumulative."
DANIEL J. BOORSTIN, Librarian of Congress
(testimony before a Congressional copyright hearing on VCRs, 1984)

"Technology used to have a 10-year life cycle. But the mean lifespan for much current technology is about 24 months, and then you have almost a whole new technology base to deal with and apply."
STANLEY E. HARRISON, CEO, BDM, a company founded by
three physicists to design, test, and evaluate U.S. defense projects
(Henderson,*Winners*, p. 195)

"Technology is so much fun but we can drown in our technology. The fog of information can drive out knowledge."
DANIEL J. BOORSTIN, Librarian of Congress (*New York Times*, July 8, 1983)

"In the struggle for freedom of information, technology not politics will be the ultimate decider."
ARTHUR C. CLARKE, science fiction writer
(quoted in Shawcross, *Murdoch*, p. 147)

TELEPHONE

"Not at all. I am its master."
EDWARD HARRIMAN, railroad tycoon, on being told he was a slave
to his telephones, which he had everywhere—
houses, offices, private rail car
(Patton, *Made in USA*, p. 340)

TELEVISION

"What we've introduced with MTV is a nonnarrative form. As opposed to conventional television, where you rely on plot and continuity, we rely on mood and emotion. We make you feel a certain way, as opposed to you walking away with any particular knowledge."

BOB PITTMAN, founder, MTV, and CEO, Quantum Media
(Tannenbaum, "A Bumpy Ride for TV's High Flyer,"
Manhattan, Inc., August 1989, p. 78)

"Television is not the truth. Television is a goddamn amusement park. Television is a circus, a carnival, a traveling troupe of acrobats, story-tellers, dancers, singers, jugglers, sideshow freaks, lion tamers and football players. We're in the boredom-killing business."

PETER FINCH ranting in *Network* (screenplay by Paddy Chayevsky)

"Why should people go out and pay money to see bad films when they can stay at home and see bad television for nothing?"

SAM GOLDWYN, film producer (*The Observer*, September 9, 1956)

"Have we the right to exist?"

JACQUES DELORS, European Community president, about European
cultural identity in the face of the popularity of *I Love Lucy, Dallas, Wheel
of Fortune*, and others (quoted in Wolff, *Where We Stand*, p. 66)

"Talk wrestling."

LARRY KING's term for ferocious talk shows like *Downey*
(Tannenbaum, "A Bumpy Ride for TV's High Flyer,"
Manhattan, Inc., August 1989, p. 79)

"I like street people. They have a reverse chic style. They are not Grant Tinker, with the $2,000 suit, the 32-inch waist and the Gucci loafers. They are big healthy guys who look more like wrestlers. They're not like studio guys who come in with their Armani shirts and have nicer tushes than their wives. I hope I never get into a barroom fight, but if I do, I hope it's with the King brothers on my side."

JIM COOPERSMITH, president, WCVB-TV in Boston,
on the King brothers (*New York Times*, July 26, 1992)

THEATER

"If I would be in this business for *business*, I wouldn't be in this business."

SOL HUROK, theatrical producer (*New York Times*, August 28, 1970)

"Because, the English theater reminds me of a glorious pool table: great legs, a beautiful green felt top and no balls!"

> English theater critic KENNETH TYNAN to David Susskind who had asked whether he preferred the English or American theater; he said the American (Randall and Mindlin, *Which Reminds Me*, p. 24)

"This is an industry that doesn't have the common cold. . . . It has cholera."

> EMANUEL AZENBERG, Broadway producer (quoted in Freedman, "The Last of the Red-Hot Producers," *New York Times*, June 2, 1985)

"A stage-doorkeeper once failed to recognize [playwright George S. Kaufman] and barred his way. Kaufman insisted, so he asked, 'I beg your pardon, sir, are you with the show?' 'Let's put it this way,' said Kaufman, 'I'm not against it.'"

> Playwright GEORGE S. KAUFMAN (Sherrin, *Cutting Edge*, p. 106)

THEFT

"They didn't even have the brains to take a couple of good pastrami sandwiches."

> LEO STEINER, on being robbed at the deli he ran for 50 years near Carnegie Hall (*New York Times*, February 7, 1986)

"Steal from yourself. Find your forte and build on it."

> HALSTON, dress designer, to Steven Gaines, author and designer (*Simply Halston*, p. 8)

"Men have been swindled by other men on many occasions. The autumn of 1929 was, perhaps, the first occasion when men succeeded on a large scale in swindling themselves."

> JOHN KENNETH GALBRAITH, economist (*The Great Crash, 1929*, 1955)

"Because I needed them."

> WILLIAM S. PALEY, chairman of CBS, on his checkbook raids in the 1940s when he lured Jack Benny, George Burns and Gracie Allen, Amos 'n' Andy, Edgar Bergen, and other radio stars to CBS from NBC (*Wall Street Journal*, Centennial Edition, 1989)

"Immature artists imitate. Mature artists steal."

> LIONEL TRILLING, critic (*The Writer's Quotation Book*, p. 40)

"Never hesitate to steal a good idea."

> AL NEUHARTH, former chairman, Gannett Company (*Confessions of an S.O.B.*, 1989)

"VAX. For those who care enough to steal the very best."
A microscopic message on the silicon chip inside one of
Digital Equipment's often stolen computer designs
(Newsweek, December 25, 1991)

"If you like something of someone else's, why not take it?"
Attributed to Igor Stravinsky, composer,
to George Ballanchine, founder, New York City Ballet

THEORY

"It's all very well in practice, but it will never work in theory."
French management saying (Forbes, December 21, 1992, p. 348)

THINKING

"Thinking without bannisters."
Hannah Arendt, political theorist, on her approach (interview, 1968)

"How can I tell what I think until I see what I say?"
E. M. Forster, writer
(quoted in Barth, Washington College Magazine, Winter, 1992, p. 11)

"The human animal resists thinking. You never think until you come to a crossroads."
Professor Philip M. Hauser, chairman of the department of sociology,
University of Chicago (quoted in Moskin, Morality in America, p. 10)

THREATS

"We're going to tee-up GM, Ford, and IBM, and make them cringe."
Michael Milken, financier (quoted in Stewart, Den, picture 2)

"My foot soldiers who go up and down Wilshire Boulevard each day will blow your brains out."
Michael Ovitz, Creative Arts Agency (CAA), to scriptwriter Joe Eszterhas
who told him he was switching agencies (Bruck, "The World of
Business," The New Yorker, October 9, 1991)

"I won't be ignored."
Glenn Close to Michael Douglas in Fatal Attraction
(screenplay by James Dearden)

"Go ahead. Make my day."
Clint Eastwood, in Dirty Harry
(screenplay by Harry Julian Fink, R. M. Fink, and Dean Riesner)

"If you're not willing to come in on Saturday, don't even *bother* coming in on Sunday."
JEFFEREY KATZENBERG, CEO, Disney Studios
to an employee (quoted in Stone, *April Fools*, p. 46)

"You're going to have to kill me."
PAUL NEWMAN as Luke to prison guard George Kennedy in
Cool Hand Luke (screenplay by Don Pearce and Frank Pierson)

"I'll be back."
ARNOLD SCHWARZENEGGER, who dies repeatedly but returns, in
The Terminator (screenplay by James Cameron and Gale Anne Hurd)

"He's gonna die because he refused to come in when I called. He didn't do nothing else wrong."
JOHN GOTTI, indicted New York gangster,
on the importance of courtesy in his organization (interview, 1991)

"Prove it."
JACK PALANCE as the villain threatening Alan Ladd in *Shane*
(screenplay by A. B. Guthrie, Jr.)

TIFFANY'S

"If you go to Paris, if you go to Duluth, the best location is called the 'Tiffany location.' That is a standard real estate phrase. And I set out to get the true Tiffany location—the location right next door to Tiffany's."
DONALD TRUMP, on buying the site next to Tiffany's
on Fifth Avenue for his Trump Tower (*New York Times*, August 26, 1980)

"Well, when I get [the blues], the only thing that does any good is to jump into a cab and go to Tiffany's. Calms me down right away. The quietness and the proud look of it. Nothing very bad could happen to you there."
AUDREY HEPBURN as Holly Golightly in
Breakfast at Tiffany's (screenplay by George Axelrod)

TIME

"Time is the friend of the wonderful company, the enemy of the mediocre."
WARREN BUFFETT, CEO, Berkshire Hathaway (annual report, 1989)

TIRED

"Well, I'm tired of you."
CASEY STENGEL, baseball manager, when a pitcher removed from a game
told him he wasn't tired (*The Gospel According to Casey*, p. 19)

"Saving New York City from bankruptcy is like making love to a gorilla. You don't stop when you're tired; you stop when he's tired."

FELIX ROHATYN, chairman, Municipal Assistance Corporation (interview, 1975)

"Tired is a disgusting word. You never say tired to a fighter, even if he's ready to drop from exhaustion. Even if he *thinks* about being tired you're dead."

ANGELO DUNDEE, heavyweight trainer (Sherrin, *Cutting Edge*, p. 205)

TOUGH

"Sure my dad is tough. But you can't be in business and be a pushover."

ED HAGGAR, on the founder of Haggar Co., clothing manufacturer (interview, 1960)

"A thick skin is a gift from God."

KONRAD ADENAUER, West German chancellor (*New York Times*, December 30, 1959)

"Business is tough; it's no kissing game."

PETER J. GRACE, CEO, W. R. Grace (interview, 1988)

TOYS

"The one who dies with the most toys wins."

Wall Street T-shirt

"He who invests in the best toys wins."

EDWARD ANTOIAN, portfolio manager, Delaware Group in Philadelphia, on the successful investment strategy of looking for winners among companies that supply his children (*Fortune*, March 9, 1992)

"As men get older, the toys get more expensive."

MARVIN DAVIS, owner, Oakland Athletics, on buying the team for a rumored $12 million (*New York Times*, December 31, 1979)

TRENDS

"Just as there is a trend toward high tech today, there is another trend toward high touch—homemade and wholesome."

MARYL GARDNER, assistant professor of marketing, New York University, on Vermont's Ben and Jerry's Ice Cream (*New York Times*, March 29, 1985)

"Beware the permanent trend. Nothing is forever. Not diamonds, not rising oil prices, not inflation, not depression, not the steady appreciation of real estate."

ANDREW TOBIAS (*Money Angles*, 1984)

"I don't think decadence is wrong. I think it's kind of kicky and cute."

ALVIN CHERESKIN, president of AC & R, advertising agency
(quoted in *The New Yorker*, 1986)

TROUBLE

"You can't save your way out of trouble; you've got to sell your way out."

LESTER MINSUK, Minsuk Macklin Stein and Associates of Princeton
Junction, New Jersey, on how companies cut back customer-service staffs
to save money (*Fortune*, March 9, 1992)

"Trouble is my business."

Raymond Chandler's PHILIP MARLOWE

"I don't mind a reasonable amount of trouble."

Dashiell Hammett's SAM SPADE (*The Maltese Falcon*, 1930)

"If you're in trouble, you're alone."

ROSS THOMAS (*Cast a Yellow Shadow*, 1967)

TRUST

"Ever since they found out that Lassie was a boy, the public has believed the worst about Hollywood."

GROUCHO MARX (*People*, February 1988)

"Murdoch used to love repeating the joke that the sun never set on the British empire because God didn't trust the Brits after dark."

WILLIAM SHAWCROSS (*Murdoch*, p. 155)

"Do not trust anyone."

JAMES B. DUKE, chairman, Duke Power and Light,
to his daughter, Doris Duke (*New York Observer*, June 8, 1992)

"Trust everybody—but cut the cards."

FINLEY PETER DUNNE, author (*Casual Observations*, 1900)

"Trust your hopes, not your fears."

Attributed to DAVID MAHONEY, chairman, Norton Simon, Inc.

"In some measure, it certainly is true, as Locke put it, that men 'live upon trust.' But the twin of trust is betrayal."

> JOHN DUNN, Trust and Political Agency
> (quoted in Malcolm, *The Journalist and the Murderer*)

"The only way to make a man trustworthy is to trust him."

> HENRY STIMSON, U.S. Secretary of War
> (*Newsweek*, August 20, 1990)

"Trust only movement. Life happens at the level of events not of words. Trust movement."

> ALFRED ADLER, psychiatrist (quoted in *Sam Walton*, p. 5)

TRUTH

"All great truths begin as blasphemies."

> GEORGE BERNARD SHAW, playwright (*Annajanska*, 1919)

"Once, when Truman started a rumor that was blatantly untrue, I told him it was immoral to make trouble where there was none. 'Never mind, Big Mama,' he replied, in that high, wispy voice. 'You just wait and see. And if you wait long enough, it'll all come true.' And it usually did."

> SLIM KEITH (*Slim: Memories of a Rich and Imperfect Life*, p. 218)

"When all else fails, tell the truth."

> Cited by DONALD T. REGAN, former White House Chief of Staff and
> former CEO, Merill Lynch (interview, 1984)

"It's still hard for me to have a clear mind thinking on it. But it's the truth, even if it didn't happen."

> KEN KESEY, writer (*One Flew Over the Cuckoo's Nest*, 1962)

"It is more important that a proposition be interesting than that it be true."

> ALFRED NORTH WHITEHEAD, theologian
> (quoted in Ashby, *Reconciling Man with the Environment*, p. 23)

"The truth is more important than the facts."

> Attributed to FRANK LLOYD WRIGHT, architect

"I don't want any yes-men around me. I want everybody to tell me the truth even if it costs them their jobs."

> Attributed to SAM GOLDWYN, film producer

"When you have eliminated the impossible, whatever remains, however improbable, must be the truth."

ARTHUR CONAN DOYLE (*The Sign of Four*, 1890)

"Life is a search for truth and there is no truth."

Chinese proverb quoted by NORTON SIMON, industrialist and philanthropist (recalled on his death, *New York Times*, June 4, 1993)

". . . variety as a positive value is a new idea. The old idea is that truth is one, error is many. To any real question, only one true answer can in principle be given; the other answers are necessarily false. The idea that there can be two sides to a question, that there may be two or more incompatible answers, any one of which could be accepted by honest, rational men—that is a very recent notion. . . . The merit of a free society is that it allows a great variety of conflicting opinions without the need for suppression—that is surely comparatively new in the West."

ISAIAH BERLIN, writer (*Conversations with Isaiah Berlin,* 1992)

"He told the truth, mainly. There were things which he stretched, but mainly he told the truth." HUCK FINN's comment about Mark Twain (quoted by David McCullough, *Truman*, 1992, p. 978)

"History warns us that it is the customary fate of new truths to begin as heresies and to end as superstitions."

T. H. HUXLEY (*The Coming of Age*, 1880)

"Truth never comes into the world but like a bastard, to the ignominy of him that brought her forth."

JOHN MILTON, poet (*Areopagitica*, 1644)

"Man will occasionally stumble over the truth, but most of the time he will pick himself up and continue on."

WINSTON CHURCHILL (quoted in Wriston, *Risk and Other Four-Letter Words*, p. 183)

"It takes two to speak the truth—one to speak, and another to listen." HENRY DAVID THOREAU (quoted in Boorstin, *Creators*, p. 265)

"A man always has two reasons for the things he does—a good one and the real one."

Attributed to J. P. MORGAN

"It's better to know nothing than to know what ain't so."
JOSH BILLINGS, nineteenth-century humorist (Proverb, 1874)

TRY

"Try to be one of the people on whom nothing is lost."
HENRY JAMES (The Art of Fiction, 1888)

UNDERDOG

"Overwhelming underdogs."
YOGI BERRA, on the 1969 Mets (It Ain't Over, 1989)

"I was very brash in my attitude, so it was difficult for people to easily latch on, but now, being the underdog, and not having been successful over the last few years, it's more easy. And I'm not going to be around that much more, let's face it."
JOHN MCENROE, former tennis champion, on his newly found popularity
during a comeback (New York Times, September 8, 1990)

UNIONS

"Economic power is not the purpose of the labor movement. Jimmy Hoffa has economic power. General Motors has economic power. The labor movement is about people—about their hopes and aspirations—their dreams."
WALTER REUTHER, labor leader
(quoted in Moskin, Morality in America, p. 141)

"Nothing comes closer to a marriage than hiring a teamster. And it's easier to get a divorce than to try to remove a teamster from a job."
ARTHUR IMPERATORE, CEO, APA Trucking Company,
on his clashes with the Newspaper and Mail
Deliverers' Union of New York and Vicinity
(New York Times, May 16, 1992)

"How many teamsters does it take to screw in a light bulb? Fifteen. You got a problem with that?"
WILLIAM NOVAK and MOSHE WALDOKS (Big Books of Humor, 1990)

"Management and union may be likened to that serpent of the fables who on one body had two heads that fighting each other with poisoned fangs, killed themselves."
PETER DRUCKER (The New Society, 1951)

"Dad strove to blur the distinction between white-collar and blue-collar workers so that unions would never crack IBM-USA."

THOMAS WATSON, JR., chairman, IBM
(Watson and Petre, *Father Son & Co.*, 1990)

"At first I had liked it when they went on strike. Well, of course I would. I liked Yeats, and medieval history, and anything strange or apocalyptic, and in law school I had even written a paper explaining how the wildcats were good: how such occasional conflict could lead, in the end, to a longer-lasting 'industrial peace.' I should say, though, that no one up in the legal department took me seriously. Up there, it was like trying to defend cholera to a bunch of doctors."

THOMAS GEOGHEGAN, UMW lawyer (*Which Side Are You On?*, p. 35)

"Pickets is bad people."

SHARON DISNEY, Walt's 4-year old daughter, on the family attitude toward the bitter strike at Disney Studios, 1941 (*The Man Behind the Magic*, p. 97)

"My own personal conclusion is that unions do not have a viable mission, except to ask for more." Professor CHRIS ARGYRIS, Yale University
(quoted in Moskin, *Morality in America*, p. 140)

"The employer puts his money into . . . business and the workman his life. The one has as much right as the other to regulate that business." CLARENCE S. DARROW, American criminal lawyer (interview, 1909)

UPWARD MOBILITY

"None of us has gotten where we are solely by pulling ourselves up from our own bootstraps. We got here because somebody—a parent, a teacher, an Ivy League crony or a few nuns—bent down and helped us pick up our boots." THURGOOD MARSHALL,
retired U.S. Supreme Court Justice, on the story of his successor,
Clarence Thomas (*Newsweek*, November 1991)

"From Poland to polo in one generation."

ARTHUR CASEAR, on Darryl Zanuck (Sherrin, *Cutting Edge*, p. 97)

"From shirt sleeves to shirt sleeves in three generations."

ANDREW CARNEGIE, financier (quoted by Jerry Goodman writing as Adam Smith, *Esquire*, December 1983, p. 223)

VIRTUE

"I've always been right-wing. It's difficult to say why, but not being a political thinker I suppose I can identify the Right with certain virtues and the Left with certain vices. All very unfair, no doubt. [Which virtues or vices?] Well, thrift, hard work, reverence, desire to preserve—those are the virtues, in case you wondered: and on the other hand idleness, greed and treason."

PHILIP LARKIN, British poet laureate (*Required Writing*, 1983)

VOTE

"Whoever you vote for, the government will get in." English graffiti

"Cartoonists have a very hard time at elections. When I go into the voting booth, do I vote for the person who is the best president? Or the slime bucket who will make my life as a cartoonist wonderful?"

MIKE PETERS, syndicated cartoonist, *Dayton Daily News*
(*Wall Street Journal*, January 20, 1993)

WALL STREET

"I offered fall, spring, and cruise lines."

KATHLEEN BROWN, Treasurer, State of California, on her successful
financing of short-term notes, long-term bonds, and revenue bonds
(speech in New York City, June 22, 1993)

"Wall Street is, at bottom, a collection of endearingly childlike innocents, always expecting the good, the beautiful, the true, and the profitable."

EMMA LATHEN (*Pick Up Sticks*, 1970)

"Along with ordinary happenings, we fellows in Wall Street now have, in addition, the fortunes of war to speculate about and that always makes great doings on a stock exchange. It's good fishing in troubled waters."

DANIEL DREW, nineteenth-century speculator
(quoted in Sharp, *The Lore and Legends of Wall Street*, p. 121)

"Wall Street is the only place people ride to in a Rolls-Royce to get advice from people who take the subway."

WARREN BUFFETT, CEO, Berkshire Hathaway
(*New York Newsday*, August 25, 1991)

WAR

"My film is not a movie. My film is not about Vietnam. It is Vietnam. The way we made it is the way Americans were in Vietnam. We had too much money, access to too much equipment, and little by little we went insane."
FRANCIS FORD COPPOLA, director, on his film,
Apocalypse Now (*Hearts of Darkness: A Filmmaker's Apocalypse*)

"Take the profit out of war."
BERNARD M. BARUCH, financier (*Atlantic Monthly*, January 1926)

"The machine overheated. You got inflation and a falling market at one end and college riots at the other and in the middle forty thousand sons of American mothers killed by shit-smeared bamboo. People don't like having Sonny killed in the jungle any more. Maybe they never liked it, but they used to think it was necessary."
John Updike's HARRY (Rabbit) ANGSTROM (*Rabbit Redux*, 1971)

"Everything in war is very simple, but the simplest thing is difficult. The difficulties accumulate and end by producing a kind of friction that is inconceivable unless one has experienced war."
KARL VON CLAUSEWITZ (*On War*, p. 119)

"The Pope! How many divisions has *he* got?"
JOSEF STALIN (quoted in Churchill, *The Gathering Storm*, 1948)

"In war there is no second prize for the runner-up."
General OMAR BRADLEY (*Military Review*, February 1950)

"Force, and fraud, are in war the two cardinal virtues."
THOMAS HOBBES, philosopher (quoted in *The Economist*, June 6, 1992)

WARNINGS

"If you're not part of the steamroller, you're part of the road."
RICH FRANK, studio president, Walt Disney Co., on the technological advances taking over Hollywood (*Wall Street Journal*, May 19, 1993)

"Basketball is a business. Pure and simple. If you want to have fun, go to the YMCA."
PAT RILEY, coach, New York Knicks (*New York*, November 25, 1991)

"To collect nothing at all is to descend below the level of magpies and marmots."

GERALD REITLINGER, collector, businessman, and writer
(*The Economist*, December 22, 1990)

"It gets so your blood turns to ketchup."

JERRY PELLETIER, assistant dean, McDonald's Hamburger University, on his devotion to hamburgers (Boas and Chain, *Big Mac*, p. 75)

"Jewelry on the beach is arriving by the pailful. Just remember before diving into the surf that sharks love shiny things."

HAL RUBENSTEIN and JIM MULLEN, "Iron, John: How to Get Dressed Better" (*New York Times Magazine*: "Men's Fashions of the Times," September 13, 1992)

"It's the economy, stupid."

James Carville, Clinton campaign manager, on why they won the presidency (*Commonweal*, February 26, 1993)

"Don't cross this field unless you can do it in 9.9 seconds. The bull can do it in 10."

Sign on the campus of the Fermi National Accelerator Laboratory, Batavia, Illinois

"You can contract AIDS from listening to too many assholes."

Graffiti at a New York City construction site

"Even if you're on the right track, you'll get run over if you just sit there."

WILL ROGERS, comedian
(quoted in Kehrer, *Doing Business Boldly*, p. 3)

"Well, George, what Jerry [Komes, Bechtel Company director] wants to tell you is a couple of things we've all learned the hard way around here. No. 1, we know how to make money. No. 2, we know how to keep it. Your experience has been in the academic world, where maybe you didn't have to think about money. And you've been in government, where you've been giving money away. So, as Steve Sr. [Bechtel] would tell you, whatever you do around here, George, *don't fuck with the money*."

BOB BRIDGES, outside counsel and member of the finance committee, Bechtel Company, to George Shultz, former Secretary of the Treasury, Secretary of State, and dean of the University of Chicago business school, while interviewing him for the presidency of Bechtel (quoted in McCartney, *Friends in High Places*, 1988)

"We don't want to skim the cream off the crop here."

> GIB LEWIS, Speaker of the Texas House, who is so well known for his
> malapropisms that his speech is called Gibberish
> (*New York Times*, October 17, 1989)

"If you quit, Henry, you'll never get a phone call from a beautiful woman again. The secret of your attraction is your proximity to power."

> WILLIAM SAFIRE, telling Henry Kissinger not to resign
> as President Nixon's national security adviser
> (quoted in Isaacson, *Kissinger: A Biography*, p. 211)

"Don't turn your back on him, or your hair will be stolen."

> OTTO PREMINGER, director, on film producer Sam Spiegel, with whom he
> had fled Austria in 1935 (*New York Review of Books*, March 17, 1988)

"Fasten your seat-belts, it's going to be a bumpy night."

> BETTE DAVIS, in *All About Eve* (screenplay by Joseph Mankiewicz)

"Don't strike a flea on a tiger's head."

> Chinese advice (quoted in Tan, *The Kitchen God's Wife*, p. 261)

"If you can't bite, don't show your teeth."

> Yiddish proverb

"Never practice two vices at once."

> TALLULAH BANKHEAD, actress (*Eat These Words*, p. 13)

"It is going to take a lot of trees so you can sharpen all those pencils."

> DON CONGDON, literary agent, to author, on delaying writing

"Champions don't smoke pipes. Pipes make you contented and champions aren't contented."

> JOE MCCARTHY, baseball manager (quoted by Heywood Hale Broun,
> *New York Times*, July 14, 1991)

"It takes dirt to grow grass."

> Governor WILLIE STARK, a character based on Huey Long
> (Robert Penn Warren, *All the King's Men*, 1946)

"You're only as good as the people you dress."

> HALSTON, dress designer (*Simply Halston*, p. 16)

"There is no trap so deadly as the trap you set for yourself."

> Raymond Chandler's PHILIP MARLOWE (*The Long Goodbye*, 1953)

"Something is wrong with our economy when the stock market is long on hamburgers and short on steel."

> Texas Senator LLOYD BENTSEN, warning in 1974 that glamour stocks like McDonald's had a book value of $200 million and a stock market value of $2.1 billion at the end of 1972 while U.S. Steel had a book value of $3.6 billion but a stock market value of only $2.2 billion (Boas and Chain, *Big Mac*, p. 71)

"Don't think there are no crocodiles because the water is calm."

> Malayan proverb (quoted in *Sam Walton*, p. 32)

"Entering a Logic-Free Zone."

> Sign for Washington, D.C. Beltway proposed by Thomas A. Schatz, president, Citizens Against Government Waste (*Business Week*, "Reinventing America," 1992, p. 208)

"A good many young writers make the mistake of enclosing a stamped, self-addressed envelope, big enough for the manuscript to come back in. This is too much of a temptation to the editor."

> RING LARDNER (*How to Write Short Stories*, 1924)

WASTE

"In Pontiac [Michigan], GM executive parking garages are heated, while the poor guys who work in the plant freeze their tails off walking to work in the snow. It costs $140,000 a year to heat one parking garage. I'd shut that thing down. It has nothing to do with cars."

> H. ROSS PEROT, founder, Electronic Data System; board member, GM (speech, Detroit Economic Club, 1987)

"Once you can afford to waste a product, it's bound to be a success."

> ALBERT LASKER, advertising man (quoted in *Wall Street Journal*, Centennial Edition, 1989)

"I find it mind-boggling. We do not shoot paper at the enemy."

> Admiral JOSEPH METCALF, on the 20 tons of paper and file cabinets on board the Navy's newest frigates (interview, 1987)

WEALTHY

"Wealth is not without its advantages and the case to the contrary, although it has often been made, has never proved widely persuasive."

> JOHN KENNETH GALBRAITH, economist (*The Affluent Society*, 1958)

"Cats of a good breed mouse better when they are fat than when they are starving; and likewise good men who have some talent exercise it to nobler ends when they have wealth enough to live well."

BENVENUTO CELLINI *(Life,* 1558)

"Wealth is the parent of luxury and indolence, and poverty of meanness and viciousness, and both of discontent."

PLATO *(The Republic* IV)

"We had a few gold coins with us. That was our fortune. And I spent that night opening the back ends of toothpaste tubes and stuffing these gold coins into the tubes. It created in me a notion of wealth that is not exactly supply-side economics, in terms of what is real. What is real to me is what I can put in the back of the toothpaste tube, or what I carry around in my head."

FELIX ROHATYN, investment banker, on his family's flight from the Nazis
(Reich, *Financier: André Meyer,* p. 81)

"It helps to be born poor. It helps to be really hungry."

Attributed to KEMMONS WILSON, founder and former chairman,
Holiday Inns of America

"The *sine qua non* of a functioning democracy is its ability to create new wealth and see to its fair distribution. The tides now running in this country are likely to do just the opposite. Wealth will be created for too few; too many will be left behind. The question of fairness will come up again and again, especially if economic growth remains anemic. When a democratic society does not meet the test of fairness . . . freedom is in jeopardy."

FELIX ROHATYN, investment banker
(commencement address, Middlebury College, 1982)

"That's it, baby! When you got it, flaunt it!"

ZERO MOSTEL yelling out the window of his shabby office at a man
emerging from a white Rolls Royce in *The Producers*
(screenplay by Mel Brooks)

"As wealth is power, so all power will infallibly draw wealth to itself by some means or other."

EDMUND BURKE, British statesman
(Commons, February 11, 1780)

"I must atone for my wealth."

Attributed to OTTO KAHN, industrialist

"If the rich could hire other people to die for them, the poor could make a wonderful living."

Yiddish proverb

"Great wealth always supports the party in power, no matter how corrupt it may be. It never exerts itself for reform, for it instinctively fears change."

HENRY GEORGE (Social Problems, 1884)

"It is beyond our power to explain either the prosperity of the wicked or the afflictions of the righteous."

The Talmud (Harper Religious and Inspirational Quotation Companion, p. 335)

WELFARE

"Bad charity drives out the good."

MARVIN OLASKY, The Tragedy of American Compassion, 1992)

"Welfare is hated by those who administer it, mistrusted by those who pay for it and held in contempt by those who receive it."

PETER C. GOLDMARK, JR., director, New York State Budget Office
(New York Times, May 24, 1977)

"Give no bounties; make equal laws; secure life and prosperity, and you need not give alms."

RALPH WALDO EMERSON, essayist (The Conduct of Life, 1860)

WESTERNERS

"Westerners seem to them by contrast a little rough, unpredictable, and immature in their frankness and ready display of emotions. In the West unpredictability in a person may be seen as amusing or spirited, but to the Japanese it is a particularly reprehensible trait."

EDWIN O. REISCHAUER, professor, Far Eastern languages
(The Japanese Today, 1988)

WIN

"We lost sight of one of the cardinal maxims of guerilla war: the guerrilla wins if he does not lose. The conventional army loses if it does not win."

HENRY KISSINGER, diplomat (Foreign Affairs, January 1969)

"If you want to win, you've got to sin bravely."

AMORY HOUGHTON, JR., chairman, Corning Glass Works

"You have to have some dislike for your opponent if you're going to win a championship."

ERVIN (Magic) JOHNSON, on the fourth game between the Phoenix Suns and the Chicago Bulls (NBC-TV, June 16, 1993)

"The difference between playing to win and playing not to lose is the difference between the successful executive and the security-hunting, mediocre man."

DAVID MAHONEY, chairman, Norton Simon, Inc. (interview, 1988)

"Just win, baby."

Los Angeles Raiders' motto

"I'm a win man myself. I don't go for place or show."

Attributed to BEAR BRYANT, football coach at the University of Kentucky, 1950

"Even when he cheated he couldn't win, because the people he cheated against were always better at cheating too."

JOSEPH HELLER, writer (Catch-22, 1961)

"The alumni are always with you, win or tie."

Attributed to DUFFY DAUGHERTY, Michigan State coach, 1965

"We can't win at home. We can't win on the road. As general manager, I just can't figure out where else to play."

PAT WILLIAMS, general manager, Orlando Magic (Sports Illustrated, January 4, 1993)

"Even if you win a rat race, you are still a rat."

Reverend WILLIAM SLOANE COFFIN, JR. (quoted in Moskin Morality in America, p. 235)

"Norman Hapgood has said of Felix Frankfurter, he liked nothing better than to win an argument, and by unfair means if possible."

DEAN ACHESON, Secretary of State (Present at the Creation, p. 62)

"I do not deserve more than half the credit for the battles I have won. Soldiers generally win battles; generals get credit for them."

NAPOLEON I (letter to Gaspard Gourgaud, St. Helena, 1818)

"You can only win one for the Gipper once."

RED AUERBACH, manager, Boston Celtics (MBA: Management by Auerbach, 1992)

"If we're going to win the pennant, we've got to start thinking we're not as good as we think we are."

> CASEY STENGEL, baseball manager, to the New York Yankees, spring 1953,
> after the team had won four straight World Championships
> (*The Gospel According to Casey*, p. 120)

"You can't win them all."

> RAYMOND CHANDLER (*The Long Goodbye*, 1953)

"Every time you win, you're reborn; when you lose, you die a little."

> GEORGE ALLEN (Michener, *Sports in America*, 1976)

WINNERS

"He favors the running game because it favors those who can administer and absorb pain, two abilities that mark life's winners. 'If it comes easy,' Hayes says, 'it isn't worth a damn.' He thinks the forward pass is a modernist heresy, worse than gun control and almost as bad as deficit spending."

> GEORGE F. WILL, on Ohio State football Coach Woody Hayes

"Winners got scars too."

> Attributed to JOHNNY CASH, singer

"There can only be one winner, folks. But isn't that the American way?"

> GIG YOUNG emceeing the dance marathon in *They Shoot Horses, Don't
> They?* (screenplay by James Poe and Robert E. Thompson)

"We don't want any losers around. In this family we want winners."

> Attributed to JOSEPH P. KENNEDY, financier

"Without losers, where would the winners be?"

> CASEY STENGEL, baseball manager (*The Gospel According to Casey*, p. 19)

WINNING

"Ballplayers are a superstitious breed, nobody more than I, and while you are winning you'd murder anybody who tried to change your sweatshirt, let alone your uniform."

> LEO DUROCHER, baseball manager (*Nice Guys Finish Last*, 1975)

"Never change a winning game; always change a losing one."

> Attributed to BILL TILDEN, tennis champion

"He was so tough to work for that winning was the easy way out."

> WILLIE DAVIS, former defensive end, Green Bay Packers, on Vince
> Lombardi (*San Francisco Chronicle*, 1984)

"Winning is a habit, gentlemen. Winning isn't everything; it's the only thing."

> VINCE LOMBARDI, on his first day coaching the Washington Redskins, who
> hadn't had a winning team since 1955 (interview, 1969)

"There are only two places in this league; first place and no place."

> TOM SEAVER, pitcher, to the New York Mets

"We like winning. We've tried both and winning is better. But don't believe that winning is really everything. It's more important to stand for something. If you don't stand for something, what do you win?"

> Attributed to LANE KIRKLAND, president, AFL-CIO

"I commenced winning pennants as soon as I got here, but I did not commence getting any younger."

> CASEY STENGEL, baseball manager (*The Gospel According to Casey*, p. 9)

". . . the shooting has started . . . history has recorded who fired the first shot. In the long run, however, all that will matter is who fires the last shot."

> FRANKLIN D. ROOSEVELT, October 27, 1941,
> following attacks by German U-boats on American destroyers

"To finish first you must first finish."

> RICK MEARS, race car driver and winner of the Indianapolis 500
> (quoted in Augustine, *Augustine's Laws*, p. 104)

WORDS

"Words are the bugles of social change. When our language changes, behavior will not be far behind."

> CHARLES HANDY, chairman, Royal Arts Society (*Age of Unreason*, p. 17)

WORK

"On the day Harry bid goodbye to Tom Pendergast in Kansas City, Pendergast had told him, 'Work hard, keep your mouth shut, and answer your mail.'"

> DAVID MCCULLOUGH, on Harry Truman's entering the U.S. Senate
> (*Truman*, p. 155)

"Work is for people who don't know how to fish."
<blockquote>Pillow in office of Paul A. Volcker, chairman, J. D. Wolfensohn and
Company (New York Times, June 8, 1992)</blockquote>

"We pretend to work. They pretend to pay us."
<blockquote>Soviet factory joke (retold by Thurow, Head to Head, p. 96)</blockquote>

"We have a blue-collar staff. They go out and work."
<blockquote>JOE TORRE, manager, St. Louis Cardinals, on the success of his pitchers
(New York Times, August 18, 1991)</blockquote>

"I was standing in the schoolyard waiting for a child when another mother came up to me. 'Have you found work yet?' she asked. 'Or are you still just writing?' Now, how am I supposed to answer that?"
<blockquote>ANNE TYLER (The Writer on Her Work)</blockquote>

"The work is the refuge."
<blockquote>JASON MILLER, actor and playwright (quoted in Brown, Shoptalk, p. 23)</blockquote>

"I don't like work—no man does—but I like what is in work—the chance to find yourself."
<blockquote>JOSEPH CONRAD (The Heart of Darkness, 1902)</blockquote>

"It was truly a splendid structure, and Yossarian throbbed with a mighty sense of accomplishment each time he gazed at it and reflected that none of the work that had gone into it was his."
<blockquote>JOSEPH HELLER (Catch-22, 1961)</blockquote>

"It's what man has aimed at all his life—getting out of work."
<blockquote>J. IRWIN MILLER, CEO, Cummins Engine
(quoted in Moskin, Morality in America, p. 48)</blockquote>

"Whoever you are, God or anybody else, you work with the materials at hand."
<blockquote>DANNY BOY (Block, Eight Million Ways to Die, 1982)</blockquote>

"I work for a government I despise for ends I think criminal."
<blockquote>JOHN MAYNARD KEYNES, economist, on his work at the Treasury
(Biographical Quotation, p. 454)</blockquote>

"If we bring a little joy into your humdrum lives, it makes us feel our work ain't been in vain for nothin'."
<blockquote>JEAN HAGEN playing a silent film star who insists on talking to her audience
in Singin' in the Rain (screenplay by Adolph Green and Betty Comden)</blockquote>

"Nothing stops the bullets like a job."
> Father GREGORY BOYLE, Jesuit and chairman, Jobs for the Future, which
> works with gang members in East Los Angeles (*Newsweek*, May 18, 1992)

"It's one of the tragic ironies of the theater that only one man in it can count on steady work—the night watchman."
> TALLULAH BANKHEAD, actress (*Tallulah*, 1952)

"What you want to do is not go to work. You're not missing a thing. The worst thing I did was start work young."
> JIMMY BRESLIN, columnist
> (Winokur, *Friendly Advice*, p. 274)

"The great thing is to last and get your work done and see and hear and learn and understand; and written when there is something that you know; and not before; and not too damned much after."
> ERNEST HEMINGWAY, writer (*Death in the Afternoon*, 1932)

"It's like two porcupines mating: one prick against a thousand others."
> WILSON MIZNER, on working conditions at Warner Bros.
> (Randall and Mindlin, *Which Reminds Me*, p. 56)

"The Yankee means to make moonlight work, if he can."
> RALPH WALDO EMERSON, essayist (*Journals*, 1848)

WORKERS

"Lazy and illiterate."
> YOSHIO SAKURAUCHI, speaker of the Japanese House,
> on American workers (*Lear's*, July 1992)

"I may be fat, but I'm not lazy."
> Detroit autoworker responding to Yoshio Sakurauchi
> (*Newsweek*, February 3, 1992)

"American workers don't work hard enough. They don't work but demand high pay."
> YOSHIO SAKURAUCHI, Japanese House speaker, on U.S. economic problems
> (*Newsweek*, February 3, 1992)

"It's ours now, let's work smarter."
> Sign put up by TWA worker outside the airline's
> overhaul base in Kansas City, Missouri
> (*New York Times*, May 16, 1993)

"Much like the *Nation* itself, the [Democratic] party has abandoned the working class in favor of the nonworking class—a kindness, to be sure, but politically lethal."

NEIL POSTMAN (*The Nation*, July 20, 1992)

WORLD

"In the fight between you and the world, back the world."

FRANK ZAPPA (Winokur, *Friendly Advice*, p. 261)

"We hope that the world will not narrow into a neighborhood before it has broadened into a brotherhood."

President LYNDON B. JOHNSON (speech at the lighting of the country's Christmas tree, December 22, 1963)

"The world is not the way they tell you it is."

ADAM SMITH (JERRY GOODMAN) (*The Money Game*, epigraph, 1968)

"Hiccups in the international business scene are not new to us. Wedgwood china has survived upheavals before—the Napoleonic Wars, the Franco-Prussian War, the world wars. We do have a sense of continuity."

ARTHUR BRYAN, CEO, Josiah Wedgwood and Sons, Ltd. (*New York Times*, March 30, 1980)

"We've moved from Ivy League football to the Big Ten."

JOSEPH L. BOWER, professor, Harvard Business School, on global industrial competition (*Wall Street Journal*, March 9, 1987)

"We have it in our power to begin the world all over again."

THOMAS PAINE (quoted in *Business Week*, "Reinventing America," 1992, p. 14)

"Two men have been supreme in creating the modern world: Rockefeller and Bismarck. One in economics, the other in politics, refuted the liberal dream of universal happiness through individual competition, substituting instead monopoly and the corporate state."

BERTRAND RUSSELL, philosopher

"The reasonable man adapts himself to the world; the unreasonable one persists in trying to adapt the world to himself. Therefore, all progress depends upon the unreasonable man."

GEORGE BERNARD SHAW, playwright (*Man and Superman*, 1902)

WORRY

"I know at last what distinguishes man from animals: financial worry."
> JULES RENARD (Plimpton, *The Writer's Chapbook*, p. 282)

"I received a card the other day from Steve Early which said, 'Don't Worry Me—I am an 8 Ulcer Man on 4 Ulcer Pay.'"
> HARRY S TRUMAN (Hillman, *Mr. President*, part 5, p. 222)

WRITERS

"Schmucks with Underwoods."
> JACK WARNER's term for screenwriters (quoted in *New York Times*, April 25, 1982)

"I'm not an author, but before I became mayor, I wasn't a mayor."
> EDWARD I. KOCH, mayor, New York City (quoted in *Publishers Weekly*, January 25, 1985)

"The highest paid secretaries in the world."
> JOSEPH L. MANKIEWICZ, screenwriter (quoted in *New York Times*, April 25, 1982)

"All the writers sit in cells in a row, and the minute a typewriter stops someone pokes his head in the door to see if you are thinking. Otherwise, it's like the hotel business."
> NATHANAEL WEST, writing a friend back East (quoted in *New York Times*, April 25, 1982)

"In America only the successful writer is important, in France all writers are important, in England no writer is important, in Australia you have to explain what a writer is."
> GEOFFREY COTTERELL (*The Writer's Quotation Book*, p. 22)

"Those big-shot writers . . . could never dig the fact that there are more peanuts consumed than caviar.
> MICKEY SPILLANE (*New York Herald Tribune,* August 18, 1961)

"He's teaching me to write, and I'm teaching him to box."
> ERNEST HEMINGWAY, writer, referring to Ezra Pound, poet, 1922
> (Baker, *Ernest Hemingway—A Life Story*, 1969)

"Writing is the only profession where no one considers you ridiculous if you earn no money."
> JULES RENARD (*The Writer's Quotation Book*, p. 23)

"The average contributor to this magazine is semi-literate; that is, he is ornate to no purpose, full of senseless and elegant variations, and can be relied on to use three sentences where a word would do."

WOLCOTT GIBBS, "Theory and Practice of Editing *New Yorker* Articles" (Thurber, *The Years with Ross*, 1957)

YES

"For God's sake, don't say yes until I've finished talking."

DARRYL F. ZANUCK, film producer (quoted in French, *The Movie Moguls*, 1969, chapter 5)

"He has so many yes-men following him around the studio, he ought to put out his hand when he makes a sharp turn."

FRED ALLEN, comedian, on Darryl F. Zanuck (*Movie Talk*, p. 221)

YESTERDAY

"Just remember, happiness is having a poor memory about what happened yesterday."

LOU HOLTZ, Notre Dame football coach (interview, 1985)

YOUTH

"Youth is not a time of life; it is a state of mind,
It is not a matter of rosy cheeks, red lips and supple knees;
It is a matter of the will,
A quality of the imagination, a vigor of the emotions;
It is the freshness of deep springs of life."

SAMUEL ULLMAN, businessman in Birmingham, Alabama, revered by many top Japanese executives, including the late Konosuke Matsushita, founder of Matsushita Electric Industrial Company, who selected this stanza as a motto (*New York Times*, November 8, 1991)

"If you refuse to be made straight when you are green, you will not be made straight when you are dry."

African proverb

"Alcibiades was telling Pericles how Athens should be governed, and Pericles, annoyed with the young man's manner, said, 'Alcibiades, when I was your age I talked just the way you are talking.' Alcibiades looked him in the face and rejoined, 'How I should like to have known you, Pericles, when you were at your best.'"

ADLAI STEVENSON, statesman (Sherrin, *Cutting Edge*, p. 146)

"Because of Mozart, it's all over after age seven."

WENDY WASSERSTEIN, playwright (Solman, *Mozartiana*, 1990)

"To exclude from positions of trust and command all those below the age of 44 would have kept Jefferson from writing the Declaration of Independence, Washington from commanding the Continental Army, Madison from fathering the Constitution, Hamilton from serving as secretary of the treasury, Clay from being elected speaker of the House and Christopher Columbus from discovering America."

President JOHN F. KENNEDY (*New York Times*, June 5, 1960)

SOURCES

Acheson, Dean. *Present at the Creation*. New York: Norton, 1969.

Adams, Douglas. *Hitch Hiker's Guide to the Galaxy*. New York: Harmony Books, 1979.

Adelman, Kenneth L., ed. *Getting the Job Done*. Knoxville: Whittle Direct Books, 1992.

Amory, Cleveland. *Who Killed Society?* New York: Harper, 1960.

Ash, Mary Kay. *Mary Kay*. New York: Harper & Row, 1981.

Ashby, Eric. *Reconciling Man with the Environment*. Stanford: Stanford University Press, 1978.

Ashe, Arthur, and Arnold Rampersad. *Days of Grace*. New York: Knopf, 1993.

Auchincloss, Louis. *Honorable Men*. Boston: Houghton Mifflin, 1985.

Auden, W. H. *A Certain World*. New York: Viking, 1970.

Auerbach, Red, with Ken Dooley. *MBA: Management by Auerbach*. New York: Macmillan, 1991.

Augarde, Tony, ed. *The Oxford Dictionary of Modern Quotations*. New York: Oxford University Press, 1991.

Bach, Steven. *Final Cut: Dreams and Disaster in the Making of Heaven's Gate*. New York: William Morrow, 1985.

Bagehot, Walter. *The English Constitution*. London: Oxford University Press, 1928 (originally published 1867).

Baida, Peter. *Poor Richard's Legacy: American Business Values from Benjamin Franklin to Donald Trump*. New York: William Morrow, 1990.

Baker, Carlos. *Ernest Hemingway—A Life Story*. New York: Scribners, 1969.

Bankhead, Tallulah. *Tallulah*. New York: Harper, 1952.

Barrett, Wayne. *Trump: The Deals and the Downfall*. New York: HarperCollins, 1992.

Bartlett, Sarah. *The Money Machine: How KKR Manufactured Power & Profits*. New York: Warner, 1991.

Bauer, Roy A., Emilio Collar, and Victor Tang, with Jerry Wind and Patrick Houston. *The Silverlake Project: Transformation at IBM*. New York: Oxford University Press, 1992.

Beard, Henry. *Latin for Even More Occasions*. New York: Villard, 1991.

Behrman, Sid. *The Lawyer Joke Book*. New York: Dorset Press, 1991.

Benedikt, Michael. *Cyberspace: First Steps*. Cambridge, Mass.: MIT Press, 1991.

Berger, Meyer. *Meyer Berger's New York*. New York: Random House, 1960.

Berkow, Ira, and Jim Kaplan, eds. *The Gospel According to Casey: Casey Stengel's Inimitable, Instructional, Historical Baseball Book*. New York: St. Martin's Press, 1992.

Berlin, Isaiah. *Conversations with Isaiah Berlin*. New York: Scribners, 1992.

Berra, Yogi, with Tom Horton. *Yogi: It Ain't Over*. New York: McGraw-Hill, 1989.

Bianco, Anthony. *Rainmaker: The Saga of Jeff Beck, Wall Street's Mad Dog*. New York: Random House, 1991.

Bierce, Ambrose. *The Devil's Dictionary*. New York: Sagamore Press, 1957 (originally published 1887).

Bjarkman, Peter C., ed. *Baseball and the Game of Life: Stories for the Thinking Fan*. New York: Vintage, 1991.

Block, Lawrence. *Eight Million Ways to Die*. New York: Arbor House, 1982.

Boas, Max, and Steve Chain. *Big Mac: The Unauthorized Story of McDonald's*. New York: Dutton, 1976.

Bolton, Sarah. *Famous Men of Science*. 4th ed., rev. New York: Crowell, 1961.

Boorstin, Daniel. *The Creators: A History of Heroes of the Imagination*. New York: Random House, 1992.

Boulding, Kenneth E. *Beasts, Ballads, and Bouldingisms*. Edited by Richard P. Beilock. New Brunswick, N.J.: Transaction Books, 1980.

Bouton, Jim. *Ball Four*. New York: Collier Books, 1990.

Bower, Tom. *Maxwell, The Outsider*. New York: Viking, 1992.

Brady, John. *The Craft of the Screenwriter*. New York: Simon & Schuster, 1981.

Brill, Jack A., and Alan Reder. *Investing from the Heart*. New York: Crown, 1992.

Broun, Heywood Hale. *Tumultuous Merriment*. New York: Marek, 1979.

Brown, Dennis. *Shoptalk*. New York: Newmarket Press, 1992.

Broyard, Anatole. *Intoxicated by My Illness: And Other Writings on Life and Death.* Compiled and edited by Alexandra Broyard. New York: Clarkson Potter, 1992.

Bryce, James. *The American Commonwealth.* New York: Putnam, 1959 (originally published 1888).

Burns, George, with Hal Goldman. *Wisdom of the 90s.* New York: Putnam, 1991.

Burrough, Bryan. *Vendetta: American Express and the Smearing of Edmond Safra.* New York: HarperCollins, 1992.

Burrough, Bryan, and John Helyar. *Barbarians at the Gate: The Fall of RJR Nabisco.* New York: Harper & Row, 1990.

Burton, Robert. *Anatomy of Melancholy.* New York: Tudor, 1955 (copyright 1927).

Cader, Michael, with Debby Roth. *Eat These Words: A Delicious Collection of Fat-Free Food for Thought.* New York: HarperCollins, 1991.

Callaghan, Morley. *That Summer in Paris.* New York: Coward-McCann, 1963.

Callahan, Daniel. *What Kind of Life?* New York: Simon & Schuster, 1990.

Capote, Truman. *The Dogs Bark.* New York: Random House, 1973.

Carlyle, Thomas. *Past and Present.* New York: New York University Press, 1977 (originally published 1843).

Cerf, Christopher, and Victor Navasky. *The Experts Speak.* New York: Pantheon, 1984.

Chandler, Raymond. *Farewell, My Lovely.* New York: Vintage, 1988 (originally published 1940).

———. *The Long Goodbye.* New York: Vintage, 1988 (originally published 1953).

———. *Trouble Is My Business.* New York: Ballantine, 1980 (originally published 1950).

Charlton, James, ed. *The Writer's Quotation Book.* New York: Penguin, 1985.

Chieger, Bob, and Pat Sullivan. *Football's Greatest Quotes.* New York: Simon & Schuster, 1990.

Clifford, Clark, with Richard Holbrooke. *Counsel to the President.* New York: Random House, 1991.

Clurman, Richard M. *To the End of Time: The Seduction and Conquest of a Media Empire.* New York: Simon & Schuster, 1992.

Cockburn, Claud. *In Time of Trouble.* London: Hart-Davis, 1956. (Published in the U.S. as *A Discord of Trumpets: An Autobiography.* New York: Simon & Schuster, 1956.)

Coffey, Frank, ed. *The Wit & Wisdom of George Steinbrenner*. New York: Penguin, 1993.

Cohen, Herb. *You Can Negotiate Anything*. Secaucus, N.J.: Lyle Stuart, 1980.

Collected Poems of Emily Dickinson. Original edition edited by Mabel Loomis Todd and T. W. Higginson. New York: Crown, 1982.

Collier, Peter, and David Horowitz. *The Fords: An American Epic*. New York: Summit, 1987.

Cooke, Alistair. *Alistair Cooke's America*. New York: Knopf, 1973.

Corey, Melinda, and George Ochoa. *The Man in Lincoln's Nose*. New York: Simon & Schuster, 1990.

Cosell, Howard. *Like It Is*. Chicago: Playboy Press, 1974.

Cramer, Richard Ben. *What It Takes: The Way to the White House*. New York: Random House, 1992.

Crichton, Michael. *Jurassic Park*. New York: Knopf, 1990.

———. *Rising Sun*. New York: Knopf, 1992.

Crowther, Bosley. *The Lion's Share*. New York: Garland, 1985 (originally published 1957).

Cutler, Henry J. *Honey Fitz: Three Steps to the White House*. Indianapolis: Bobbs-Merrill, 1962.

D'Aguilar, George C., trans. *Military Maxims of Napoleon*. New York: Macmillan, 1988.

Dannen, Frederic. *Hit Men: Power Brokers and Fast Money Inside the Music Business*. New York: Random House, 1990.

Darwin, Charles. *The Descent of Man*. New York: Modern Library, 1936 (originally published 1871).

Davis, Adelle. *Let's Eat Right to Keep Fit*. Rev. ed. New York: Harcourt Brace Jovanovich, 1970 (originally published 1954).

Davis, Patti. *The Way I See It*. New York: Putnam, 1992.

Dickens, Charles. *A Tale of Two Cities*. London: Oxford University Press, 1949 (originally published 1859).

Dickson, Paul. *Baseball's Greatest Quotations*. New York: Harper, 1991.

Drucker, Peter F. *The New Society*. New York: Harper & Row, 1962.

———. *Post-Capitalist Society*. New York: HarperCollins, 1993.

Dunne, John Gregory. *The Studio*. New York: Simon & Schuster, 1969.

———. *Crooning: A Collection*. New York: Simon & Schuster, 1990.

Durocher, Leo. *Nice Guys Finish Last*. New York: Simon & Schuster, 1975.

Eigen, Lewis D., and Jonathan P. Siegel. *The Macmillan Dictionary of Political Quotations*. New York: Macmillan, 1993.

Eisler, Kim. *Shark Tank: Greed, Politics, and the Collapse of Finley Kumble*, 1990.

Ellis, John. *The Social History of the Machine Gun*. New York: Pantheon, 1975.

Emerson, Ralph Waldo. *The Works of Ralph Waldo Emerson: Four Volumes in One*. New York: Tudor.

Evans, Peter. *Ari*. New York: Summit, 1986.

Exley, Frederick. *A Fan's Notes*. New York: Vintage, 1985 (originally published 1968).

Fadiman, Clifton. *The Little Brown Book of Anecdotes*. Boston: Little Brown, 1985.

Farago, Ladislas. *The Last Days of Patton*. New York: McGraw-Hill, 1981.

Farmer's Almanac. Dublin, N.H.: Yankee Publishing, various years.

Fisk, Jim, and Robert Barron, eds. *Official MBA Handbook of Great Business Quotations*. New York: Simon & Schuster, 1982.

Fitzgerald, F. Scott. *The Great Gatsby*. New York: Scribners, 1958 (originally published 1925).

———. *The Last Tycoon*. New York: Scribners, 1941.

Flower, Joe. *Prince of the Magic Kingdom: Michael Eisner and the Re-Making of Disney*. New York: Wiley, 1991.

Flynn, John Thomas. *God's Gold*. Westport, Conn.: Greenwood Press, 1971 (originally published 1932).

Forster, E. M. *Howard's End*. New York: Vintage, 1961 (copyright 1921).

———. *Commonplace Book*. Stanford, Calif.: Stanford University Press, 1985.

Fox, Paula. *The Widow's Children*. San Francisco: North Point Press, 1986.

French, Philip. *The Movie Moguls*, 1969.

Friedman, Milton, with assistance of Rose D. Friedman. *Capitalism and Freedom*. Chicago: University of Chicago Press, 1962.

Frommer, Myrna Katz, and Harvey Frommer. *It Happened in the Catskills*. New York: Harcourt Brace Jovanovich, 1991.

Gaines, James R. *Wit's End: Days and Nights of the Algonquin Roundtable*. New York: Harcourt Brace Jovanovitch, 1977.

Gaines, Steven. *Simply Halston: The Untold Story*. New York: Putnam, 1991.

Galbraith, John Kenneth. *The Great Crash, 1929*. Boston: Houghton Mifflin, 1955.

———. *American Capitalism*. Boston: Houghton Mifflin, 1956.

———. *The Affluent Society*. Boston: Houghton Mifflin, 1958.

————. *Age of Uncertainty*. Boston: Houghton Mifflin, 1983.

————. *The Culture of Contentment*. Boston: Houghton Mifflin, 1992.

Game Day USA: NCAA College Football. Produced by Rich Clarkson. Charlottesville, Va.: The Professional Photography Division of Eastman Kodak Company and Thomasson-Grant, 1990.

Gardner, Erle Stanley. *The Case of the Singing Skirt*. Cambridge, Mass.: R. Bentley, 1981 (originally published 1959).

Gardner, John. *The Art of Fiction*. New York: Knopf, 1984.

Gash, Jonathan. *The Vatican Rip*. New Haven: Ticknor & Fields, 1981.

Geneen, Harold, with Alvin Moscow. *Managing*. New York: Doubleday, 1984.

Genva, Robert. *Managing Your Mouth: An Owners Manual for Your Most Important Business Asset*. New York, 1993.

Geoghegan, Thomas. *Which Side Are You On?* New York: Farrar, Straus, 1991.

George, Henry. *Social Problems*. New York: Robert Schalkenbach Foundation, 1934 (originally published 1884).

————. *The Science of Political Economy*. New York: Robert Schalkenbach Foundation, 1962 (originally published 1897).

Getty, J. Paul. *Getty on Getty: Conversations with Somerset de Chair*. London: Cassell, 1989.

Geyelin, Philip L. *Lyndon B. Johnson and the World*. New York: Praeger, 1966.

Ghent, W. J. *Our Benevolent Feudalism*, microfilm. New York: Macmillan, 1902.

Gies, Joseph. *Bridges and Men: The History and Lore of Bridges from the First Vines Thrown across Streams to the Verrazano-Narrows Bridge across the Entrance to New York Harbor*. Garden City, N.Y.: Doubleday, 1963.

Ginzberg, Eli, and George Vojta. *Beyond Human Scale: The Large Corporation at Risk*. New York: Basic Books, 1985.

Goldman, Peter Louis. *The Death and Life of Malcolm X*. New York: Harper & Row, 1973.

Goldman, William. *Adventures in the Screen Trade*. New York: Warner, 1983.

Goodman, Jerry [Adam Smith]. *The Money Game*. New York: Random House, 1968.

Gould, Richard. *Sacked: Why Good People Get Fired and How to Avoid It*. New York: Wiley, 1986.

Green, Benny, ed. *A Hymn to Him: The Lyrics of Alan Jay Lerner*. New York: Limelight, 1987.

Greene, Katherine and Richard. *The Man Behind the Magic, The Story of Walt Disney*. New York: Viking, 1991.

Grobel, Lawrence. *The Hustons*. New York: Scribners, 1989.

Gunther, John. *Inside U.S.A.* rev. ed. New York: Harper, 1951 (originally published 1947).

Hacker, Andrew. *Two Nations: Black and White, Separate, Hostile, Unequal*. New York: Scribners, 1992.

Hackett, Pat, ed. *The Andy Warhol Diaries*. New York: Warner, 1989.

Halberstam, David. *The Making of a Quagmire*. New York: Ballantine, 1964.

———. *The Best and the Brightest*. New York: Random House, 1969.

———. *The Reckoning*. New York: William Morrow, 1986.

Half, Robert. *Robert Half on Hiring*. New York: Crown, 1985.

Hamilton, Alexander, John Jay, and James Madison [Publius]. *The Federalist*. New York: New American Library, 1961 (originally published, 1787–78).

Hammer, Michael, and James Champy. *Reengineering the Corporation: A Manifesto for Business Revolution*. New York: Harper, 1993.

Hammett, Dashiell. *The Maltese Falcon*. San Francisco: North Point Press, 1930.

Handy, Charles. *The Age of Unreason*. Boston: Harvard Business School Press, 1990.

Hannan, Michael T., and John Freeman. *Organizational Ecology*. Cambridge, Mass.: Harvard University Press, 1989.

Hardy, Godfrey Harold. *A Mathematician's Apology*. London: Cambridge University Press, 1967 (originally published 1940).

Harris, Ruth. *Modern Women*. New York: St. Martin's, 1989.

Hartley, L. P. *The Go-Between*. Leicester, England: Charnwood, 1981 (originally published 1953).

Haun, Harry, ed. *Movie Quote Book*. New York: Crown, 1986.

Hawke, David Freeman. *John D.: The Founding Father of the Rockefellers*. New York: Harper & Row, 1980.

———. *Nuts and Bolts of the Past: A History of American Technology, 1776–1860*. New York: Harper & Row, 1988.

Heiler, Joseph. *Catch-22*. New York: Delacorte Press, 1972 (originally published 1961).

Hemingway, Ernest. *Death in the Afternoon*. New York: Scribners, 1932.

———. *For Whom the Bell Tolls*. New York: Scribners, 1940.

———. *Men at War*. New Complete Ed. New York: Bramhall House, 1942.

———. *The Sun Also Rises*. New York: Scribners, 1970 (originally published 1926).

————. *The Old Man and the Sea*. Three Novels. New York: Scribners, 1952.

Henderson, Carter. *Winners: The Successful Strategies Entrepreneurs Use to Build New Businesses*. New York: Holt, 1985.

Hillman, William, ed. *Mr. President: the First Publication from the Personal Diaries, Private Letters, Papers and Revealing Interviews of Harry S Truman*. 1952.

Hiss, Tony. *The Experience of Place*. New York: Knopf, 1990.

Hoffer, Eric. *Beyond the Sabbath*. New York: Harper & Row, 1979.

Holmes, Oliver Wendell. *The Autocrat of the Breakfast Table*. New York: Heritage Press, 1955 (originally published 1858).

Holovak, Mike. *Violence Every Sunday—The Story of a Professional Football Coach*, 1967.

Horning, Jane E., ed. *Mystery Lovers Book of Quotations, The*. New York: Mysterious Press, 1988.

Howells, William Dean. *The Rise of Silas Lapham*. Bloomington: Indiana University Press, 1971 (originally published 1885).

Hughes, Dorothy B. *Erle Stanley Gardner*. New York: William Morrow, 1978.

Hughes, Robert. *Culture of Complaint: The Fraying of America*. New York: Oxford University Press, 1993.

Hyman, Dick. *Washington Wind & Wisdom: Jokes, Lies, and True Stories about America's Politics and Politicians*. Lexington, Mass.: Stephen Greene Press, 1988.

Iacocca, Lee, with William Novak. *Iacocca: An Autobiography*. New York: Bantam, 1984.

Isaacson, Walter, and Evan Thomas. *The Wise Men*. New York: Simon & Schuster, 1986.

Israel, Lee. *Estee Lauder: Beyond the Magic*. New York: Macmillan, 1985.

Ivins, Molly. *Molly Ivins Can't Say That, Can She?* New York: Random House, 1991.

Jackley, John. *Hill Rat: Blowing the Lid Off Congress*. Washington, D.C.: Regnery Gateway, 1992.

Jacobs, Herbert. *Frank Lloyd Wright*. New York: Harcourt Brace, 1965.

Johnston, Alva. *The Great Goldwyn*. New York: Arno Press, 1978 (originally published 1937).

Josephson, Matthew. *The Robber Barons: The Great American Capitalists*. New York: Harcourt, Brace & World, 1962 (originally published 1934).

Kanter, Rosabeth Moss. *Men and Women of the Corporation*. New York: Basic Books, 1977.

Kaufman, Herbert. *Time, Chance, and Organizations: Natural Selection in a Perilous Environment.* Chatham House, 1991.

Kearns, David. *Prophets in the Dark.* New York: Harper, 1992.

Kehrer, Daniel. *Doing Business Boldly: Essential Lessons in the Art of Taking Intelligent Risks.* New York: Simon & Schuster, 1989.

Keith, Slim, with Annette Tapert. *Slim: Memories of a Rich and Imperfect Life.* New York: Simon & Schuster, 1990.

Kenin, Richard, and Justin Wintle. *The Dictionary of Biographical Quotation.* New York: Knopf, 1978.

Kerr, Jean. *Please Don't Eat the Daisies.* Garden City, N.Y.: Doubleday, 1957.

Kesey, Ken. *One Flew Over the Cuckoo's Nest.* New York: Viking, 1962.

Keynes, John Maynard. *The Economic Consequences of the Peace.* New York: Harcourt Brace, 1919.

———. *The General Theory of Employment, Interest, and Money.* New York: Harcourt Brace & World, 1936.

———. *The End of Laissez-Faire.* New York: Harcourt Brace, 1962.

Klinkenborg, Verne. *Making Hay.* New York: Vintage, 1986.

Korda, Michael. *Power! How to Get It! How to Use It!* New York: Random House, 1975.

———. *Success!* New York: Random House, 1977.

Lapham, Lewis. *Money and Class in America: Notes and Observations on Our Civil Religion.* New York: Weidenfeld & Nicolson, 1988.

Larkin, Philip. *Required Writing.* New York: Farrar, Straus, 1983

Lathen, Emma. *Pick Up Sticks.* Bath, England: Chivers Press, 1990 (originally published 1970).

Lehrer, Jim. *A Bus of My Own.* New York: Putnam, 1991.

Lenzner, Robert. *The Great Getty.* New York: Crown, 1985.

Leopold, Aldo. *A Sand Country Almanac: And Sketches Here and There.* London: Oxford University Press, 1949.

———. *The River of the Mother of God and Other Essays.* Madison: University of Wisconsin Press, 1991.

Lerner, Max. *The Mind and Faith of Justice Holmes.* Boston: Little Brown, 1943.

Lewis, Alfred, and Constance Woodsworth. *Miss Elizabeth Arden.* New York: Coward, McCann & Geoghegan, 1972.

Lewis, Michael. *Liar's Poker: Rising Through the Wreckage on Wall Street.* New York: Norton, 1989.

Lewis, Sinclair. *Babbitt.* New York: Harcourt Brace & World, 1961 (originally published, 1950).

Lifton, Robert Jay. *Home from the War.* New York: Simon & Schuster, 1974.

Lombardi, Vince, with W. C. Heinz. *Run to Daylight*. New York: Simon & Schuster, 1989.

Love, John F. *McDonald's: Behind the Arches*. Toronto: Bantam Books, 1986.

Lurie, Alison. *The Language of Clothes*. New York: Vintage, 1983.

Lutz, William. *Doublespeak*. New York: Harper & Row, 1989.

Lynch, Peter. *Beating the Street*. New York: Simon & Schuster, 1993.

Lyons, Nick. *The Sony Vision*. New York: Crown, 1976.

Macdonald, Ross. *The Moving Target*. South Yarmouth, Mass.: Curley Press, 1979 (originally published 1949).

———. *The Drowning Pool*, South Yarmouth, Mass.: Curley Press, 1979 (originally published 1950).

Mackay, Harvey. *Swim with the Sharks Without Being Eaten Alive*. New York: William Morrow, 1988.

Macrone, Michael. *By Jove! Brush Up Your Mythology*. New York: HarperCollins, 1992.

Mahon, Gigi. *The Last Days of The New Yorker*. New York: McGraw-Hill, 1988.

Mahoney, David, with Conarroe, Richard. *Confessions of a Street-Smart Manager*. New York: Simon & Schuster, 1988.

Malcolm X, with Alex Haley. *The Autobiography of Malcolm X*. New York: Grove Press, 1964.

Malcolm, Janet. *The Journalist and the Murderer*. New York: Knopf, 1990.

Marion, John L., with Christopher Andersen. *The Best of Everything: The Insider's Guide to Collecting—For Every Taste and Every Budget*. New York: Simon & Schuster, 1989.

Marx, Karl. *Capital*. New York: Dutton, 1930 (originally published 1887).

Maybury-Lewis, David. *Millennium: Tribal Wisdom and the Modern World*. New York: Viking, 1992.

Mayer, Martin. *The Bankers*. New York: Weybright and Talley, 1974.

Mayer, Mayer. *Stealing the Market: How the Giant Brokerage Firms, with Help from the SEC, Stole the Stock Market from Investors . . .* New York: Basic Books, 1992.

McCartney, Laton. *Friends in High Places*. New York: Simon & Schuster, 1988.

McCullough, David. *Truman*. New York: Simon & Schuster, 1992.

McLellan, Diana. *Ear on Washington*. New York: Arbor House, 1982.

McWilliams, Carey. *Southern California Country*. Freeport, N.Y.: Books for Libraries Press, 1970 (originally published 1946).

Michaels, Louis. *The Humor and Warmth of Pope John XXIII*. New York: Pocket Books, 1965.

Michener, James A. *Sports in America*. New York: Random House, 1976.

Miller, Arthur. *Death of a Salesman*. New York: Viking, 1949.

Mingo, Jack, and John Javna. *Primetime Proverbs: The Book of TV Quotes*. New York: Harmony Books, 1989.

Moore, Wilbert. *The Conduct of the Corporation*. New York: Vintage, 1962.

Morgan, James, and J. Jeffrey Morgan. *Cracking the Japanese Market: Strategies for Success in the New Global Economy*. New York: Free Press, 1991.

Morgan, Robin. *Sisterhood Is Powerful: An Anthology of Writings from the Women's Movement*. New York: Random House, 1970.

Morgan, Ted. *Maugham*. New York: Simon & Schuster, 1980.

Morra, Umberto. *Conversations with Berenson*. Boston: Houghton Mifflin, 1965.

Moskin, J. Robert. *Morality in America*. New York: Random House, 1966.

Mumford, Lewis. *My Work and Days*. New York: Harcourt, Brace, Jovanovich, 1979.

Nash, Ogden. *I Wouldn't Have Missed It: The Selected Poems of Ogden Nash*. Selected by Linell Smith and Isabel Eberstadt. Boston: Little Brown, 1975.

Neuharth, Al. *Confessions of an S.O.B.* New York: Doubleday, 1989.

Nofziger, Franklin C. *Nofziger*. Washington, D.C.: Regnery Gateway, 1992.

Noonan, Peggy. *What I Saw at the Revolution: A Political Life in the Reagan Era*. New York: Random House, 1990.

Novak, William, and Moshe Waldoks. *Big Books of Humor*. New York: Harper, 1990.

O'Brien, Conor Cruise. *The Great Melody: A Thematic Biography and Commented Anthology of Edmund Burke*. Chicago: University of Chicago Press, 1992.

O'Brien, Joseph F., and Andris Kruns. *Boss of Bosses, the Fall of the Godfather: The FBI and Paul Castellano*. New York: Simon & Schuster, 1991.

Ogilvy, David. *Ogilvy on Advertising*. New York: Vintage, 1985.

———. *The Unpublished David Ogilvy*. New York: Crown, 1987.

Olasky, Marvin. *The Tragedy of American Compassion*. Washington, D.C.: Regnery Gateway, 1992.

Olive, David. *Business Babble*. New York: Wiley, 1990.

O'Rourke, P. J. *Parliament of Whores*. New York: Atlantic Monthly Press, 1991.

Orwell, George. *Animal Farm*. San Diego: Harcourt Brace Jovanovich, 1982.

Parkinson, C. Northcote. *Inlaws and Outlaws: And Parkinson's Third Law*. Boston: Houghton Mifflin, 1962.

———. *Parkinson's Law: And Other Studies in Administration*. New York: Ballantine, 1971.

Patton, George. *War as I Knew It*. Boston: Houghton Mifflin, 1947.

Patton, Phil. *Made in USA: The Secret Histories of the Things That Made America*. New York: Grove Weidenfeld, 1972.

Pepper, Margaret, ed. *The Harper Religious & Inspirational Quotation Companion*. New York: Harper & Row, 1989.

Peter, Laurence. *The Peter Principle*. New York: William Morrow, 1969.

———. *The Peter Plan*. New York: William Morrow, 1976.

Peters, Thomas J. *Thriving on Chaos: Handbook for a Management Revolution*. New York: Knopf, 1987.

———. *Liberation Management: Necessary Disorganization for the Nanosecond Nineties*. New York: Knopf, 1992.

Peters, Thomas J., and Robert H., Waterman, Jr. *In Search of Excellence: Lessons from America's Best Run Companies*. New York: Harper & Row, 1982.

Petras, Ross and Kathryn, eds. *The 776 Stupidest Things Ever Said*. New York: Doubleday, 1993.

Plimpton, George. *The Writer's Chapbook*. New York: Viking, 1989.

Porter, Michael. *The Comparative Advantage of Creating and Sustaining Superior Performance*. New York: Free Press, 1985.

Price, Richard. *Clockers*. Boston: Houghton Mifflin, 1992.

Queen, Ellery. *The Roman Hat Mystery*. Leicester, England: Ulvescroft, 1981 (originally published 1929).

Rachlis, Eugene, and John E. Marqusee. *The Land Lords: An Informal History—from Astor to Zeckendorf—of the Men Whose Adventures in Real Estate Changed the Face of America*. New York: Random House, 1963.

Randall, Tony, and Michael Mindlin. *Which Reminds Me*. New York: Bantam, 1990.

Reich, Robert. *The Work of Nations*. New York: Knopf, 1991.

Reischauer, Edwin O. *The Japanese Today*. Cambridge, Mass.: Harvard University Press, 1988.

Ricardo, David, *Principles of Political Economy, V*, 1817.

Robertson, Nan. *The Girls in the Balcony*. New York: Random House, 1991.

Roddick, Anita, and Miller. *Body and Soul: Profits with Principles*. New York: Crown, 1991.

Roth, Philip. *Portnoy's Complaint*. New York: Random House, 1967.

Rothchild, John. *Going for Broke: How Robert Campeau Bankrupted the Retail Industry, Jolted the Junk Bond Market, and Brought the Booming Eighties to a Crashing Halt*. New York: Simon & Schuster, 1991.

Safire, William, and Leonard Safir, eds. *Good Advice*. New York: Times Books, 1982.

———. *Safire's Words of Wisdom*. New York: Simon & Schuster, 1989.

Sampson, Anthony. *The Anatomy of Britain*. Harper & Row, 1962.

———. *The Sovereign State of ITT*. Greenwich, Conn.: Fawcett, 1973.

Samuelson, Paul. *Economics*. 8th ed. New York: McGraw-Hill, 1970.

Sante, Luc. *Low Life: Lures and Snares of Old New York*. New York: Farrar Straus, 1991.

Sarnoff, David. *The Wisdom of David Sarnoff and the World of RCA*. New York: McGraw-Hill, 1968.

Schlesinger, Arthur M., Jr. *A Thousand Days*. Boston: Houghton Mifflin, 1965.

———. *The Cycles of American History*. Boston: Houghton Mifflin, 1986.

Schumacher, E. F. *Small Is Beautiful*. New York: Harper & Row, 1973.

Secrest, Meryle. *Frank Lloyd Wright: A Biography*. New York: Knopf, 1992.

Seidel, Michael. *Ted Williams*. Chicago: Contemporary Books, 1991.

Seidman, L. William, and Steven L. Skancke. *Productivity: The American Advantage. How 50 U.S. Companies Are Regaining the Competitive Edge*. New York: Simon & Schuster, 1989.

Serrin, William. *Homestead: The Glory and Tragedy of an American Steel Town*. New York: Random House, 1992.

Shapley, Deborah. *Promise and Power: The Life and Times of Robert McNamara*. Boston: Little, Brown, 1993.

Sharp, Robert M. *The Lore and Legends of Wall Street*. Homewood, Ill.: Dow Jones-Irwin, 1989.

Shawcross, William. *Murdoch*. New York: Simon & Schuster, 1992.

Sherrin, Ned. *Cutting Edge*. London: J. M. Dent, 1984.

Shipman, David, ed. *Movie Talk*. New York: St. Martin's, 1989.

Sloan, Alfred P. *My Years with General Motors*. Garden City, N.Y.: Doubleday, 1964.

Smith, Adam. *The Wealth of Nations*. Chicago: University of Chicago Press, 1976 (originally published 1776).

Smith, Frank. *Insult to Intelligence: The Bureaucratic Invasion of Our Classrooms*. New York: Arbor House, 1986.

Smith, Sally Bedell. *In All His Glory: The Life of William S. Paley, The Legendary Tycoon and His Brilliant Circle*. New York: Simon & Schuster, 1990.

Snow, C. P. *Strangers and Brothers*. New York: Scribners, 1985 (originally published 1940).

Solman, Joseph, ed. and illus. *Mozartiana: Two Centuries of Notes, Quotes and Anecdotes about Wolfgang Amadeus Mozart*. New York: Vintage, 1990.

Souhami, Diana. *Gertrude and Alice*. London: Pandora, 1991.

Sperber, Murray. *College Sports Inc.: The Athletic Department vs the University*. New York: Henry Holt, 1990.

Spooner, John D. [Brutus]. *Confessions of a Stockbroker*. Boston: Little Brown, 1972.

Squire, Jason E. *The Movie Business Book*. Englewood Cliffs, N.J.: Prentice-Hall, 1983.

Steinberg, Alfred. *Sam Johnson's Boy*. New York: Macmillan, 1968.

Sternberg, Janet, ed. *The Writer on Her Work*. New York: Norton, 1980.

Stevenson, Robert Louis. *Virginibus Puerisque*. New York: Scribners, 1912.

Stone, Dan G. *April Fools*. New York: Donald I. Fine, 1990.

Stout, Rex. *Fer-de-lance*. Boston: G. K. Hall, 1981.

Strasser, J. B., and Laurie Becklund. *Swoosh: The Unauthorized Story of Nike and the Men Who Played There*. New York: Harper, 1993.

Sun Tzu. *The Art of War*. New York: Delacorte Press, 1983.

Tan, Amy. *The Kitchen God's Wife*. New York: Putnam, 1991.

Tartikoff, Brandon, and Charles Leerhsen. *The Last Great Ride*. New York: Turtle Bay Books, 1992.

Taylor, William R. *In Pursuit of Gotham: Culture and Commerce in New York*. New York: Oxford University Press, 1992.

Teichmann, Howard. *George S. Kaufman: An Intimate Portrait*. New York: Atheneum, 1972.

Thomson, David. *Showman: The Life of David O. Selznick*. New York: Knopf, 1992.

Thurber, James. *The Years with Ross*. Boston: Atlantic Little Brown, 1957.

Thurow, Lester. *Head to Head: The Coming Economic Battle Among Japan, Europe, and America*. New York: William Morrow, 1992.

Tobias, Andrew. *Getting by on $100,000 a Year (and Other Sad Tales)*. New York: Simon & Schuster, 1980.

———. *Money Angles*. New York: Simon & Schuster, 1984.

Townsend, Robert. *Further Up the Organization*. New York: Knopf, 1984.

Truman, Harry S. *Memoirs*. New York: Doubleday, 1955.

Trump, Donald. *The Art of the Deal*. New York: Random House.

Tuchman, Barbara. *A Distant Mirror: The Calamitous 14th Century*. New York: Knopf, 1978.

———. *Practising History*. London: MPapermac, 1983.

Tuleja, Thaddeus F. *Beyond the Bottom Line: How Business Leaders Are Turning Principles into Profits*. New York: Facts on File, 1985.

Updike, John. *Rabbit Redux*. New York: Knopf, 1971.

Veblen, Thorstein. *Absentee Ownership*. New York: Viking, 1923.

———. *An Inquiry into the Nature of Peace and the Terms of Its Perpetuation*. New ed. A. M. Kelley, 1964 (originally published 1919).

Veeck, Bill. *Veeck as in Wreck*. New York: Simon & Schuster, 1989 (originally published 1962).

Vidal, Gore. *Screening History*. Cambridge, Mass.: Harvard University Press, 1992.

Volcker, Paul, and Toyoo Gyothen. *Changing Fortunes: The World's Money and the Threat to American Leadership*. New York: Times Books, 1992.

von Clausewitz, Klaus. *On War*. Princeton: Princeton University Press, 1984.

Walton, Sam, with John Huey. *Sam Walton: Made in America*. New York: Doubleday, 1992.

Watson, Thomas J., and Peter Petre. *Father Son & Co.: My Life at IBM and Beyond*. New York: Bantam, 1990.

White, Theodore H. *The Making of the President, 1964*. New York: Atheneum, 1965.

Whittingham, Richard, ed. *Bears: In Their Own Words: Chicago Bear Greats Talk about the Team the Game the Coaches, and the Times of Their Lives*. Chicago: Contemporary Books, 1991.

Who Built America? Working People and the Nation's Economy, Politics, Culture, and Society, Vol. One: From Conquest and Colonization Through Reconstruction and the Great Uprising of 1877. American Social History Project, City University of New York, under direction of Herbert G. Gutman. New York: Pantheon, 1989.

Wilde, Oscar. *Phrases and Philosophies for the Use of the Young*. 1894

Wilk, Max. *The Wit and Wisdom of Hollywood*. New York: Atheneum, 1971.

Winokur, Jon, ed. *The Portable Curmudgeon*. New York: New American Library, 1987.

Winokur, Jon. *Friendly Advice*.

————. *True Confessions*. New York: Dutton, 1992.

Wolff, Michael, with Peter Rutten, Albert F. Bayers III, and the World Rank Research Team. *Where We Stand: Can America Make It in the Global Race for Wealth Health and Happiness?* New York: Bantam, 1992.

Wriston, Walter. *Risk and Other Four-Letter Words*. New York: Harper & Row, 1986.

Wurman, Richard Saul. *Follow the Yellow Brick Road: Learning to Give, Take, & Use Instructions*. New York: Bantam, 1992.

Zierold, Norman. *Moguls*. New York: Coward-McCann, 1969.

INDEX OF NAMES

INDEX OF CROSS-TOPICS

About the Authors

The compilers of this volume treasure the well-chosen quote. They have mined widely and laboriously to find the more than 5,000 nuggets offered here. Julia Vitullo-Martin has written hundreds of speeches and articles for the nation's leading business executives, foundation heads, and political leaders. She has written extensively for many publications, including *Fortune*, the *New York Review of Books*, and *New York* magazine. J. Robert Moskin has written five books and hundreds of magazine articles, and has served as an editor of *Look* and other major magazines, and as the editorial director of both The Aspen Institute and The Commonwealth Fund. His writings have received many awards.